AN OUTLINE OF
EUROPEAN
ARCHITECTURE

AN OUTLINE OF
EUROPEAN
ARCHITECTURE

By

NIKOLAUS PEVSNER

✴

NEW YORK
CHARLES SCRIBNER'S SONS

FIRST
AMERICAN EDITION
1948

NA 950
P 51 o

Made and Printed in Great Britain by
Hazell, Watson & Viney, Ltd., London and Aylesbury

Contents

Acknowledgments

Author and Publisher wish to thank the following for permission to reproduce photographs:

Messrs. Aerofilms, pl. xcɪɪɪ; Fratelli Alinari, pls. xxɪɪ, xLvɪ; Messrs. Anderson, pls. xLvɪɪ, xLɪx, ɪ, ɪɪv, ɪxɪɪ, ɪxv, ɪxvɪ, ɪxvɪɪɪ; Architectural Press, fig. 38; Archives Photographiques, pls. xɪɪa, xvɪɪ, xvɪɪɪ, xxv, xxvɪɪ; Mr. F. L. Attenborough, pl. xxxɪv; Messrs. B. T. Batsford, fig. 77, pls. xLɪ, ɪxx; Professor K. J. Conant, pl. xɪɪɪ; Country Life Ltd., pls. xLɪɪ, ɪxxvɪɪɪ, xcɪɪ, xcvɪ, xcvɪɪ; Mr. F. H. Crossley, pl. xxxvɪ; E.N.A., pl. cɪɪɪ; Mr. H. Felton, pl. xxxɪɪɪ; Fox Photos, pls. cɪ, cɪɪ; Mr. Charles Holden, fig. 100; Kunstgeschichtliches Seminar, Marburg, pl. ɪxxɪv; Rijksbureau voor de Monumentenzorg, The Hague, pl. ɪxxxv; Sir John Soane Museum, pl. xcvɪɪɪ; The Spanish Embassy, pl. ɪxɪx; Mr. V. Turl, pl. xxxv; Warburg Institute, University of London, pl. c; Mr. F. Reece Winstone, pl. vɪɪɪ; Mr. F. R. Yerbury, pl. xcv.

List of Illustrations

FIGURES IN TEXT

List of Plates

(AT THE END OF THE BOOK)

xi

Foreword

A HISTORY of European architecture in two hundred pages can achieve its goal only if the reader is prepared to concede three things.

He must not expect to find a mention of every work and every architect of importance. If this had been attempted, the space available would have been filled with nothing but names of architects, names of buildings and dates. One building must be accepted as sufficient to illustrate one particular style or one particular point. This means that in the picture which the reader is going to see gradations are eliminated, and colour is set against colour. He may regard that as a disadvantage, but he will, it can be hoped, admit that the introduction of subtler differences would have doubled or trebled the bulk of the book. Thus the nave of Lincoln will be discussed but not the nave of Wells, and Sto. Spirito in Florence but not S. Lorenzo. Whether St. Michael's, Coventry, is really a more complete or suitable example of a Perpendicular parish church than Holy Trinity, Hull, the Palazzo Rucellai of the Italian Renaissance than the Palazzo Strozzi, is of course debatable. Unanimity cannot be achieved on matters of that kind. Yet, as architectural values can be appreciated only by describing and analysing buildings at some length, it was imperative to cut down their number and devote as much space as possible to those finally retained.

Besides this limitation, two more have proved necessary. It was out of the question to treat European architecture of all ages from Stonehenge to the 20th century, or the architecture of all the nations which make up Europe to-day. Neither would, however, be expected of a volume called European Architecture. The Greek temple, most readers probably feel, belongs to the civilisation of Antiquity, not to what we usually mean when we talk of European civilisation. It will also be agreed, though for quite different reasons, that the architecture of, say, Bulgaria need not be dealt with in these pages. The main reasons here are that Bulgaria in the past belonged to the Byzantine and then to the Russian orbit, and that her importance now is so marginal as to make her omission pardonable. So everything will be left out of this book that is only of marginal

xvi

interest in the development of European architecture, and everything that is not European or—as I thus propose using the term
European—Western in character. For Western civilisation is a distinct unit, a biological unit, one is tempted to say. Not for racial
reasons certainly—it is shallow materialism to assume that—but for
cultural reasons. Which nations make up Western civilisation at any
given moment, at what juncture a nation enters it, at what juncture
a nation ceases to be of it—such questions are for the individual
historian to decide. Nor can he expect his decision to be universally
accepted. The cause of this uncertainty regarding historical categories
is obvious enough. Though a civilisation may appear entirely clear
in its essential characteristics when we think of its highest achievements, it seems blurred and hazy when we try to focus its exact out-
lines in time and space.

Taking Western civilisation, it is certain that prehistory is not
part of it, as the prehistory of every civilisation—the word expresses
it—is a stage *præ*, i.e. before that civilisation itself is born. The birth
of a civilisation coincides with the moment when a leading idea, a
leitmotiv, emerges for the first time, the idea which will in the course
of the centuries to follow gather strength, spread, mature, mellow,
and ultimately—this is fate, and must be faced—abandon the civilisation whose soul it had been. When this happens, the civilisation
dies, and another, somewhere else or from the same soil, grows up,
starting out of its own prehistory into its own primitive dark age,
and then developing its own essentially new ideology. Thus it was,
to recall only the most familiar example, when the Roman Empire
died, and Western civilisation was born out of prehistoric darkness,
passed through its Merovingian infancy, and then took shape first
under Charlemagne and finally during the reign of Otto the Great in
the 10th century.

Now, besides prehistory and Antiquity, nearly all that belongs to
the first thousand years A.D. has had to be left out, because the events
of that age, centred in the Eastern Mediterranean—i.e. the oriental-
isation of the Roman Empire, early Christianity, early Talmudism,
early Mohammedanism and the Byzantine Empire, with its successor
civilisations in the Balkans and Russia—make up a separate civilisation of its own, of a character fundamentally different from the Greek
and Roman as well as the Western.

So these three omissions—all omissions in time—will, it is to be
hoped, be considered justifiable. As for limitations in space, a few

words will suffice. Whoever makes up his mind to write a short history of European architecture, or art, or philosophy, or drama, or agriculture, must decide in which part of Europe at any time those things happened which seem to him to express most intensely the vital will and vital feelings of Europe. It is for this reason that, e.g. Germany is not mentioned for her 16th-century but for her 18th-century buildings, that Spain's rôle in Western Mohammedan architecture is left out, but her rôle in Western Christian architecture considered, that buildings in the Netherlands are only touched upon, and Scandinavian buildings not mentioned at all. The only positive bias towards the work of one nation which has been permitted (and needs no special apology) is towards British examples, where they could be introduced without obscuring the issue, instead of examples from abroad. The issue, to say it once more, is Western architecture as an expression of Western civilisation, described historically in its growth from the 9th to the 19th century.

Most of the drawings in the text of this edition were specially drawn by Miss Margaret Tallet. The index is the work of Pamela Reekie; the author wishes cordially to thank her for having given up so much of her limited spare time to its compilation. He also wishes to place on record his gratitude to Margaret Whinney and Anthony Blunt for reading the text of the whole book in typescript and improving it in many ways.

LONDON, 1948   N P.

Introduction

A BICYCLE SHED is a building; Lincoln Cathedral is a piece of architecture. Nearly everything that encloses space on a scale sufficient for a human being to move in, is a building; the term architecture applies only to buildings designed with a view to æsthetic appeal. Now æsthetic sensations may be caused by a building in three different ways. First, they may be produced by the treatment of walls, proportions of windows, the relation of wall-space to window-space, of one story to another, of ornamentation such as the tracery of a 14th-century window, or the leaf and fruit garlands of a Wren porch. Secondly, the treatment of the exterior of a building as a whole is æsthetically significant, its contrasts of block against block, the effect of a pitched or a flat roof or a dome, the rhythm of projections and recessions. Thirdly, there is the effect on our senses of the treatment of the interior, the sequence of rooms, the widening out of a nave at the crossing, the stately movement of a baroque staircase. The first of these three ways is two-dimensional; it is the painter's way. The second is three-dimensional, and as it treats the building as volume, as a plastic unit, it is the sculptor's way. The third is three-dimensional too, but it concerns space; it is the architect's own way more than the others. What distinguishes architecture from painting and sculpture is its spatial quality. In this, and only in this, no other artist can emulate the architect. Thus the history of architecture is primarily a history of man shaping space, and the historian must keep spatial problems always in the foreground. This is why no book on architecture, however popular its presentation may be, can be successful without ground plans.

But architecture, though primarily spatial, is not exclusively spatial. In every building, besides enclosing space, the architect models volume and plans surface, i.e. designs an exterior and sets out individual walls. That means that the good architect requires the sculptor's and the painter's modes of vision in addition to his own spatial imagination. Thus architecture is the most comprehensive of all visual arts and has a right to claim superiority over the others.

This æsthetic superiority is, moreover, supplemented by a social superiority. Neither sculpture **nor** painting, although both are

CHAPTER I

Twilight and Dawn

THE Greek temple (pl. I) is the most perfect example ever achieved of architecture finding its fulfilment in bodily beauty. Its interior mattered infinitely less than its exterior. The colonnade all round conceals where the entrance lies. The faithful did not enter it and spend hours of communication with the Divine in it, as they do in a church. Our Western conception of space would have been just as unintelligible to a man of Pericles's age as our religion. It is the plastic shape of the temple that tells, placed before us with a physical presence more intense, more alive than that of any later building. The isolation of the Parthenon or the temples of Pæstum, clearly disconnected from the ground on which they stand, the columns with their resilient curves, strong enough to carry without too much visible effort the weight of the architraves, the sculptured friezes and sculptured pediments—there is something consummately human in all this, life in the brightest light of nature and mind: nothing harrowing, nothing problematic and obscure, nothing blurred.

Roman architecture also thinks of the building primarily as of a sculptural body, but not as one so superbly independent. There is a more conscious grouping of buildings, and parts are less isolated too. Hence the all-round, free-standing columns with their architrave lying on them are so often replaced by heavy square piers carrying arches. Hence also walls are emphasised in their thickness, for instance, by hollowing niches into them; and if columns are asked for, they are half-columns, attached to, and that is part of, the wall. Hence, finally, instead of flat ceilings—stressing a perfectly clear horizontal as against a perfectly clear vertical—the Romans used vast tunnel-vaults or cross-vaults to cover spaces. The arch and the vault on a large scale are engineering achievements, greater than any of the Greeks, and it is of them as they appear in the aqueducts, baths, basilicas (that is public assembly halls), theatres and palaces, and not of temples that we think, when we remember Roman architecture (pl. II).

However, with very few exceptions, these grandest creations of

I

the Roman sense of power, mass and plastic body belong to a period later than the Republic, and even the Early Empire. The Colosseum is of the late 1st century A.D., the Pantheon of the early 2nd, the Baths of Caracalla of the early 3rd, the Basilica of Maxentius (usually called of Constantine) of the early 4th.

By then a fundamental change of spirit and no longer only of forms had taken place. The relative stability of the Roman Empire was overthrown after the death of Marcus Aurelius (180); rulers followed each other at a rate such as had been known only during short periods of civil war. Between Marcus Aurelius and Constantine, in 125 years, there were forty-seven emperors; less than four years was the average duration of a reign. They were no longer elected by the Roman Senate, that enlightened body of politically experienced citizens, but proclaimed by some provincial army of barbarian troops, often barbarians themselves, rude soldiers of peasant stock, ignorant of and unsympathetic to the achievements of Roman civilisation. There was constant internecine warfare, and constant attacks of barbarians from outside had to be repulsed. Cities declined and were in the end deserted, their market-halls and baths and blocks of flats collapsed. Soldiers of the Roman army sacked Roman towns. Goths, Alemans, Franks, Persians sacked whole provinces. Trade, seaborne and landborne, came to an end, estates and farms and villages became self-supporting once again, payments in money were replaced by payments in kind; taxes were often paid in kind. The educated bourgeoisie decimated by wars, executions, murder and a lower and lower birthrate had no longer a share in public affairs. Men from Syria, Asia Minor, Egypt, from Spain, Gaul and Germany, held all the important positions. The subtle political balance of the Early Empire could no longer be appreciated and was no longer maintained.

When a new stability was brought about by Diocletian and Constantine about 300, it was the stability of an oriental autocracy with a rigid oriental court ceremonial, with a merciless army and far-reaching State control. Soon Rome was no longer the capital of the Empire; Constantinople took her place. Then the Empire fell into two: that of the East to prove mighty, that of the West to become the prey of Teutonic invaders, the Visigoths, the Vandals, the Ostrogoths, the Lombards, and then for a while to be part of the Eastern—the Byzantine—Empire.

Now during these centuries the massive walls, arches, vaults, niches and apses of Roman palaces and public buildings with their grossly inflated decoration grew up all over the vast Empire. But whilst this new style left its mark on Trier as much as on Milan, its centre was the Eastern Mediterranean: Egypt, Syria, Asia Minor, Palmyra—that is the country in which the Hellenistic style had flourished in the last century B.C. And the Late Roman Style is indeed the successor to the Late Greek or Hellenistic.

The Eastern Mediterranean led in matters of the spirit too. From the East came the new attitude towards religion. Men were tired of what human intellect could provide. The invisible, the mysterious, the irrational were the need of that orientalised, barbarised population. The various creeds of the Gnostics, Mithraism from Persia, Judaism, Manichæism, found their followers. Christianity proved strongest, found lasting forms of organisation, and survived the danger under Constantine of an alliance with the Empire. But it remained Eastern in essence. Tertullian's: "I believe in it because it is absurd" would have been an impossible tenet for an enlightened Roman. Augustine's "Beauty cannot be beheld in any bodily matter" is equally anti-antique. Of the greatest of the late Pagan philosophers, Plotinus, his pupil and biographer said that he walked like one ashamed of being in the body. Plotinus came from Egypt, St. Augustine from Libya. St. Athanasius and Origen were Egyptians; Basil was born and lived in Asia Minor, Diocletian was a native of Dalmatia, Constantine and St. Jerome came from the Hungarian plains. Judged by the standards of the age of Augustus, none of them was a Roman.

Their architecture represents them, their fanaticism and their passionate search for the invisible, the magic, the immaterial. S.

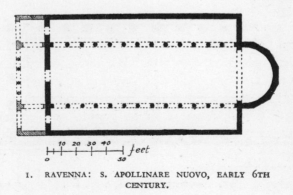

1. RAVENNA: S. APOLLINARE NUOVO, EARLY 6TH
CENTURY.

3

Apollinare Nuovo in Ravenna (pl. III and fig. 1) was built early in the 6th century by Theodoric, ruler of the Ostrogoths in Italy. Yet there is nothing specifically Teutonic in it; it belongs wholly to that universal but, in its essentials, Eastern style that goes under the name of Early Christian. The functional elements of a Christian church are here already so completely established that neither a Gothic nor a present-day church has gone beyond it. The church is taken as the visible symbol of the way of the faithful towards the mystery of the Real Presence. The altar under the apse and the miracle of the Real Presence are the goal. There may be a transept as a halt between nave and apse—a rare motif incidentally, confined mainly to some major churches of Rome built under Constantine and his immediate successors (Old St. Peter's, S. Paolo fuori le mura, S. Giovanni in Laterano, S. Maria Maggiore). With or without transepts, the main axis of propelling movement is indicated by the nave with its un-interrupted sequence of columns dividing off the aisles. It is this that drives us irresistibly on towards the East. There is no articulation in that long colonnade to arrest our eyes, nor in the long row of window after window up in the clerestory; and the solemn and silent mosaic figures of martyrs and holy virgins, with their motionless faces and stiff garments, march with us. One monotonous mesmerising rhythm fills the whole of the church—no secondary motifs weaken its fanatical single-mindedness. This type of plan and spatial develop-ment is so fitting that one feels tempted to regard it as a Christian invention. That is, however, not so. Basilica is the name under which such churches with nave, lower aisles and apse are known to this day. We have met it before meaning a public hall in Rome or the

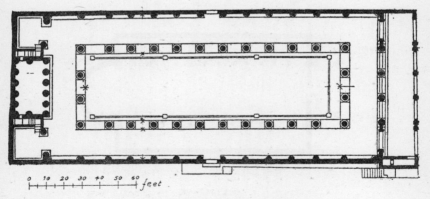

0 10 20 30 40 50 60 feet

2. POMPEII: BASILICA, c. 100 B.C.

4

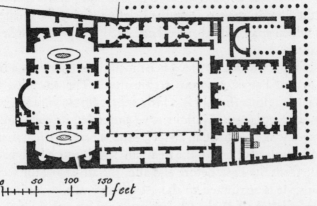

3. ROME: PALACE OF THE FLAVIAN EMPERORS, LATE 1ST CENTURY A.D.

Roman Empire. The word is Greek and means royal. So it may
have come to Rome with Hellenistic regal pomp. But Roman
basilicas are in no surviving form the immediate predecessors of the
Early Christian church building. They usually have colonnades not
only between "nave" and "aisles", but also on the narrow sides, that
is a complete ambulatory, like a Greek temple turned inside out—or
rather outside in (fig. 2). Apses were not uncommon; even two apses
are found; but they are as a rule cut off from the main body by the
colonnades. Thus as a general term for a large-aisled hall the word
basilica may have been transferred from Pagan to Christian, but
hardly the building type as such. Other guesses have been made: the

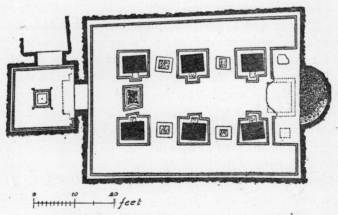

4. ROME: "BASILICA" OF PORTA MAGGIORE, 1ST CENTURY A.D.

scholæ, or the private halls in large houses and palaces (for instance, that of the Flavian emperors on the Palatine (fig. 3))—smaller apsed rooms, which may indeed have been used for private worship by Christians.

But since 1917 we know of a much more direct connection between Christian and Pagan religious architecture. The so-called Basilica of Porta Maggiore (fig. 4) is a little subterranean building of only about forty feet length. With its nave and aisles, its piers and apse it looks exactly like a Christian chapel. Stucco reliefs reveal that it was the meeting-place of one of the many mystical sects which had come to Rome from the East, before and after the advent of the sect of the Christians. It is attributed to the 1st century A.D. Considering the close dependence of Early Christian thought on that of the other oriental religions believing in a saviour, in sacrifice and re-birth, the basilica of Porta Maggiore is the most convincing single source of Early Christian architecture yet found.

During the 4th century Constantine and his successors built vast basilicas in East and West; by the 5th century Christian churches existed everywhere—even in England (Silchester). Most of them are varieties of the basilican plan. An exception were baptisteries and memorials or mausoleum chapels for which, on a Roman precedent, centrally planned buildings were preferred. On a large scale central planning was developed chiefly in Byzantium itself. It culminated in Justinian's two large churches, St. Sergius and Bacchus and then St. Sophia (532–37). On Italian soil a reflection of these, and a resplendent one indeed, is found at Ravenna, which after the fall of the Ostrogoths had become the capital of Byzantine Italy. S. Vitale was built by the same Justinian and completed in 547 (pl. IV and fig. 5). It is an octagon with a two-storied octagonal ambulatory, a chancel and apse added at the east end, and at the west end a narthex or anteroom for the congregation to collect before entering the House of God. The spatial motif that determines the character of the room, a motif of purely æsthetic, i.e. no functional purpose, is the use of the niches into which the central octagon expands. As these niches are not enclosed by walls, but open out with arcades into the ambulatories on the ground floor and the first floor, no clear distinction exists between the two main parts of the building. The central space flows into the ambulatory, and the ambulatory becomes a senseless shape if looked at as an independent unit. The same sensation of uncertainty, of a dreamlike floating, is created, where solid walls remain, by the

6

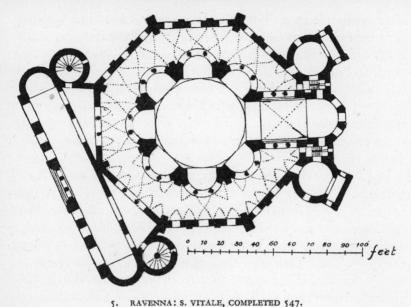

5. RAVENNA: S. VITALE, COMPLETED 547.

mosaics covering them. These glowing surfaces with austere, gaunt figures in sombre tints, seem just as immaterial, as magical and weightless as the surging and drooping curves of the octagon.

The Franks in Gaul, the Angles and Saxons in Britain, the Visigoths in Spain could not possibly appreciate the complexity and sophistication of such churches. Theirs was still the outlook of native tribes, although Clovis had accepted in 496 what he understood as Christianity. With the same merciless cruelty in which the Anglo-Saxon warrior revelled in England, all but exterminating what had remained of civilisation on the island, the princes of the Merovingians sought to exterminate whole families of rivals. The pages of Gregory of Tours, who wrote in the second half of the 6th century, are full of assassination, rape and perjury. Yet this is how our own civilisation began, and how all civilisations begin—in the darkness of tribal barbarism. The Church was the only tie between these shifting kingdoms and the spiritual achievements of the South. Thus Anglo-Saxon brutality was tamed by Irish monasticism (inspired in some obscure way by the Coptic Church of Egypt) in the North and by missionaries from Rome in the South, until, early in the 8th century, the Venerable Bede and the circle around him attained a height of education unparalleled anywhere else in Europe. What they built

7

seems primitive to us, but descriptions seem to indicate that large churches reflected more faithfully early Italian magnificence. Eddius in his Life of Wilfrid calls Hexham a building "columnis variis et porticibus multis suffultum, mirabili longitudine et altitudine", and Ripon also "variis columnis et porticibus suffultam", and Alcuin speaks of York as possessing thirty altars, and again many columns and arches, beautiful ceilings and many *porticus*, whether these mean outer colonnades, or galleries, or aisles, or indiscriminately all of them.

Yet what survives or has been excavated does not bear out such accounts. Churches appear small throughout the country, more Mediterranean in form in the South-East, more original in the North. At Canterbury and elsewhere in Kent apses were, it seems, usual, in Northumberland and the neighbouring counties there are long, narrow unaisled buildings, for instance at Monkwearmouth and Jarrow, founded in 674 and 685. Chancels are separate, and the effect of the interiors is of a tall, tight gangway leading towards a small chamber. Externally masonry is rude and primeval. Geographically between the two regions lies Brixworth in Northamptonshire, the only partly preserved aisled basilica, built with the use of Roman bricks probably in the 7th century.

Amongst the Franks of present-day France and the West of Germany the position was very much the same. There are a few odd Merovingian survivals, small in scale and of debased Roman and Early Christian forms (St. Jean Poitiers, Baptistery Venasque, etc.), and there are plenty of descriptions of buildings seemingly much more ambitious and accomplished—for instance, of the 6th century in Gregory of Tours's *History of the Franks*. A change which we can follow from buildings still upright or which can be reconstructed in our minds with some certainty came only with Charlemagne, heralded perhaps by a few major enterprises of his father, Pepin the Short. Charlemagne had grown up illiterate; he never wrote with ease. But he had a conscious programme of educating his people or peoples to a conception of Roman urbanity and Roman grandeur in a new Christian guise. Hence he gathered round his person the flower of European scholarship and poetry, men from England, Spain, France and Italy—all ecclesiastics, of course. Hence he built for himself palaces with hall, chapel and large ranges of rooms, all as clearly organised in their relative positions as the palaces of the Roman emperors on the Palatine, and all connected by vast

8

colonnades of evidently Roman Eastern derivation (fig. 6). To visualise these palaces we have to rely on excavations and description. Only in one case a substantial piece of one of Charlemagne's palaces still stands: the Chapel Palatine of Aachen (Aix-la-Chapelle),

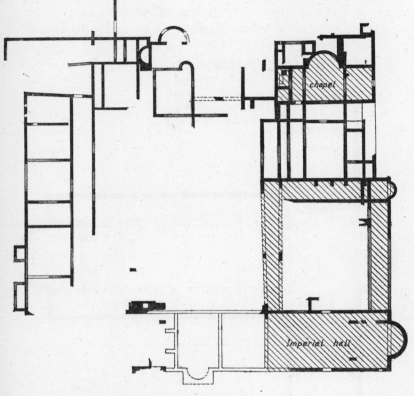

6. INGELHEIM: CHARLEMAGNE'S PALACE, EARLY 9TH CENTURY.

one of the emperor's principal residences. It was originally connected with the Great Hall (not now traceable beyond parts of the foundation walls) by colonnades nearly 400 feet long (pl. v). An equestrian statue of Theodoric, believed to be Constantine, looted from Rome, was significantly placed in this colonnaded forecourt, and columns of the chapel also came from Italy. So did undoubtedly its ground plan. There can be little doubt that the architect took his inspiration from S. Vitale. But he could see no sense in the curved-out niches, so he flattened them out, thus re-establishing the straightforward division between central octagon and ambulatory. He also eliminated the columns on the ground floor. Simple wide openings alternate with short, sturdy piers. The plainness and massiveness of this ground floor (and also of the giant niche of the facade) strike a note utterly different from the subtle spatial harmonies of S. Vitale. Yet the upper floors with their polished antique columns, superimposed in two orders, re-echo something of the transparency, and the floating of space from one unit into another, which make the beauty of Justinian's churches.

Aachen sums up the historic position of Carolingian architecture

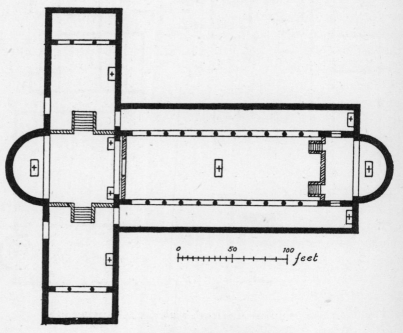

7. FULDA: ABBEY CHURCH, BEGUN 802.

at the extreme end of Early Christian and at the beginning of Western developments. Roman-Christian intentions—it is eminently significant that on Christmas Day of the year 800 Charlemagne made the Pope crown him with the crown of a new Holy Roman Empire—are everywhere traceable but appear marred or in other cases rejuvenated by the naïve vigour of an unskilled, but very determined, somewhat barbarous youth. Of the major churches of which we know some are in plan surprisingly pure Early Christian—St. Denis and Fulda derive directly from St. Peter's and the other Roman basilicas with transepts.[1] Fulda was begun in 802 (fig. 7), the other one, St. Denis, even before Charlemagne came to the throne, about 760.

Centula (or St. Riquier near Abbeville), on the other hand (fig. 8), is in most features unprecedented. The church which was built in 790–99 no longer stands, and is known to us only by an old engraving and a still older description. First of all it had in its exterior just as much accent on the west as on the east parts. Both were strongly emphasised by towers over the crossings rising in several stages and by additional lower staircase towers—a group, varied and interesting, and very different from the simple detached campanile or clock-tower which Early Christian churches occasionally possessed. Then there were two transepts, one in the east and one in the west. Also the east apse was separated from the transepts by a proper chancel. This became almost a matter of course in the coming centuries. The Western part has a complicated spatial organisation, with a low, probably vaulted entrance hall and a chapel above, open towards the nave. Such a Westwork, as it is called in Germany, was also a popular feature of later churches, especially in Germany, as was the bold grouping of manifold blocks with manifold towers. However, we cannot trace a direct uninterrupted connection from Centula to the 11th and 12th centuries.

Some of the ideas of Centula appear again in an immensely interesting original plan on vellum which, about the year 835, had been sent by some bishop or abbot close to the emperor's court to the Abbot of St. Gall as an ideal scheme ('exemplar') for the rebuilding of his monastery. But then, under the grim frosts of the later 9th and the 10th centuries the premature flowering of Carolingian thought and imagination withered away. Less than thirty years after Charlemagne's death in 814 the Empire was divided. France and Germany henceforth took separate courses. But internal struggles, earl against earl, duke against duke, shook both. And from outside, the Vikings ravaged the North-West—Normans they called them in France, Danes in England —the Hungarians menaced the East, the Saracens, i.e. Mohammedan Arabs, the South. No progress was possible in art and architecture. What we know is almost as primitive as Merovingian work, although forms taken up under Charlemagne and his immediate successors

---

[1] The plan may have suggested itself to the Carolingian rulers on a Northumbrian precedent, if the published plans of excavations at Hexham (apparently badly handled and recorded) are at all reliable. They show a large church of the same type of plan, and there is no reason not to assume that it is Wilfrid's, that is a building of the 7th century.

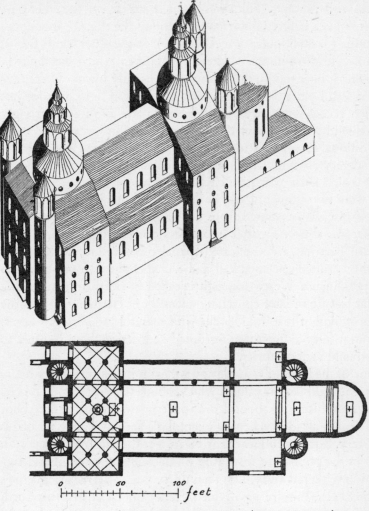

8.   CENTULA: ABBEY CHURCH, 790–99 (RECONSTRUCTION).

were still used. But the spirit in which they were used was blunt and crude. And since during the pre-Carolingian centuries intercourse with Roman architecture had not entirely ceased, the period between about 850 and 950 seems even more barbaric.

Not much of this dark age has stood the ravages of war and the zeal of later builders in France and Germany. To see greater numbers of 9th- and 10th-century buildings in anything like their original state one must go to the borderlands of Western civilisation, to Spain and Britain.

12

In Spain the Visigoths, rulers from the 5th to the early 8th century, had built churches of an oddly mutilated basilican type. S. Juan de Baños, for example, dedicated in 661, consisted originally (fig. 9 shows the plan before the later alterations) of a short nave separated from the aisles by arcades with horseshoe arches, exaggeratedly projecting transepts, a square apse, two rectangular eastern chapels or vestries inorganically detached from the apse and, as another inorganic appendix, a rectangular west porch. There is no spatial flow nor even a unity of plan in this minute building. The exterior colonnades originally running along the north, south and west walls are of Late Antique-Oriental origin, as incidentally is the horseshoe arch.

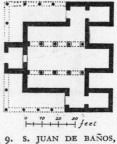

9. S. JUAN DE BAÑOS, DEDICATED 661. THE EAST PARTS HAVE LATER BEEN ALTERED.

This motive however the Arabs, when they conquered the South of Spain in the 8th century, made so much their own that for several centuries to come it remained the hall-mark of Mohammedan and Mozarabic, i.e. Christian Spanish, architecture under Arab influence. The Arabs, as against the Vikings and Hungarians, were far from uncivilised. On the contrary, their religion, their science and their cities, especially Cordova with her half-million inhabitants, were far ahead of those of 8th-century Franks in France or Asturians in Northern Spain. The Mosque at Cordova (786–990), a building of eleven aisles, each twelve bays long, with interlaced arches and complicated star-ribbed vaults, has a filigree elegance more in keeping with the spatial transparency of S. Vitale than of the sturdy uncouthness of the North.

Owing to their proximity to Mohammedan sophistication, the Asturias show a certain airiness here and there which is absent in any other contemporary Christian buildings. At S. Maria de Naranco near Leon, for example (pl. VI and VII) the fluted buttresses outside—as a structural device and a decorative motif still remotely evocative of Rome—and the slender arcade inside which now separates nave from choir are in a strange contrast to the heavy tunnel-vault, the odd shield-like or seal-like medallions from which spring the transverse arches of the vault and the clumsy spiral shafts with their crude block capitals along the walls.

The building incidentally is of very special interest, in so far as in all probability it was designed between 842 and 848 as a Royal Hall for Ramiro I of Asturias—the only surviving early mediæval example of such a building. It has a low vaulted cellar or crypt, and above this the hall proper, now the nave of the church. This is reached by flights of outside steps leading to porches in the centres of both the long sides of the building. On the east and the west there were originally open loggias, communicating with the main room by arcades, of which one, as has been said before, survives. The present choir is in fact one of the loggias blocked up towards the outside.

In British 9th- and 10th-century architecture one would look in vain for such subtleties. Where buildings are preserved complete or nearly complete, we can see that their ground plans were just as elementary. At Bradford-on-Avon (fig. 10), e.g., the nave has no aisles. The chancel is accessible from the nave only by a narrow door with crudely worked joints. The porches on the north and south sides are also separated from the main room. Compartment is added to compartment, very much as in the Visigothic churches of Spain. Anglo-Saxon decoration is just as elementary. The craftsmen who worked the Ruthwell Cross in Bede's time seem superior to those who, one or two generations before the Conquest, decorated the tower of Earl's Barton. The only structural part of its decoration is the emphasising of the three stories by plain string courses (pl. VIII). All the rest, the wooden-looking strips arranged in rows vertically like beanstalks, or higher up in crude lozenge patterns, is structurally senseless. Yet they are in a similar relation to Carolingian architecture as Asturian decoration was to the Muslim style. But while the day-to-day proximity of Arab to Spanish civilisation created the mixed idiom of Naranco and the Mozarabic style of the 10th century, the British builders reduced the Romanising motifs of Carolingian decoration to ungainly rusticity. The so-called long-and-short work up the edges of Earl's Barton tower, and so many other contemporary English towers, is another indication of the rawness of the minds and the heaviness of the hands of these late Anglo-Saxon architects, if architects they can be called.

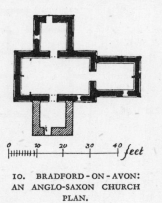

10. BRADFORD - ON - AVON:
AN ANGLO-SAXON CHURCH
PLAN.

CHAPTER II

The Romanesque Style

c. 1000–c. 1200

YET during these dark and troubled years the foundations of mediæval civilisation were laid. The feudal system grew, one does not know from what roots, until it had became the framework round which all social life of the Middle Ages was built, a system as characteristic and unique as mediæval religion and mediæval art, strictly binding lord and vassal, and yet so vague, so dependent on symbolical gestures that we to-day can hardly recognise it as a system at all. By the end of the 10th century it had received its final form. By then political stability too had been re-established in the Empire. Otto the Great was crowned in Rome in 962. At the same time the first of the reform movements of monasticism set out from Cluny in Burgundy. The great abbot Majeul was enthroned in 965. And again at the same time the Romanesque style was created.

To describe an architectural style it is necessary to describe its individual features. But the features alone do not make the style. There must be one central idea active in all of them. Thus several essential Early Romanesque motifs can singly be traced in Carolingian architecture. Their combination however is new and determines their meaning.

The most significant innovations of the late 10th century are those in the ground plan—three above all—and all three caused by a new will to articulate and clarify space. This is most characteristic. Western civilisation was only just beginning to take shape, but already at that early stage its architectural expression was spatial, as against the sculptural spirit of Greek and Roman art—and spatial in an organising, grouping, planning way, as against the magic floating of space in Early Christian and Byzantine art. In France the two chief plans for the east ends of Romanesque churches were conceived; the radiating plan somewhere near the future centre of the country (probably at St. Martin's in Tours, begun after a fire in 997, dedications in 1014 and 1020[1]), and the staggered plan at Cluny apparently in

---

[1] But some French archæologists attribute the same plan to the rebuilding of Notre Dame at Clermont Ferrand in 946, and even claim it for an earlier building of St. Martin's, Tours, a building of about 915. The case is uncertain and would require further investigations on the spot.

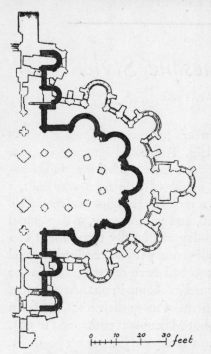

11. TOURS: ST. MARTIN'S. THE THICK BLACK LINES ARE THE WALLS OF THE CHURCH BEGUN SHORTLY AFTER 997, DEDICATIONS IN 1014 AND 1020.

Abbot Majeul's rebuilding dedicated in 981 (figs. 11 and 12). The functional reason for both was the growing worship of saints, with its ensuing need for more altars. To find accommodation for them, chapels in the eastern parts, i.e. the parts reserved for the clergy, were added to the original one centre chapel or apse. One can imagine how crudely Anglo-Saxon or Asturian architects would have added them. The architect of the new age groups them into one coherent unified entity, either by laying an ambulatory round the apse and adding radiating chapels, or by running the aisles on past the transepts, finishing them in small apses parallel or nearly parallel with the main apse and, in addition, placing one, two or even three apses along the east wall of each transept.

Almost exactly at the time when the French began to evolve these new schemes, in Saxony, the centre province of Otto's empire, just north of the Harz mountains, another and even more thorough

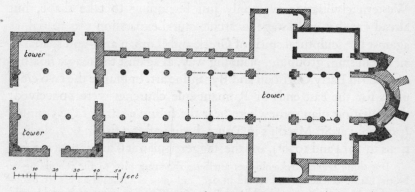

12. CLUNY: ABBEY CHURCH, AS BEGUN *c.* 960 AND DEDICATED IN 981. (BLACK—EXISTING FOUNDATIONS; OUTLINED—HYPOTHETICAL.)

16

"metrical system" was found to articulate the whole of a church, the system followed by Central European architects for the next two centuries. St. Michael's at Hildesheim (fig. 13) was begun immediately after the year 1000. It had (for now, alas, it is completely gutted) two transepts, two chancels and two apses, a logical development of ideas first tried out in a rudimentary form at Centula. Thus the monotony of the Early Christian arrangement was replaced by a grouping less single-minded and rhythmically more interesting. And St. Michael's went decisively beyond Centula in dividing the

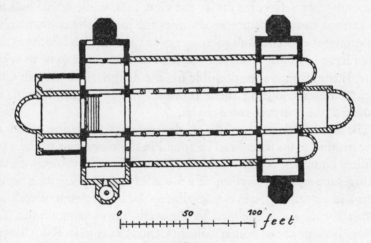

13.   HILDESHEIM: ST. MICHAEL'S, BEGUN SHORTLY AFTER 1000.

nave into exactly three squares, with aisles separated from the nave by arcades that have an alternation of supports, pillars to stress the corners of the squares, columns in between. Each transept again consisted of a centre square flanked by a rectangle. The centre squares were clearly singled out by means of chancel arches not only to the east and west, but also to the north and south. In later buildings each transept was to be square too, and the aisles consisted of sequences of squares. On the east side at Hildesheim a square chancel was inserted between crossing and apse. Chapels branched off the transepts parallel to the main apses—a complex ground plan, yet fully ordered by an active conquering power of reason.

Who conceived this "metrical system" we do not know. What we do know, however, and have no reason to question, is the fact, recorded by his biographer, that St. Bernward, the bishop who was responsible for the building of St. Michael's, was "foremost in

17

writing, experienced in painting, excellent in the science and art of bronze founding and in all architectural work." Similarly we know, e.g., of Aethelwold, the great English bishop, that he was a "theoreticus architectus", well versed in the building and repairing of monasteries, of Benno, Bishop of Osnabruck in the 11th century, that he was "an outstanding architect, a skilful planner ('dispositor') of masonry work". We also possess the plan of about 835 for St. Gall, which has been mentioned before, and was obviously the sender's— that is a bishop's or abbot's—conception. Such and many similar contemporary references justify the view that, while actual building operations were of course at all times the job of the craftsman, the designing of churches and monasteries in the early Middle Ages may often have been due to clerics—at least to the same extent to which Lord Burlington was responsible for the design of his villa in Chiswick. After all, during those centuries nearly all the literati, the educated, the sensitive were clerics.

The same tendency towards an elementary articulation which the new ground plans reveal can be found in the elevations of the 11th-century churches. At St. Michael's, Hildesheim, the system of alternating supports, the rhythm of *a b b a b b a* (*a* representing square piers and *b* columns), serves to divide up the long stretch of wall, and ultimately the space enclosed by the walls, into separate units. This system became the customary one in Central European Romanesque architecture. In the West, and especially in England, another equally effective method was developed for achieving the same aim. It had been created in Normandy early in the 11th century. The Normans by then had lived in the North-West of France for a hundred years and from being Viking adventurers had become rulers of a large territory, clear-minded, determined and progressive, adopting French achievements where they saw possibilities in them—this applies to the French language, suppler than their own, to feudalism and to the reform of Cluny—and imbuing them with the energy of their native spirit. They conquered Sicily and parts of Southern Italy in the 11th and 12th centuries and created an eminently interesting civilisation there, a blend of what was most advanced in the administration of Normandy and in the thought and habits of the Saracens. In the meantime they had also conquered England, to replace there by their own superior mode of life that of the Northern invaders who had come before them. The Norman style in architecture, the most consistent variety of the Romanesque style in the West, strongly influenced France during the 11th century; in England it did more than that: it made English mediæval architecture. One cannot discuss the Romanesque style without taking into consideration English Norman cathedrals and abbey churches. French writers too often forget that. The fulfilment of what had been initiated at Jumièges about 1040 (pl. xiia) and Caen about 1050 lies at Ely, at Winchester, at Durham, to mention only a few.

The new principle was the separation of bay from bay by tall shafts running through from the floor to the ceiling—a flat ceiling everywhere; for the art of vaulting the width of a nave was all but lost. Thus again an articulation was achieved that conveys to us at once a feeling of certainty and stability. There is no wavering here—as there was none in the ruthless policy of William the Conqueror in subduing and normanising England. Blunt, massive and overwhelmingly strong are the individual forms which architects used in these early buildings, sacred as well as secular. For the Norman keep (pl. ix), the other architectural type which the Normans brought from France, has got the same compactness, the same disdain of embellishment as the Norman church. There were, of course, reasons of defence for the bareness of the keep, but it was a matter of expression, i.e. of æsthetics, too, as a comparison with such a piece of building as the transept of Winchester Cathedral (c. 1080–90) proves. At Winchester (pl. x) the solid wall, though opened up in arcades on the ground floor and the gallery floor and again in a passage-way in front of the clerestory window, remains the primary fact. We feel its mighty presence everywhere. The tall shafts are bound to it and are themselves massive, like enormous tree-trunks. The columns of the gallery openings are short and sturdy, their capitals rude blocks (cf. fig. 14), the simplest statement of the fact that here something of round section was to be linked up with something of square section. If the elementary block form of the capital is given up, it is replaced by fluting, the future favourite motif of the Anglo-Norman capital, in its most primitive form (fig. 17). This plainness is typical of the 11th century, a plainness of statement expressed in terms of the plainest of forms.

By the end of the century changes began to appear, all pointing towards a new differentiation. More complex, more varied, more lively forms can be found everywhere. There is perhaps less force in them, but more individual expression. Now comes the age of St. Bernard of Clairvaux (died 1153), who called it his aim as a preacher

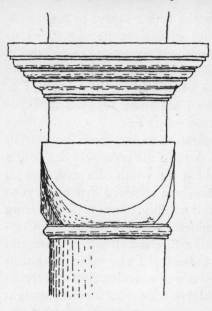

14. BLOCK CAPITAL FROM ST. MICHAEL'S, HILDESHEIM, EARLY 11TH CENTURY.

(and he was one of the greatest of mediæval preachers) to move hearts, not to expound scripture, the age of Abelard (died 1142), the first to write an autobiographical account of his personal problems of love and scholarship, and in England the age of Henry II and Thomas Becket (died 1170). They stand before us as human beings; William the Conqueror as a natural phenomenon, irresistible and relentless. [Just before 1100—when Western Christianity rallied round the banners of the first Crusade—the pioneer work was done in architecture; Early Romanesque was transformed into High Romanesque. Durham is the crucial monument in England, begun in 1093, the east parts vaulted in 1104, the nave *c.* 1130 (pl. XI). The nave appears higher than it is, because, instead of the flat ceiling usual until then and usual in England for some time to come, it is covered by a rib-vault. As our eyes follow the lines of the shafts upwards, this movement does not come to a standstill where the walls end, but is carried farther up with the ribs. The vaults of Durham choir (now renewed) are the earliest rib-vaults of Europe. In this lies Durham's eminence in the history of building construction.]

Engineering skill had developed considerably during the century between the earliest examples of the Romanesque style and 1100. To vault in stone naves of basilican churches was the ambition of the craftsmen, for reasons of safety against fires in church roofs as well as for reasons of appearance. The Romans had known how to vault on a large scale; but in the West there were before the late 11th century only vaulted apses, tunnel- or cross-vaulted aisles or narrow tunnel-vaulted naves without aisles (for instance Naranco), and even smaller tunnel-vaulted naves with aisles (St. Martin de Canigou in French Catalonia of 1009; in its historical importance enormously overrated by M. Puig y Cadafalch, and the so-called crypt of St. Wipert at Quedlinburg in Saxony of *c.*930). Now the vaulting of the wider naves of major churches was mastered, and—as always happens when an innovation is the full expression of the spirit of an age —mastered independently by several ingenious architects in several centres of building activity at about the same time. Burgundy remained faithful to massive tunnel-vaults. The earliest that can be dated seem to belong to about 1065; those at Cluny, when this mightiest monastery of Europe was rebuilt, about 1100, had the widest span anywhere. Speyer, the imperial cathedral on the Rhine, received her first cross-vaults in the eighties. And then there is Durham. A good deal of controversy still remains about dates of early vaults (especially concerning S. Ambrogio in Milan, whose rib-vaults some count amongst the pioneer works, while others date them about the second and third quarters of the 12th century). The new powerful initiative of the late 11th century however is beyond doubt.

Now the most remarkable fact about the vaults of Durham is that rib-vaults as against ribless cross-vaults are accepted as one of the *leitmotivs* of the Gothic style. Their structural advantages, just like those of pointed arches and buttresses, lie in the fact that they concentrate thrusts along specially chosen lines and leave the masonry between stretched out like the canvas of a tent from post to post. Thus great saving in stone and in solid timber centering could be achieved. Hence the Gothic style appears to most people as a constructional affair exclusively. Durham proves this materialistic theory to be wrong. The ribs here are not built up independently, the filling masonry is not lighter. The motif is there, but its constructional application has not yet been discovered. The reason of the Durham builders for introducing so telling a feature must have been the very fact that it is so telling, that it represents the ultimate fulfilment of that tendency towards articulation which had driven Romanesque architects forward for over a hundred years. Now the bay has become a unity not only by the two-dimensional means of lines of demarcation along the walls, but by the three-dimensional means of those diagonal arches set across. Where the two arches meet, where later architects inserted their bosses, there each unified bay has its centre. We move along through the cathedral, not driven towards the altar without halt as in Early Christian churches but stepping from spatial compartment to spatial compartment in a new measured rhythm.

15. DECORATED BLOCK CAPITAL FROM THE CRYPT OF CANTERBURY CATHEDRAL, EARLY 12TH CENTURY.

The rib-vault imparts indeed to the whole structure an alertness opposed to the weight of inert wall so oppressive in 11th-century interiors. This alertness is taken up in the more animated expression of the arcades and their mouldings, and the introduction of a few sharp ornamental forms, the zig-zag above all. Still, in spite of this quickening of rhythm Durham is far from playful or busy. The circular pillars of the arcades are still of overpowering strength, their sheer bulk being emphasised by the elementary decoration, lozenges, zig-zags, flutes exquisitely carved into their surfaces. The fact, incidentally, that all ornament at Durham is abstract, is typical only of Norman architecture in England and Normandy, not of Romanesque architecture in general. In France many types of foliated decoration, especially of capitals, exist. The best-known instance in England is characteristically enough in the crypt of Canterbury, the gateway through which a Continental style had passed once before, about 600, and another one was going to pass in 1175. The capitals here (fig. 15) have foliated decoration, and some even beasts. But nature had no immediate influence on these. They derive from sample-books kept in the lodges of the masons and based on illuminated manuscripts, ivories, previous work of the lodge, etc. Originality was a conception unknown, so was observation of nature. Style as a restrictive force of discipline ruled as unchallenged as authority in religion. Still, Durham seems more humane than Winchester, and 12th-century capitals more humane than the block shapes of the 11th, just as the sermons of St. Bernard seem more humane and more personal than those of the theologians before him.

The exterior of Durham Cathedral is one of the most magnificent sights of England. There it stands, flanked on one side by the Bishop's Castle, on the top of its steep wooded hill with its mighty tower over the crossing and the two slenderer western towers to balance its weight. They are not Norman in their present form, the western towers dating from the 13th, the central tower (originally with a spire) from the 15th century. But towers were planned from the beginning, and where they were carried out, they ended in spires of moderate pitch such as those at Southwell. The outside appearance of Romanesque churches thus differed just as widely from that of Early Christian churches as their interiors. While at S. Apollinare Nuovo the exterior hardly mattered—even church

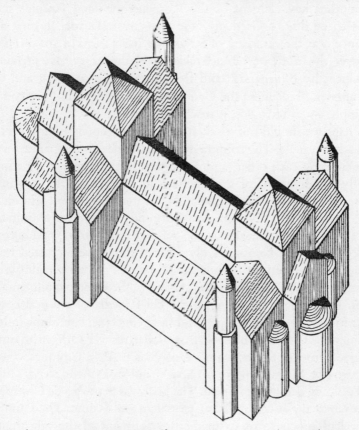

16. HILDESHEIM: ST. MICHAEL'S, BEGUN SHORTLY AFTER 1000 (AXONO-
METRIC RECONSTRUCTION OF THE ORIGINAL STATE).

towers, when they were introduced, stood separate from their churches—a few Carolingian and then most larger Romanesque churches were designed to display variety and magnificence outside as well as inside. St. Michael's at Hildesheim with its two choirs, towers over both crossings and staircase turrets on both ends of both transepts, is the earliest surviving example of a truly Romanesque exterior (fig. 16).

Altogether Germany was eminently important for the development of art and architecture in the early 11th century. It was the years of Ottonian and Salian power, the years before the Emperor Henry IV had to humiliate himself before a Cluniac pope. There is nothing in the arts of Italy or France to emulate the bronze doors of Hildesheim Cathedral. Similarly, in architecture the introduction of yet another key element of the Romanesque (and Gothic) style seems to be due to Germany: the two-tower facade. Its first appearance is at the cathedral of Strassburg in its form of 1015. Then, however, the motif was at once taken up by the most active province of France: by Normandy; and from Jumièges (1040–67), and the two abbeys of William the Conqueror at Caen (Holy Trinity and St. Stephen's, *c.* 1065–80), it reached Britain.

Perhaps we should not speak at all of France concerning the 11th and 12th centuries. The country was still divided into separate territories fighting each other, and consequently there was no one universally valid school of architecture, as, thanks to the Norman kings, there already was in England. The most important schools in France are those of Normandy, Burgundy, Provence, Aquitaine (or rather, broadly speaking, the whole South-West), Auvergne and Poitou. Their comparatively static customs were crossed by a strong current from the North and West of France right down to the far North-West of Spain, the current of the principal pilgrimage routes. Pilgrimages were one of the chief media of cultural communication in the Middle Ages, and their effects on church planning are evident. They can be seen from Chartres via Orléans, Tours, Poitiers, Saintes to Spain; from Vézelay via Le Puy, Conques, or via Périgueux to Moissac and on to Spain; and from Arles to St. Gilles and Toulouse and then to Spain. The goal was Santiago de Compostela, a sanctuary as celebrated as Jerusalem and Rome. The Cluniac Order had much to do with the development of the pilgrimage routes, and characteristics of Cluny can be found in the chief monasteries all the way along. What these were, we can read from the many surviving Cluniac houses—the Order, according to Dr. Joan Evans's calculations, possessed some 1,450 priories at the height of its power—and also from the excavations and reconstruction of Cluny itself, carried out for the Mediæval Academy of America by Professor Conant.[1] Cluny, as rebuilt at the end of the 11th century and early in the 12th and destroyed by the French themselves in 1810, had

[1] I am greatly indebted to Professor Conant for allowing me to illustrate his reconstruction.

two transepts (as later became the rule in English cathedrals), each with an octagonal tower over the crossing. The more important of these, the one farther west, had octagonal towers to the right and left of the crossing as well (one of these survives), and two eastern apses to each arm. The eastern transept had four apses too. Moreover, the chancel apse had an ambulatory with five radiating chapels. Thus one saw looking at the church from the east (pl. xiii) a graded development in many carefully proportioned steps from the low radiating chapels over the ambulatory, the main apse, the chancel roof, the tower over the eastern crossing, to the tallest tower farther west—a structure so complex, so polyphonous, as earlier centuries in the West could not have conceived, and the Greeks would have detested, but the ideal expression no doubt of that proudest moment in mediæval Christianity, when the Reform had conquered the throne of the popes, asserted the superiority of the papal tiara over the imperial crown, and called up the knights of Europe to defend the Holy Land in the first Crusade (1095).

Of the architectural elements of Cluny, it was especially the tunnel-vaulted naves with galleries (pl. xiib) and the stepped-up east ends which appear in the great churches of the Order and on the pilgrimage route: St. Stephen's in Nevers, St. Martial's in Limoges (destroyed), St. Faith in Conques, St. Sernin in Toulouse (the grandest in its exterior, pl. xiv) and Santiago itself. The motif of the radiating chapels, it need hardly be added, had been used at Tours long before any of these churches took it over. Regional modifications of this pilgrimage style make the individual churches all the more fascinating.

Of the main regional characteristics only a few can here be mentioned. Of Normandy with its basilicas, flat-roofed or with plain cross-vaults or rib-vaults, and with galleries, we have already spoken (pl. xiia). The school of Provence liked tunnel-vaulted churches without any aisles, or occasionally with aisles the same height as the nave. In Poitou the same height for tall naves and tall narrow aisles was the rule —a proportion very different from that of the South and Provence. In Auvergne aisles are also as a rule as high as the nave, but they do not look it, because they have galleries. Burgundy (in accordance with her geographical position between Provence, the North Italian sphere of influence and the Rhineland) kept to the basilican tradition and used for vaulting either tunnel-vaults or cross-vaults. Cluny belonged to the first kind; Vézelay, begun in 1096 and completed, it seems, in 1132, is the supreme example of the second (pl. xvii).

The church was supposed to possess the relics of the Magdalen; they made it a favourite goal of pilgrimages. It lies majestically on a hill over-shadowing the houses of the minute town. The main entrance is through an aisled narthex or galilee of three bays (a Cluniac motif, for Vézelay was Cluniac too), and on through one of the wildest of Romanesque figure portals. The nave has nothing of that violence. With its later and lighter choir in the far distance, its length of about 200 ft. between narthex and crossing, its unusually high nave vaults, its arches of alternating grey and white courses and its inexhaustible profusion of capitals with sacred stories, it possesses a quick and lively rhythm and a proud magnificence without being less robust than Durham.

One more school must be mentioned, with a system quite apart from all the others: the school of Aquitaine, with Angoulême and Périgueux as its centres. They preferred aisleless churches—only occasionally are there aisles of nave height—consisting of several domed bays, with or without transept. Their simplicity and grave majesty are unparalleled (pl. xv). The centralising tendency which is apparent wherever domes are used, culminates at St. Front in Périgueux (pl. xvi), where during the second quarter of the 12th century the decision was taken to create a purely central building—a great rarity in the Middle Ages—by leaving without the western bay of its nave an Aquitanian aisleless church which had already its transepts. Thus a Greek cross resulted, with a square for the centre and four squares for the arms. Each square has in its turn again short arms and is covered by a vast dome. The interior (for the exterior is badly restored) is the classic expression of Romanesque clarity and determination.[1] There is no sculptural decoration anywhere except for some arcading along the walls. The system is copied from S. Mark's in Venice, begun in 1063. There, however, where it stands in the centre of the most oriental and most romantic of European cities, as an outpost of Byzantine architecture, it has all the magic of the East, mosaics, luxuriant capitals, arcades to separate centres from arms and concealed spatial relations in the sense which we have seen at Ravenna. At Périgueux it is stripped of all that

[1] The term *classic* is used throughout in this book with a meaning different from *classical*. *Classical* applies to anything inspired by, or copied from, the style of Antiquity, *classic* to the short moments of perfect balance achieved by many styles. When we say of a work of literature or art that it is *a classic*, we mean something similar, namely that it is perfect of its kind, and universally accepted as such.

suspicious glamour and appears pure and sheer, great for its architectural nobility and none other. There is something strikingly Roman in this bareness. No wonder that the ground plan was re-invented in almost identical form by the Italians of the Renaissance.

So much of France. Germany could not do better than develop the theme set at Hildesheim, and the cathedrals and monastery churches of the central Rhineland, notably Speier, Mainz, Worms and Laach, make a splendid display of towers over their crossings and staircase towers, of double transepts and double chancels in an unending variety of proportion and detail (pl. XXI). The second main school of German Romanesque architecture is that of Cologne. Of the Saxon school something has already been said—the others are more provincial. Cologne, until five years ago, possessed an unrivalled number of churches dating back to the 10th, 11th, 12th and early 13th centuries. Their loss is one of the most grievous casualties of the war. Their hall-mark (since St. Mary in Capitol, consecrated in 1065) is a resolutely centralising scheme for the east ends, a scheme in which both transepts and the chancel end in identical apses. Oriental influence has been presumed. The exteriors were as glorious and as varied as any higher up the Rhine.

North Italy has one church of the same type: S. Fedele at Como. Some have tried to construct a dependence of Cologne on Como, but it is now certain that if there is any relation it must have operated the other way. In other respects the connections between Lombardy and the Rhine are still controversial. Nobody can deny them; but priority in types and motifs will scarcely ever be established beyond doubt. The most likely answer to the question is that along the routes of the Imperial campaigns into Italy there was a continuous give and take of ideas and workmen. Probably Saxony and the Rhine were leading to the end of the 11th century, and North Italy in the 12th. At that time gangs of Lombard masons must have travelled far and wide, just as they did again in the Baroque. We find their traces in Alsace as well as in Sweden, and one man from Como appears in Bavaria in 1133. The *leitmotiv* of this Lombardo-Rhenish style is the dwarf-gallery, that is the decoration of walls, and especially those of apses, high up under the eaves with little arched colonnades.

In her ground plans North Italy was less enterprising. Some of the most famous churches have not even a projecting transept, that is, keep close to Early Christian traditions. This applies, for instance, to the cathedral of Modena and S. Ambrogio in Milan. S. Ambrogio is the most impressive of them all (pl. **xxii**), with its atrium and its austere front, its low squat nave, its massive piers, its wide domed cross-vaults and its broad primitive ribs (on these see p. 21). Generally speaking the interior characteristics of these Lombard cathedrals are cross-vaults or rib-vaults, galleries in the aisles, polygonal domes over the crossings, their outside characteristics isolated towers (*campanile* is their Italian name), and those miniature arcadings already referred to. The extreme case of such decorative arcading is the front and the leaning tower of the cathedral of Pisa in Tuscany, both of the 13th century.

Pisa strikes one altogether as of rather an alien character—Oriental more than Tuscan. Similarly alien is the style of Venice with its Byzantine and of Sicily with its Arab connections. To see the Italian Romanesque at its most Italian, that is at its most purely Tuscan, one has to look to such buildings as S. Miniato al Monte in Florence (pl. **xxiii**), which, in spite of its early date (its ground floor may even be contemporary with the transept of Winchester, pl. **x**), possesses a delicacy of treatment, a civilised restraint in sculptural decoration and a susceptibility to the spirit of Antiquity unparalleled anywhere in the North—a first synthesis of Tuscan intellect and grace with Roman simplicity and poise.

Yet in those parts of France in which classical remains abound and men, climate and scenery strike one as so akin to Italy, a new sympathy with the heritage of Rome also appeared with the 12th century. The most important monuments of this blend of the Romanesque and the Roman stand in Burgundy and Provence. The Burgundian church of St. Lazare at Autun (pl. **xviii**) has fluted pilasters, and Autun as well as Vigilay and others possess capitals in which the debased "Corinthian" of the earlier Romanesque style (fig. 18) is restored to something like its original meaning by a new live understanding of the vegetal and decorative character of the acanthus leaf (fig. 19). A similar understanding, not of Roman detail, but of Roman architecture as a whole distinguishes the facade of St. Gilles in Provence (pl. **xix**). For while its three round-headed porches and the manifold mouldings to their arches are unmistakably Romanesque, the columns in front of the walls between the doorways have straight entablatures, a feature of antique, never of Western architecture, and luxuriant Corinthian capitals. Moreover, there are figures of saints standing upright in straight-headed recesses. Life-size sculpture had

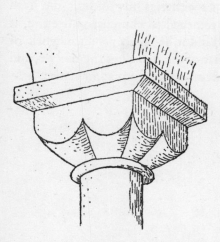

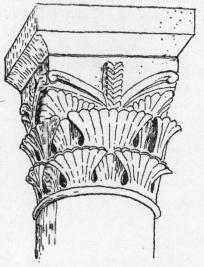

17. FLUTED CAPITAL FROM WINCHESTER CATHEDRAL, LATE 11TH CENTURY.

18. DEBASED CORINTHIAN CAPITAL FROM ST. STEPHEN'S, NEVERS, LATE 11TH CENTURY.

19. CAPITAL FROM VÉZELAY, c. 1120: REVIVED INTEREST IN ANTIQUITY.

20. CROCKET CAPITAL FROM LAON, c. 1175: EARLY GOTHIC RESILIENCE.

been the greatest achievement of Classical Antiquity. In the days of S. Apollinare Nuovo it had all but disappeared. There is no large-scale Carolingian figure sculpture either. Only during the 11th century, when the plastic sense returned to church architecture, it reappeared; only towards its end did it begin to produce work of an æsthetic standard equalling that of the buildings themselves, and only centuries later did it gain independence from architecture.

CHAPTER III

The Early and Classic Gothic Style

c. 1150–c. 1250

IN 1140 the foundation stone was laid for the new choir of St. Denis Abbey near Paris (fig. 21). It was consecrated in 1144. Abbot Suger, the mighty counsellor of two kings of France, was the soul of the enterprise. There are few buildings in Europe so revolutionary in their conception and so rapid and unhesitating in their execution. Four years was an exceptionally short time in the 12th century for rebuilding the choir of a large abbey church. Whoever designed the choir of St. Denis, one can safely say, invented the Gothic style, although Gothic features had existed before, scattered here and there, and, in the centre of France, the provinces around St. Denis, even developed with a certain consistency.

The features which make up the Gothic style are well enough known, too well in fact, because most people forget that a style is not an aggregate of features, but an integral whole. Still, it may be just as well to recapitulate them and re-examine their meaning. They are the pointed arch, the flying buttress and the rib-vault. The pointed arch conveys weight down on to walls or piers at a more reasonable angle than the semicircular arch, and had for this purpose already been used frequently in the Romanesque buildings of Burgundy and Poitou. The other and at least equally important advantage of the pointed arch, the advantage that it enables masons to vault bays of other than square plan without getting into trouble about level heights for their arches, had not been understood in the West before

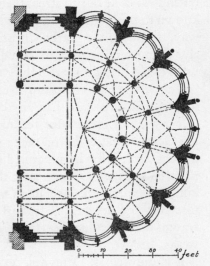

21. ST. DENIS: ABBEY CHURCH, CONSE-
CRATED 1144.

St. Denis. With rounded arches the mason who is dealing with a narrow rectangular bay has to stilt some of his arches or depress some to achieve level heights. Now all this could be adjusted by varying the degree of pointing. Ribs we have met as early as about 1100 at Durham. But the discovery how by means of ribs stone vaults can be reduced to a few strong supporting lines holding each other in position, with light thin panels of masonry between, belongs to the Gothic style. Flying buttresses were invented to transfer the vertical thrust from the vault on to the more distant buttresses of the aisles instead of leaving it to press downwards vertically on the clerestory walls and the arcades of the nave beneath. As such they had already been used, though hidden by aisle roofs at Durham, in the Auvergne and elsewhere. But only the Gothic style realised that thanks to buttresses—a device to strengthen walls at regular intervals already known to the Romans and carried on, though in a somewhat weakly way, through the Early Christian and Romanesque centuries—and flying buttresses, piers could be made taller and slimmer and walls could be built more lightly than ever before.

The whole Gothic system is more logical and ingenious, more scientific and abstract than any constructional device of antiquity. Yet it was not created for technical reasons. It is wrong to say that the Gothic style is the outcome of such material innovations. On the contrary, it has been pointed out that the understanding of the material advantages came later than the spiritual desire for a new kind of expression. Architects wished to enliven inert masses of masonry and to quicken spatial motion. For these and no other reasons they introduced shafts to articulate walls and ribs to articulate vaults.

It is only at St. Denis (pl. xxiv) that Gothic construction and Gothic motifs are linked up with each other to form a Gothic system. The consequence is at once obvious. Rib-vaults cover the varying shapes of bays, buttresses replace the massive walls between the radiating chapels which now form a continuous wavy fringe to the ambulatory. Their side walls have disappeared entirely. If it were not for the five-ribbed vaults, one would feel like walking through a second, outer ambulatory, with exceedingly shallow chapels. The effect inside the church is one of lightness, of air circulating freely, of supple curves and energetic concentration. No longer is part demonstratively separated from part. The transept, recent excavations have shown, was not intended to project beyond the nave and chancel walls as it had always done until then.[1] Articulation remains; but it is a far more sophisticated articulation. Who was the great genius to conceive this? Was it Abbot Suger himself who so proudly wrote a little book about the building and consecration of his church? Hardly; for the Gothic, as against the Romanesque style, is so essentially based on a co-operation between artist and engineer, and a synthesis of æsthetic and technical qualities, that only a man of profound structural knowledge can have invented such a system. We are here at the beginning of a specialisation that has gone on splitting up our activities into smaller and smaller competencies, until to-day the patron is not an architect, the architect not a builder, the builder not a mason, let alone such distinctions as those between the quantity surveyor, the heating engineer, the air-conditioning engineer, the electrical installation expert and the sanitation expert.

The new type of architect to whom St. Denis and the later French and English cathedrals must be ascribed is the master craftsman as a recognised artist. Creative master craftsmen had of course existed before, and probably always designed most of what was built. But their status now began to change. It was a very gradual development. Suger in his book does not say one word about the architect of St. Denis, nor in fact about the designer of the church as such. It seems curious; surely he must have known very well what a daring work he had put up. To explain his silence one must remember the often-quoted and often-misunderstood anonymity of the Middle Ages. It does not mean of course that cathedrals grew like trees. They were all designed by someone. But in the earlier mediæval centuries the names of these men, immortal as their work seemed, did not count. They were content to be workmen working for a cause greater than their own fame. However, during the 12th and, above all, the 13th centuries the self-confidence of the individual grew, and personality came to be appreciated. The names of the architects of Rheims and Amiens cathedrals were recorded in a curious way on the pavement of the naves. A preacher complained that master-masons got higher wages than others by simply going about with their staffs in their hands and giving orders, and—he adds—"nihil laborant". A century after this the King of France was godfather to the son of one of these men and made him a considerable present in gold to enable him to study at a university. But two hundred years had to elapse after the time of Suger to make such intimacy possible.

[1] See *College Art Journal*, vol. 6, 1947, p. 236.

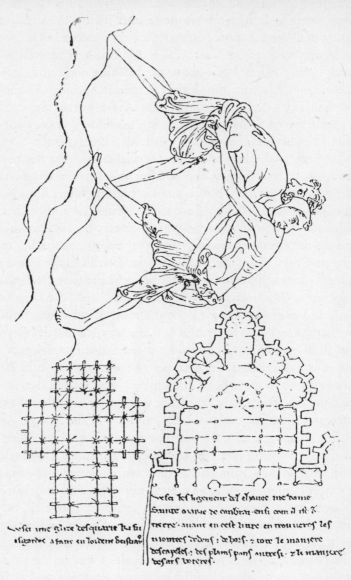

22. PAIR OF WRESTLERS, A CISTERCIAN CHURCH PLAN, AND THE PLAN OF
THE CATHEDRAL OF CAMBRAI. FROM VILLARD DE HONNECOURT'S TEXTBOOK,
c. 1235.

One of the earliest cases in which we can form a live impression
of the personality of one of the great master-masons of the early
Gothic style is that of William of Sens, architect to the choir of
Canterbury Cathedral—a work as revolutionary in England as St.
Denis was in France. A fire had destroyed the old choir in 1174, as

we are told by Gervase, the chronicler of the cathedral, who had himself lived through the events he relates. There was great despair amongst the brethren until after a while they began to consult "by what method the ruined church might be repaired. Architects, both French and English, were assembled; but they disagreed. Some suggested repair, while others insisted that the whole church must be taken down, if the monks wished to dwell in safety. This overwhelmed them with grief. Among the architects there was one, William of Sens, a man of great abilities and a most ingenious workman in wood and stone. Dismissing the rest, they chose him for the undertaking. And he, residing many days with the monks and carefully surveying the burnt walls . . . did yet for some time conceal what he found necessary to do, lest the truth should kill us in our hopelessness. But he went on preparing all things that were necessary, either himself or by the agency of others. And when he found that the monks began to be somewhat comforted, he confessed that the damaged pillars and all that they supported, must be destroyed, if the monks wished to have a safe and excellent building. At length they agreed . . . to take down the ruined choir. Attention was given to procure stones from abroad. He made the most ingenious machines for loading and unloading ships, and for drawing the mortar and stones. He delivered also to the masons models (cut-out wooden templates) for cutting the stones. . . ." Then the chronicler tells us exactly what during each of the following four years was done. At the beginning of the fifth year, however, William, while on the scaffolding, fell down to the ground from a height of fifty feet. He was badly hurt and had to "entrust the completion of the work to a certain ingenious monk who was overseer of the rough masons . . .". But though lying in bed, he gave orders "what was first and what was last to be done. . . . At length, finding no benefit from the skill of his surgeons, he went to France to die at home", and an English successor was appointed.[1]

So here we have the craftsman, equally skilled in masonry and engineering work, diplomatic with his patrons and appreciated by them, but never while conducting work abroad forgetting the land of his youth. At Sens, wherefrom he came, a new cathedral had been begun about thirty years before he went over to Canterbury, a cathedral with certain features evidently imitated at Canterbury.

[1] The quotations are from Mr. Charles Cotton's edition (*Canterbury Papers* No. 3. Published by the Friends of Canterbury Cathedral, 1930).

We are fortunate in possessing at least one even more complete record of the personality and work of a Gothic architect, a notebook, or rather textbook, prepared about 1235 by Villard de Honnecourt, an architect from the Cambrai region of Northern France. This text-

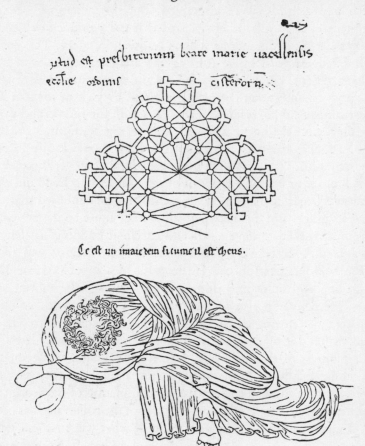

23. ANOTHER CISTERCIAN PLAN, AND A DISCIPLE ON THE MOUNT OF OLIVES. FROM VILLARD DE HONNECOURT'S TEXTBOOK, *c.* 1235.

book, preserved at the National Library in Paris, is an eminently personal document. Villard addresses his pupils. He promises them tuition in masonry and carpentry, drawing of architecture and figures, and geometry. Of all this the book contains examples, drawn and briefly described. It is invaluable as a source of information on the methods and attitude of the 13th century. Villard, although an architect, draws a Crucifixion, a Madonna, and figures of the sleeping disciples as they

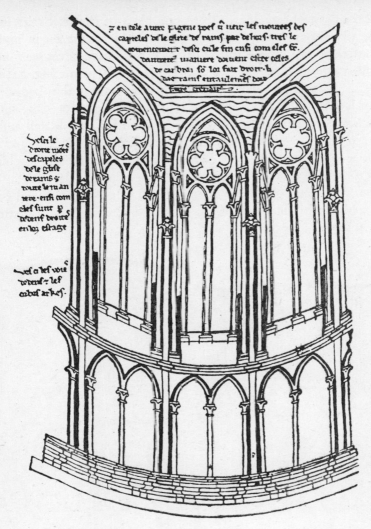

24. ONE OF THE RADIATING EAST CHAPELS OF RHEIMS CATHEDRAL. FROM
VILLARD DE HONNECOURT'S TEXTBOOK, *c.* 1235.

were represented in the scene on the Mount of Olives (fig. 23), all
these evidently for stone carvers to work from. He also drew figures
of Pride and Humility, the Church Triumphant and the Wheel of
Fortune. But there are worldly scenes too, wrestlers (fig. 22), men on
horseback, a king with his retinue. Then there are many animals,
some surprisingly realistic, others quite fantastic. There are simple
geometrical schemes for drawing human heads and animals. He

37

records parts of buildings, the ground plans of church choirs (fig. 22), a tower of Laon Cathedral (he says: "I have been in many countries as you can see from this book, but I have never seen such another tower"), windows from the choir of Rheims (fig. 24; he says: "I was on my way to Hungary, when I drew this, because I liked it best"), and a rose window at Lausanne. He traces a labyrinth, and draws foliage. He designs a foliated end for a choir stall and a lectern with three evangelists. He has diagrams of mouldings and of timber construction. He adds proudly a good many pieces of machinery, a sawmill, a device for lifting heavy weights, and also such automata as a lectern eagle that turns its head, or a heatable metal orb for a bishop to hold in his hand. He even notes a recipe for getting rid of superfluous hair.

25. ELEVATION OF THE NAVE OF NOYON
CATHEDRAL, DESIGNED *c.* 1150.

26. ELEVATION OF THE NAVE OF LAON
CATHEDRAL, DESIGNED *c.* 1170.

Such was the range of knowledge and experience of the men who built the great Gothic cathedrals. They were invited abroad as the bringers of the new Gothic style, the "opus francigenum", as it is called in a German record of that time; they kept their eyes open while they travelled, and noted buildings, sculptures and paintings with the same eagerness. They knew as much of the carving of figures and ornaments as of building construction, although their drawing technique was still elementary.

St. Denis must owe its novelty to a master-mason of this calibre. And many a bishop and an architect burned with ambition to emulate Suger and St. Denis. Between 1140 and 1220 new cathedrals were begun on an ever-growing scale at Sens, Noyon, Senlis, and then Paris (Notre Dame, c. 1163 seqq.), Laon (c. 1170 seqq.), Chartres (c. 1195 seqq.), Rheims (1211 seqq.), Amiens (1220 seqq.) and Beauvais (1247 seqq.). These are by no means all; there are many more all over France. We must, however, here confine ourselves to a brief analysis of the main development in the Ile de France and the surrounding regions, which just then became the centre of a national French kingdom. It is a development as consistent and as concise as that of the Greek temple.

27. PROBABLE ORIGINAL ELEVATION OF THE NAVE OF NOTRE DAME, DESIGNED c. 1170.

Of St. Denis we possess only the choir and, very restored, the west front. This is of the two-tower type of Caen which became now *de rigueur* for North French cathedrals, but, against Caen, enriched by a still round-headed triple portal. Chartres followed St. Denis at once. Of the cathedral of about 1145 only the west portals remain, gloriously vigorous, alert and human in their sculpture, as against the rest of France. We can guess what the naves of St. Denis and Chartres were like from the cathedrals of Sens and especially Noyon. At Noyon, the walls are enriched, as against the Norman system of arcade, gallery and clerestory, by a low wall-passage or triforium between gallery and clerestory. This division of the wall into four zones instead of three does away with much that had remained inert before. The arcades have alternating supports, composite piers as major and round ones as minor divisions. In accordance with this the vaults are sex-partite as they had been in some Norman and Romanesque churches. That means that between two transverse arches ribs run across diagonally from composite to composite pier, while the shafts on the round piers are followed up by subsidiary ribs parallel with the transverse arches and meeting the diagonal ribs in the centre of the whole bay. The effect again is more lively than we know in the Romanesque style (fig. 25).

However, the architects of the two immediately following cathedrals must have felt that in the walls, piers and vaults of Noyon there was still too much left of Romanesque weight and stability. The alternating supports and sex-partite vaults especially produced square, that is static, bays. So at Laon (pl. **xxv** and fig. 26), after some experimenting with alternating supports, all the piers are circular, although on the upper floors an alternating between groups of five and of three thin shafts rising from the circular piers is still preserved, and there are still sex-partite vaults. The many thin shaft-rings, or annulets, round the shafts also still emphasise the horizontal. All the same, in walking along the nave the halting at every major support is avoided. That was a decisive step to take. Notre Dame in Paris goes yet one step farther (pl. **xxvi** and fig. 27). The shafts on the circular piers are no longer differentiated, and the shaft-rings are left out. But the wall was still, it seems, originally in four stages, with gallery and then, instead of the triforium, a row of circular windows below those of the clerestory. However, the proportions have now changed sufficiently to show what tendency lay behind these gradual modifications. The gallery arcades have coupled openings in the choir—

as was the Norman tradition—but trebled, that is much slimmer, openings in the slightly later nave, and the separating colonnettes are exceedingly slender.

Still more daring than the elevation of Notre Dame is its ground plan (fig. 28). Already at Sens and Noyon a slightly centralising tendency can be noted: at Sens by a lengthening of the chancel between transept and ambulatory, at Noyon by semicircular endings of the transepts to the north and south. Now in Paris the architect has placed his transept almost exactly half-way between the two west towers and the east end. He has adopted the most ambitious plan

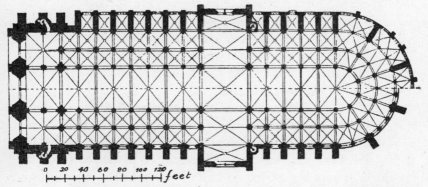

28. PARIS: NOTRE DAME, BEGUN c. 1163. TOP HALF—GROUND-FLOOR; LOWER HALF—UPPER FLOOR. THE CHAPELS BETWEEN THE BUTTRESSES OF THE NAVE WERE BEGUN c. 1235, AROUND THE EAST END IN 1296.

for nave and chancel, the one with double aisles, familiar from Old St. Peter's in Rome as well as from Cluny. His transepts project very little beyond the outer aisles, and there were originally no radiating chapels at all. The present ones, as well as the present chapels between the buttresses of nave and chancel, are a later addition. The resulting spatial rhythm is much smoother than that of Romanesque cathedrals or of Noyon. It is no longer split into numerous units which one has to add up mentally, as it were, to summarise the spatial totality, but concentrated in a few, in fact three, sections: west, centre, east. The transept acts as the centre of the balance. The facade and the double ambulatory round the apse are the two scales. Within this rhythm the evenness of the narrowly spaced arcade columns is most important. It leads you on towards the altar as forcibly as did the columns of Early Christian basilicas.

The movement which had grown from St. Denis to Noyon and from Noyon to Paris reached maturity in the cathedrals designed from the end of the 12th century onwards. Early Gothic changed into High Gothic. Chartres was rebuilt after a fire in 1194 (fig. 29). The new choir and nave at last do away with the sex-partite vault and return to vaults with only diagonal ribs. But whereas the Romanesque rib-vaults were placed over square or squarish bays, the bays now are roughly half that depth. The speed of the eastward drive is thereby at once doubled. The piers remain circular, but they have on each side a circular attached shaft. Towards the nave this shaft reaches right up to where the vault starts (as the shafts of Winchester and Normandy had already done). So the isolation of the circular column is overcome. Nothing at arcade level stops the vertical push. And the wide and tall gallery has disappeared. There is now only a low triforium, dividing the tall arcades from the tall clerestory windows. These innovations constitute the High Gothic style. The plan is less radical than that of Paris, but has the transept also mid-way between the west front and the choir end.

Once Chartres had introduced the new type of piers, the three-storied elevation and the simplified vaulting, Rheims, Amiens and Beauvais did nothing more than perfect it and carry it to the boldest and most thrilling extremes (figs. 30 and 31). As in the plans so in the interiors a balance is achieved no doubt but not the happy, seemingly effortless and indestructible balance of the Greeks. High Gothic balance is a balance of two equally vehement drives towards two opposite directions. One's first impression is of breathtaking height. In Durham the relation between width and height of nave had been 1 : 2·3, in Chartres 1 : 2·6, in Paris 1 : 2·75. In Amiens it has become 1 : 3, and in Beauvais 1 : 3·4. The absolute height in Durham had been approximately 80 feet. In Paris it is 115 feet, in Rheims 125, in Amiens 140 and in Beauvais 157. The drive upward is just as forcible as, or, owing to the slenderness of all members, even more forcible than was the drive eastward in Early Christian churches. And the eastward drive has not by any means slackened either. The narrowness of the arcades and the uniform shape of the piers do not seem to call for even a momentary change of direction. They accompany one on one's way, as closely set and as rapidly appearing and disappearing as telegraph poles along a railway line. There is not time at first to stop and ad-mire them. Yet in pressing forward, the transept halts us and diverts our eyes to the right and left. Here we stop, here we endeavour for the first time to take in the whole. In an Early Christian church nothing of this kind was provided, in a Romanesque church so much of it that movement went slowly from bay to bay, from compartment to compartment. At Amiens (pl. **xxvii** and fig. 31) there is only one such halt, and it cannot be long. Again nave and aisles, now of the chancel, close round us, and we do not come to an ultimate rest until we have reached the apse and the ambulatory, gathering with

29.   ELEVATION OF THE NAVE OF CHARTRES CATHEDRAL, DESIGNED *c.* 1195.

43

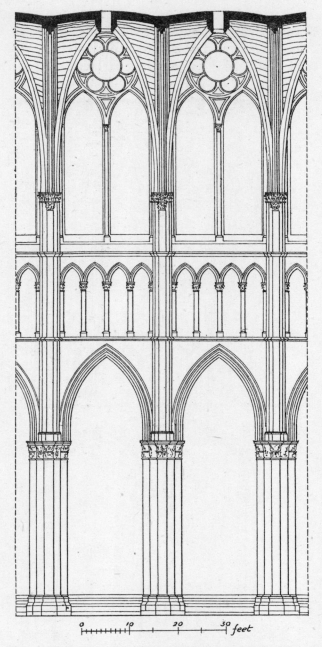

30. ELEVATION OF THE NAVE OF RHEIMS CATHEDRAL, DESIGNED *c.* 1211.

0   10   20   30 feet

31. ELEVATION OF THE NAVE OF AMIENS CATHEDRAL, BEGUN 1220.

splendid energy the parallel streams of east-bound energy and concentrating them in a final soaring movement along the narrowly spaced piers of the apse and the narrow east windows up to the giddy heights of the vault ribs and vaulting bosses.

This description is an attempt at analysing a spatial experience, ignoring of course the fact that a normal 13th-century church-goer would never have been admitted to the chancel. What will have become evident from it is how spectacularly Rheims, Amiens and Beauvais are the final achievement of an evolution which had begun back in the 11th century in Normandy and at Durham and had worked one after another, seemingly small, but very significant changes at St. Denis, Noyon, Laon, Paris and Chartres. This final achievement is, to say it once more, far from reposeful. It possesses the tension of two dominant directions or dimensions, a tension transformed by a supreme feat of creative energy into a precarious balance. Once one has felt this, one will recognise it in every detail. The piers are slender and erect, part of the upward drive. Yet they are round, firm and shapely, with their exquisite realistic foliage (cf. pl. XXXIV). The mouldings of the arcades are sharp and manifold with rolls and deep hollows, high lights and black but precise shadows. The clerestory is all opened up into vast sheets of glass. Yet they are subdivided by vigorously moulded shafts and by geometrical tracery. The introduction of tracery, an invention of the Gothic style, is especially telling. Its development can be traced from Chartres to Rheims and from Rheims to Amiens in figs. 29, 30 and 31. Before Rheims tracery is just a punching of pattern into the wall, the wall itself remaining intact as a surface. At Rheims, for the first time, we find what is called bar tracery as against plate tracery. The stress now rests on the lines of the pattern, not on the surface of the wall. Each two-lighted window is crowned by a circle with a sexfoil ornament —repose at the end of forceful action. Amiens is an enrichment of Rheims, with four lighted windows and three circles instead of one. The same energetic vitality appears in the vaults. Each boss signifies Gothic balance—the firm knotting of four lines of energy, conducted by shafts and then by ribs.

This balance of high tensions is the classic expression of the Western spirit—as final as the temple of the 5th century B.C. was that of the Greek spirit. Then it was rest and blissful harmony, now it is activity, only just for one moment held in suspense. And it requires concentrated effort to master the contrasts and partake of the balance. Like a Bach fugue, a Gothic cathedral demands all our emotional and intellectual powers. Now we find ourselves lost in the mystical ruby and azure glow of translucent stained glass, and now called back to alert attention by the precise course of thin yet adequately strong lines. What is the secret of these vast temples? Is it in their miraculous interiors with vast stone vaults at an immense height, walls all of glass and arcades much too slim and tall to carry them? The Greek architect achieved a harmony of load and support convincing at once and for ever, the Gothic architect, far bolder constructionally, with his Western soul of the eternal explorer and inventor, always lured by the untried, aims at a contrast between an interior all spirit and an exterior all intellect. For inside the cathedral we cannot and are not meant to understand the law governing the whole. Outside we are faced with a frank exposition of the complicated structural mechanism. The flying buttresses and buttresses, though by no means without the fascination of intricate pattern, will chiefly appeal to reason, conveying a sensation similar to that of the theatre-goer looking at the stage apparatus behind the scenes.

One need hardly point out in so many words how exactly the Gothic cathedral re-echoes in all this the achievements of Western thought in the 13th century, the achievements, i.e. of classic scholasticism. Scholasticism is the name for the characteristically mediæval blend of divinity and philosophy. It grew up with the Romanesque style, the centuries before the 11th having in the main not done more than simplify, regroup and, here and there, modify the doctrines of the Fathers of the Church and the philosophers and poets of Rome. During the 12th century, when the Gothic style was created and spread, scholasticism developed into something just as lofty and at the same time just as intricate as the new cathedrals. The first half of the 13th century saw the appearance of the compendia of all worldly and sacred knowledge, St. Thomas Aquinas's *Summa*, and the works of Albert the Great and St. Bonaventura, the *Specula* of Vincent of Beauvais, and in poetry Wolfram's *Parsifal*.

One of these encyclopædic tomes, the *De Proprietatibus Rerum* by the English Dominican Bartholomæus Anglicus, written about 1240, begins with a chapter on the essence, unity and the three persons of God. The next chapter deals with the angels, the third with Man, his soul and senses. There follow chapters on the elements and temperaments, on anatomy and physiology, on the Ages of Man, on food, sleep, and similar physical needs, on diseases, on sun, moon, stars and zodiac, on time and its divisions, on matter, fire, air, water, on the birds of the air, the fishes of the water, the beasts of the land, on geography, on minerals, trees, colours, tools. Vincent of Beauvais, who writes about 1250, divides his work into the Mirrors of Nature, of Doctrine, and of History. And just as the Mirror of Nature starts from God and Creation, so the Mirror of History starts from the Fall of Man, and leads up to the Last Judgment. The cathedral was—besides being a strictly architectural monument of the spirit of its age—another *Summa*, another *Speculum*, an encyclopædia carved in stone. The Virgin stood at the centre post of the centre portals of Rheims Cathedral (pl. xxviii). Figures were placed into the jambs of this portal representing such scenes as the Annunciation, the Visitation, the Presentation. High up in the gables of the three portals appear the Crucifixion, the Coronation of the Virgin and the Last Judgment. But there are also in the Gothic cathedrals the lives of Christ, the Virgin and saints told in the stained glass of the windows, and, spread over the plinths, the jambs, the voussoirs and, up against the buttresses, saints with their attributes by which they are recognised—St. Peter with the key, St. Nicholas with the three golden balls, St. Barbara with the tower, St. Margaret with the dragon—and scenes and figures from the Old Testament, the Creation of Man, Jonah with the Whale, or Abraham and Melchisedek, and the Roman Sibyls who had foretold, it was believed, the coming of Christ, and the Wise and the Foolish Virgins, and the Seven Liberal Arts, and the months of the year with their occupations—the grafting of trees, sheep-shearing, harvesting, pig slaughtering—and the signs of the zodiac, and the elements. The profane and the sacred—a compendium of knowledge; but everything, as St. Thomas puts it, "ordered towards God". For Jonah is represented, not because he comes into the Old Testament, but because his three days inside the whale represent the resurrection of Christ, as Melchisedek offering bread and wine to Abraham represented the Last Supper. To the mediæval mind everything was a symbol. The meaning that mattered lay behind the outward appearance. The simile of the two swords, the emperor's and the pope's, was a symbolic expression of political theories. To Gulielmus Durandus the cruciform church represented the Cross, and the weathercock on the spire the preacher who rouses the sleeping from the night of sin. The mortar, he says, consists of lime, that is love, sand that is earthly toil which love has taken upon itself, and water uniting heavenly love and our earthly world.

All this one must keep in mind to realise how alien this world is to ours, despite all enthusiasm for the cathedrals and their sculptures. We are liable to a reaction in these vast halls which is far too romantic, nebulous, sentimental, whereas to the cleric of the 13th century everything was probably lucid. Lucid, but transcendental. That is the antagonism which defeats us in our age of agnosticism. In the 13th century the bishop and the monk, the knight and the craftsman believed firmly—though each to the measure of his capacity—that nothing exists in the world which does not come from God, and derive its sense and sole interest from its divine meaning. The mediæval conception of truth was fundamentally different from ours. Truth was not what can be proved, but what conformed to an accepted revelation. Research was not conducted to find truth, but to penetrate more deeply into a pre-established truth. Hence authorities meant more to the mediæval scholar than to anyone now, and hence also the faith of the mediæval artist in the 'exemplar', the example to be copied. Neither originality nor the study of Nature counted for much. Even Villard de Honnecourt copied in nine out of ten of his pages. Innovations came by degrees and much less deliberately than we can imagine.

Yet the Gothic style surely was a deliberate innovation and the work of strong and self-confident personalities. Its forms allow us to assume that, and we find in fact within scholasticism, as the chief innovation of the 13th century, a marked departure from the purely transcendental attitude of the Romanesque and earlier centuries. St. Peter Damiani, in the first half of the 11th century, had said: "The world is so filthy with vices that any holy mind is befouled by even thinking of it". Now Vincent of Beauvais exclaims: "How great is even the humblest beauty of this world! I am moved with spiritual sweetness towards the Creator and Ruler of this world, when I behold the magnitude and beauty and permanence of His creation". And beauty according to St. Thomas Aquinas (or a close follower of his philosophy) "consists of a certain consonance of diverging elements".

But it is never—not yet—the beauty of the world as such that is praised. It is the beauty of God's creation. We can enjoy it wholeheartedly; for God Himself "rejoices in all things, because everyone is in actual agreement with His Being" (St. Thomas). Thus stone-carvers could now portray the loveliest leaves, the thorn, the oak, the maple, the vine (pl. XXXIV). When St. Peter Damiani wrote, ornament was abstract or severely stylised. Now youthful life pulses in it, as it pulses in shafts and ribs. But the ornament of the 13th century is even at its most naturalistic, neither petty, nor pedantic. It is still subordinate, never forward, always ministering to a greater cause, that of religious architecture.

Yet it would not have been possible at an earlier age than that of St. Francis's song to Brother Sun and Sister Earth and Brother Wind, than that of the *"dolce stil nuovo"*, and the French epics of chivalry. The earlier monastic orders had lived in the seclusion of their cloisters, the new orders of the 13th century, the Dominicans and Franciscans, had their monasteries in towns and preached to the burghers. The first Crusades had been called up to liberate the Holy Land, the fourth, the one of 1203, was deflected by the Venetians to Constantinople, which they needed for the benefit of their commerce. But still in the fifth there was in the person of the French King Louis IX, St. Louis, a true Christian knight, a hero in whom the ideals of religion and chivalry burned with equal ardour. Wolfram's *Parsifal* is the greatest epic of the 13th century. Here at the moment when Rheims Cathedral was begun, the young knight is taught to "keep his soul pledged to God, without losing his hold on the world". And he is taught that "in joy and in grief right measure" should always be his guide. That sounds like the Greek "Nothing in excess", but it is not. It is just as in architecture, a balance gained as the ultimate prize by him who indefatigably strives for his redemption. A noble and upright ideal worthy of the great cathedrals and the superb sculptures of their portals. At Chartres, under the name of St. Theodore, one can see him, the knight of the Parsifal virtues, standing in the porch of the south transept, and at Rheims, as an unknown king, under a canopy of one of the buttresses, and on horseback at Bamberg, and again with the most beautiful young women that Western sculptors ever carved, women both vigorous and maidenly, around the choir of Naumburg Cathedral.

In England the emissaries of Henry VIII and of Cromwell have destroyed the majority of what there was of cathedral sculpture. A few pieces that are left, such as a headless figure at Winchester, are of the same character and quality as 13th-century sculpture in France. But neither the facade of Wells nor the surviving statues at Lincoln and Westminster are up to the standards of Chartres and Rheims.

The English are not a sculptural race. Their architecture, however, the style which they evolved, is just as exquisite as that of the French cathedrals, and at the same time typically English, known under the name of Early English.

Originally it came from France, as did the Gothic style in all countries. The Cistercians, the new reformed order of the 12th century, to which St. Bernard belonged, favoured it. Cistercian houses in England were amongst the first to use pointed arches. Into cathedral architecture it was introduced by William of Sens at Canterbury. Details there are French in character. What is, however, unusual in France, is the duplicating of the transepts as we find it at Canterbury and then at Lincoln, Wells, Salisbury and many more cathedrals. It is not a feature invented in England. Cluny, the centre of the most influential Benedictine order before the foundation of the Cistercians, had it—not in the 10th-century shape of the church which is illustrated (fig. 12), but as it was rebuilt in 1095 seqq. (pl. XIII). The fact that this duplication remained solitary in France but became so popular in England is eminently characteristic of the different approach to architecture in the two countries. The Gothic style in France, as we have seen, tends all to spatial concentration. The Early English style lacks that quality. A cathedral such as Salisbury with its square east end and its square double transepts (fig. 32) is still the sum, as it were, of added units, compartment joined to compartment. Looking at, say, Lincoln and then at Rheims (pls. XXX and XXIX), this difference comes out most eloquently. Rheims seems vigorously pulled together, Lincoln comfortably spread out. The same contrast can be found in the west facades. The English ones are comparatively insignificant. Porches, added to the naves and developed sometimes into superb pieces of independent decorative architecture, serve as main entrances instead. And where there are fully developed facades, as at Wells and Lincoln, they have an existence unrelated to the interiors behind, are screens, as it were, placed in front of the church proper, and not the logically designed outward projection of the inside system, as are French facades. It has been said that this seemingly conservative attitude of English architects was due to the survival of so many big Norman cathedrals, the foundations and walls of which were used in the rebuilding. But this materialistic explanation, like so many of the same kind, does not hold good. Salisbury was a new foundation. There was nothing on the site when the first stone was laid in 1220 (the same year in which

Amiens Cathedral was begun), yet the ground plan is of the same type as Lincoln (fig. 32). The preference for the "additive" plan must therefore be accepted as a national peculiarity; and once one has realised that, one will recognise its essential similarity to the Anglo-Saxon ground plans of churches such as Bradford-on-Avon (fig. 10), and also its harmony with the specifically national qualities in Early English elevations.

Canterbury cannot unreservedly be called English; Wells and Lincoln are. Wells was begun just before 1191, Lincoln in 1192. If one compares the nave of Lincoln roofed in 1233 (pl. xxxib) with that of Amiens, the national contrast is obvious. Yet both cathedrals are of the aristocratic, youthful yet disciplined, vigorous yet graceful spirit of the 13th century. The bays in Lincoln are wide, while they are narrow in Amiens, the piers are of comfortable proportions; no shafts run right through from bottom to top. Those supporting the ribs of the vaults rest on corbels just above the capitals of the piers—an illogical arrangement from the French point of view. The triforium gallery has broad, low openings and pointed arches, so low that they seem round[1]—another inconsistency, a French critic would say. And most curious of all to anybody thinking in terms of Amiens or Beauvais is the vault. For while the French vault is the logical termination of the bay system, the vault of Lincoln has besides the transverse ribs separating bay from bay, and the four cross ribs, a ridge-rib running all along the centre of the vault parallel to the

[1] Though not as exaggeratedly depressed as they are at Salisbury a little later (fig. 33).

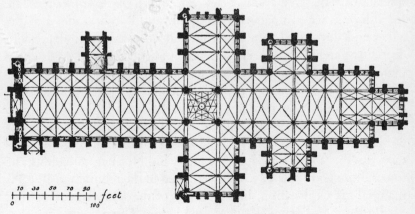

10 30 50 70 90
0   100 *feet*

32. SALISBURY CATHEDRAL, BEGUN 1220.

arcades, and so-called tiercerons, i.e. ribs springing from the same capitals as the cross ribs, but leading up to other points along the ridge or at right angles to the ridge. Thus the vault in Lincoln assumes the shape of a sequence of stars—more decorative but less reasonable than the French system.

In all this, the Early English style appears the true representative of a national character that seems scarcely changed to this day. There is still the same distrust of the consistent and logical and the extreme and uncompromising. Now it has not been possible to discover these peculiarly English qualities in Norman architecture, and it is worth mentioning in this context that just about the middle of the 13th century there are other indications as well of an awakening of national consciousness. The Provisions of Oxford of 1258 are the first official document with a text not only in French (or Latin) but also in English. And they declare that no royal fiefs shall in future go to foreigners, and that the commanders of royal castles and ports must in future all be English. It is known that Simon de Montfort's revolt was a national movement, and that Edward I was influenced by Simon's ideas to a considerable extent. The same tendency towards national differentiation can incidentally be noticed during the same period in other European countries. It may be connected with the experiences of the Crusades. Here the knights of the West, though united in a common enterprise, must for the first time have become aware of the contrasts of behaviour, feelings and customs of the nations.

As far as architecture is concerned, the Crusades have had, beyond this, one more immediate effect. They caused a complete reform in the planning and building of castles. Instead of the Norman reliance for defence on the keep, a system of concentric curtain walls with towers at intervals was now adopted. It came from the mighty castles (such as Le Crak des Chevaliers) built by the Crusaders in Syria and the Holy Land. The Crusaders took it from the Turks, who in their turn had derived it from Roman military architecture. The Tower of London, as enlarged by Henry III and his successors, is an instance of this concentric plan. What is, however, more specially important here, is the fact that the new functional standard is accompanied at least in a number of cases by a new æsthetic standard. To the architects who designed the Edwardian castles of Wales the appearance of the Norman castle, with its irregular bailey and its keep on a mount in one corner, was haphazard and untidy. They re-

33. ELEVATION OF THE NAVE OF SALISBURY CATHEDRAL, DESIGNED *c.* 1220.

discovered symmetry as a possible planning principle for castles—rediscovered, because Rome had known it. Just as they designed newly founded towns (New Winchelsea, e.g.) on the chessboard pattern, they ventured to make of Harlech and Beaumaris completely symmetrical configurations (fig. 34). The effect, in Harlech especially, is one of overwhelming majesty. Far too few people know that here, in Wales, the most consummate masterpieces of European military architecture are to be found. For grandeur and daring of conception, only the Emperor Frederick II's slightly earlier Castel del Monte in South Italy can be compared, again a synthesis of Roman, Eastern and Gothic elements.

In English religious architecture the achievement that lends itself most readily to a comparison with Harlech and Beaumaris is the 13th-century chapter-house, again something specifically English, again something hardly known abroad and—owing to the British inferiority complex in matters of art—insufficiently appreciated over here. Salisbury Chapter-house of about 1275 (pl. XXXIII) is centrally planned, an octagon with a central pillar and spacious windows filling the walls entirely except for the arcade strip just above the stone benches for the members of the Chapter. But while in France such glass walls give a sensation of a rapturous union with a mysterious world beyond ours, the proportions of the windows at Salisbury with their generously sized tracery circles keep the interior in safe and happy contact with the ground. A sunny breadth is achieved which makes Amiens feel both over-pointed and over-excited.

At the same time the Early English style has just as much refinement, crispness and *noblesse* in every individual motif as the French style of the great cathedrals. It is in fact this essential similarity of detail that reminds one all the time of the ultimate identity of spirit behind French and English 13th-century architecture. To feel this, it is only necessary to look at the central pier at Salisbury or the piers of the nave arcade in Lincoln with their slender detached shafts and their resilient crocket capitals (of a type equally characteristic of *c.* 1200 in England and France, cf. fig. 20), or at the clarity and erectness of the English lancet window (English in that it presupposes a solid wall into which it is placed as against the French elimination of the whole wall), or at the masterful carving of the leaves around the capitals of Southwell Chapter-house (pl. XXXIV) throbbing with life, yet kept under the strict discipline of architecture, economic in treatment, nowhere fussy or ostentatious and of a precision of surface only to be compared with the classic Greek art of the Parthenon.

But the Classic is only a moment in the history of a civilisation. The most progressive had reached it in France and England at the end of the 12th century. The most progressive were tired of it and embarked on new adventures shortly after the middle of the 13th. In France, however, the magnificent creative impulse soon flagged —after the Sainte Chapelle in Paris and the gigantic choir of Beauvais there was nothing for a long time with such intensity of life. England on the other hand kept up her creative energy for another century. In fact, the architecture of England between 1250 and 1350 was, although the English do not know it, the most forward, the most important and the most inspired in Europe.

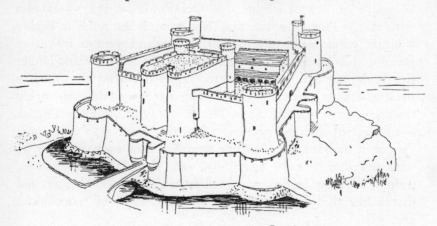

34. HARLECH CASTLE, CHIEFLY 1286–90.

CHAPTER IV

The Late Gothic Style

c. 1250–c. 1500

LATE Gothic, though by the predominant use of the pointed arch still part of the Gothic style, is essentially different from the High Gothic of the great French cathedrals of Paris, Rheims and Amiens, and the English cathedrals of Salisbury and Lincoln. Its coming can clearly be traced within Lincoln Cathedral. The retro-choir, or Angel Choir (pl. XXXII), was begun in 1256. It is of supreme beauty, but it possesses no longer the freshness of spring or early summer; this abundance of rich and mellow decoration has the warmth and sweetness of August and September, of harvest and vintage. But what generous fulfilment in the luxuriant foliage of the corbels and the gallery shafts and capitals, the full mouldings of the arcades and tracery of the gallery, and, above all, the two gorgeous layers of tracery up in the clerestory: one in the windows and one separating the wall-passage from the interior.

While here there is still breadth and fullness, in other equally advanced work of the same date a tendency becomes noticeable towards the more sophisticated and at the same time the more complicated. This tendency runs parallel with the dominant tendency in contemporary philosophy—the abstruse intricacies of Duns Scotus (born c. 1270) and his pupil Occam (died c. 1347)—and also with that in French architecture. But whereas the result in France is on the whole lean and retrospective, England went on inventing forms with amazing profuseness, forms merely decorative, no longer strictly architectural. The most perfect expression of this new spirit is in the kind of tracery which is called flowing as against the geometrical tracery of 1230 to about 1300. The economy of the Early English —a feature of all classic phases—is in strong contrast to the infinite variety of the Decorated. Where there had been exclusively circles with inscribed trefoils, quatrefoils, etc., there are now pointed trefoils, and ogee or double curved arches, shapes like daggers and shapes like the *vesica piscis*, and whole systems of reticulations (fig. 35).

To study this new English flow in terms of space, one must go to

35.   SELBY ABBEY, EAST WINDOW, *c.* 1325.

one west country and one east country church: the cathedral (then abbey church) of Bristol, and the cathedral of Ely. The chancel of Bristol was begun in 1298 and chiefly built during the first third of the 14th century (pl. xxxv). It differs in four significant things from all English cathedrals of the preceding period. It is an aisled hall, not a basilica—that means that its aisles are as high as its nave, so that no clerestory exists. This type of church elevation had existed in Romanesque South-western France (see p. 25), but it had then nowhere attempted what it now does: the creation of a unified room with piers inserted, instead of the classic Gothic principle of a staggered elevation from aisle to nave. This tendency towards the unified room has its origin in the refectories and dormitories of monastic architecture and such retrochoirs as that of Salisbury. Its introduction into the body proper of the church made the Bristol architects change, with a self-certainty remarkable at such an early date, the shapes of both piers and vaults. The piers, a peculiarity exceptional before the 15th century, have no capitals, the vaults no special emphasis on the transverse arches. That means that no halt stops the flow up these shafts and into the ribs, and the flow along the star-like formations of the primary and secondary ribs. There appears in this a deliberate break with the classic Gothic principle of functional articulation all the way through from pier base to vault boss. Moreover, to support the weight of the nave vault, which in a basilican Gothic church is conducted down by flying buttresses to the roof of the aisles and then by buttresses to ground level, the aisles are crossed at the level of the springing of their vaults by curiously ingenious and yet naïve struts or bridges thrown across below the transverse arches. From their centres ribs sprout up to help in forming transverse pointed tunnel-vaults to abut the nave vault. The device may thus have been thought out for technical reasons: it is æsthetically most effective all the same. A classic Gothic interior is meant to affect us in two directions only: the facade-altar direction and the other, at right angles to it, which make us see the sheets of stained glass and the tracery on the right and the left. At Bristol our eyes are lured all the time into glimpses diagonally up and across.

The same effect can be studied on a larger scale in Wells Cathedral, where in 1338 an enormous arch or strut of similar design and function was placed between nave and crossing to support the crossing tower. It is grossly baffling, but undeniably impressive. At Bristol itself the cathedral architect has given a more playful version of the same spatial motifs in the sacristy of the cathedral. Here the ribs of the little vault are accompanied by a skeleton of secondary flying ribs starting at a lower level than the others, shooting through the air and meeting the primary ones at the central boss. The effect is again one of deliberate and pleasing confusion. Classic Gothic ribs, just like classic Gothic arches, keep strictly to the strata of space assigned to them; they never stray into others.

At Ely more than anywhere else the new attitude towards space has found an adequate form. Between 1322 and 1342 the crossing of the cathedral was rebuilt in the form of an octagon. The choice of this shape by the designer, who probably was the King's carpenter, Master William de Hurle, can have been nothing but a deliberate attempt at breaking the 13th-century's discipline of right angles. The diagonal axes, with their large windows and flowing tracery, destroy the precise dividing lines between nave, aisles, transepts and choir which had been the groundwork in the plan and elevation of a classic Gothic church. It has been argued that the glass of Amiens or the Sainte Chapelle also breaks this logicality of the earlier Middle Ages by opening the room towards a mysterious transcendental world. That is not so; the sheets of glass may give a diaphanous character to the enclosure, but it is an enclosure all the same. It doesn't really allow the eye to wander into dim, incomprehensible distances. The octagon of Ely has this very effect, an effect of surprise and ambiguity.

The Lady Chapel at Ely (1321–49) achieved the same aim by subtler and more delicate means. The rectangular chapel isolated from the main building, as only chapter-houses usually are, has all the way round an exquisite arcading with crocketed ogee arches gathered together by larger three-dimensional or nodding ogee arches (pl. XXXVI). Ogee-curved quatrefoils with seated figures fill the spandrels. The arches are covered with a luxuriant growth of vegetation, no longer as crisp as that of the 13th century, but with its undulations of knobbly leaves and its intricacy of minute detail at once more sophisticated and, strangely enough, more uniform in its general appearance. This is due to a treatment that makes it impossible to isolate part from part, as one could in looking at the leaves of Southwell. Now all one sees is an incessant ripple and flow, lights and shadows whisking over bossy surfaces, fascinating but far removed from the clarity of a hundred years ago.

The three-dimensional ogee arch is a motif of great significance. It does what the octagon does in Ely Cathedral, and the piers without capitals, the vaults without transverse arches and the bridges in the aisles did in Bristol—it sets space into a motion, quicker, more complicated and less single-minded than any to be experienced in Early English churches. Its immediate forerunner in the three-dimensional treatment of a wall is the chapter-house of York Cathedral, *c.* 1290, where the seats around the walls have not blind arcades behind, as at Salisbury (pl. XXXIII) about fifteen years before, but are placed into tiny polygonal niches. Their forty-four times repeated projection causes a spatial ripple too slight still to be felt as breaking the continuity of the wall, but quite noticeable, once one is aware of the coming of this new tendency.

This tendency was by no means exclusively English. Continental countries experienced it too, though considerably later. France especially did not fully wake up to the spatial and ornamental implications of the Late Gothic style until the end of the 15th century. Only in the *midi* there exists work of European significance, culminating in the Cathedral of Albi (begun 1282). Albi, a fortified church, is a mighty compact block from outside without any of the elaborate articulation of classic Gothic exteriors, and inside consists of a single nave with side chapels—originally fully as high as the nave—placed between the buttresses. Thus spatial unity is achieved, though a unity of plainness and not of complex interwoven movement as at Bristol.

This tendency towards inner and outer plainness, as characteristic of the change-over from High to Late Gothic as the intricacies of the Decorated in England, is chiefly an outcome of the influence of the new Orders of Preachers, the Franciscans and Dominicans or Grey Friars and Black Friars, founded in 1209 and 1215, and spreading from 1225 onwards at a rate only comparable to those of the Cluniac and Cistercian spreads in their respective centuries. The 13th-century churches of the friars, in whatever country they were built, were, in accordance with the reformed rules of the new orders, of simple and useful plan, large, and with very little to suggest a specifically ecclesiastical atmosphere. They did not need much in the way of eastern chapels, as many of the friars were not priests, but they could not do without very spacious naves to house the large congregations which came to listen to their popular sermons.

The friars, it is known, where the orders of the people. They liked strong effects and active lives. They scorned the sheltered and leisurely existence of the other orders on their country estates, chose busy towns to settle in and there developed their preaching technique as a medium of religious propaganda to a degree never attempted since the days of the Crusades.

Thus all they needed was halls of vast dimensions, a pulpit and an altar. Beyond that their church plans differ in the various countries. In Italy, the land of their origin, they were at first aisleless halls, barns as it were, with an apseless choir and smaller chapels along a transept, on one of the standard early Cistercian patterns. The size of such churches as those of the Franciscans and Dominicans at Siena is enormous, 300 feet in length and more. In the north we find aisleless as well as aisled friars' churches, and in Germany some hall churches too. Their bare long walls without any towers can be most impressive (Erfurt). The English Franciscans and Dominicans relieved this exterior monotony by a tower or spire over the bay between nave and choir. Otherwise there was often no structural division between the two parts at all. But hardly anything survives of complete friars' churches in England, and one may therefore easily underestimate the influence their style must have had about 1300. Of this more will be said later.

This international tendency towards plainness in the architecture of the new orders seems at first glance in contrast to the spatial adventures of Bristol and Ely. In fact, however, the Friars' style and the Decorated style of England both belong to the same general trend. The connection between the two can in some ways best be pointed out by a look at the Late Gothic style in Germany, since it combines the principle of the plain enclosure with that of a *Waldweben* inside. In Germany, too, the friars were instrumental in disseminating the new style. It was, however, created in parish churches, and parish churches are its chief monuments, the parish churches of the 14th and 15th centuries in which, as in the friars' churches, the sermon grew more and more to be the centre of the service. The movement away from High Gothic principles started later than in England and Italy, about 1350, and culminated as late as in France: about 1500. Its favourite vehicle was the aisled hall, an exception—in spite of Bristol—in English (and also in French) church architecture. For 14th- and 15th-century Germany it became almost a matter of course, especially in Westphalia, in the brick districts of the Hanseatic coast towns and of Bavaria, and, after the discovery of silver, in the newly founded, newly prospering towns of Upper Saxony. It had had a long national history, going back much further than the date of Bristol. There are occasional Romanesque aisled halls in Germany, even one (on a small scale) as early as 1015. It may thus not be necessary to suppose connections with the aisled halls of South-West France. Aisled halls in Gothic forms were built directly the style had been taken over. As in England, the new inspiration came probably from the refectories and chapter-houses of German (chiefly Cistercian) monasteries. The type spread during the second half of the 13th century, and assumed its German characteristics: wide arcades and wide aisles. These, needless to say, invite the eye, even more than the narrower opening of Bristol, to wander off the main Gothic lines of vision. Diagonal vistas spread on all sides. Space seems to flow directionlessly around us while we walk in the church. A proof of the master builders' conscious development are the cases in which a choir in the new Late Gothic style was added without any æsthetic mediation to an earlier nave. This is for instance the case at St. Lawrence's, Nuremberg, of 1445–72 (pl. XLIV). Having walked along the nave in the rigidly prescribed way of the Romanesque or earlier Gothic basilica, the entrance into the wider and higher choir with nave and aisles of identical width comes as a startling surprise. Bays are wider, piers slenderer, vaults of a rich star-like configuration (as created by the English nearly 200 years before), weighing down the vertical push of the piers. These have no capitals (again a motif of English priority), and so the streams of energy conducted upwards flew away undammed into ribs extending in all directions.[1] The sculptural decoration of the choir emphasises its spatial freedom. The magnificent stone spire of the tabernacle (now, I understand, destroyed by a bomb) rises in an asymmetrical position into the vault, and the huge locket of Veit Stoss's wood-carved Annunciation hangs down, joyful and transparent, into the space in front of the altar, so that you see it against the light of the central upper window. There are two rows of windows all the way round, and this, as the close pattern of the star-vault, adds weight to the horizontals. The classic Gothic *excelsior* is effectively (and no doubt consciously) broken. The earth claims her own against heaven. The clouds of the Reformation were gathering. Luther was born before

---

[1] Some of the latest and best German churches of this period (e.g., Annaberg) have octagonal piers with concave sides—a particularly clear indication of the tendency to make the space of nave and aisles surge up from all directions against the stone divisions. The same type of piers occurs in Cotswold churches (Chipping Campden). Flying ribs as in the sacristy of Bristol, incidentally, are also a speciality of the boldest of these Late Gothic German churches.

the tabernacle and the Annunciation were commissioned. The discrepancy between interiors of undulating flow, in which the individual may lose himself as between the trees of a forest, and exteriors of powerful solidity with unbroken walls and two rows of windows, heralds the mood of the German Reformation, torn between mystical introspection and a hearty new thrust into this world. Moreover, the new rooms of German Late Gothic had a practical advantage—the same as the aisleless halls of the Italian friars: they were evidently much better suited for listening to long sermons than the old interiors with parallel and separated avenues.

However, practical considerations alone did not create the new style, nor can it be said that the spirit of the coming Reformation alone created it. For it is just as noticeable in Spain as in Germany. In Spanish architecture of the 15th century there was a good deal of German influence. Masters from Cologne and Nuremberg were called to Burgos and established such German motifs as star-vaults and net-vaults. But these masons and stone-carvers from the North would hardly have been so successful if there had not been an indigenous Spanish trend towards the new Late Gothic expression. The star-vaults seemed no more than a variation of the theme of the Mohammedan dome with its flying ribs forming stars of many kinds. The conciseness of the classic French cross-vaults and indeed classic French ideals altogether had not appealed to Spaniards. As in Germany, imitation of French Gothic is rare, and as in Germany there are wide aisles, although they are lower than the nave (that is basilican), and side chapels between the buttresses so that the exteriors seem flat and less articulated than those of the 13th century —again two clear proofs of the tendency towards one unified room (fig. 36).

This tendency is nowhere more obvious than in Catalonia, not until 1479 united with Central and Northern Spain. The typical Catalan plan of the 14th and 15th centuries—closely connected with Southern French plans such as that of Albi—is a wide aisleless or aisled hall with side chapels between the buttresses and a very wide shallow apse. The exteriors are bare as in Germany, the interiors spacious and plain, the right kind to hold the large congregations of the prosperous trading towns of the Catalan coast. Again this practical advantage may have had something to do with the plan chosen. But it is hardly enough to explain the interesting case of Gerona Cathedral, which had been begun in the French way with a choir, ambulatory and radiating chapels in 1312. When these eastern parts were complete, work for some reason stopped, and it was not until 1416 that the then master-mason, Guillermo Boffiy, suggested the adding of a new nave. His daring suggestion was a nave without aisles the width of apse and ambulatory put together. There was opposition amongst

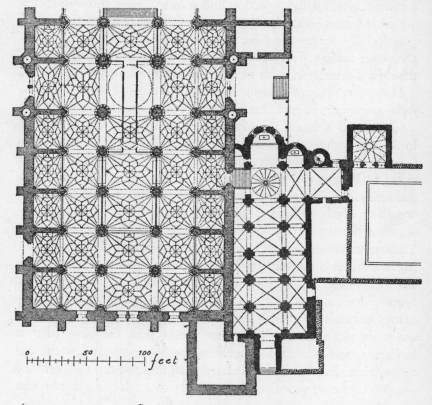

36. JUAN GIL DE HONTAÑON: SALAMANCA CATHEDRAL, BEGUN 1512. ON THE RIGHT THE OLD CATHEDRAL.

the cathedral authorities, and so—a curiously modern idea—a commission was appointed to decide. Its members were twelve leading architects. Their answers have been preserved. Seven members were in favour of continuing the basilican scheme westward, but five were taken with Boffiy's idea. In 1417, in fact, Boffiy was committed to start on his scheme. It is a masterpiece of building technique, with a clear span of 73 feet, one of the widest vaulted rooms of mediæval Europe (fig. 37). The weight of the vaults is in the usual Spanish way carried by internal buttresses with chapels in

the interstices. The room is somewhat bare, as the friars' churches of
Tuscany, but it has a great power, and it certainly is, with its sharp
contrast of one room in the west and a system of three spatial units
of staggered height and width in the east, the most convincing proof
of the change of style from High to Late Gothic.

But when did the one phase end and the other begin? Our Spanish
and German examples were of the 15th century, our examples from

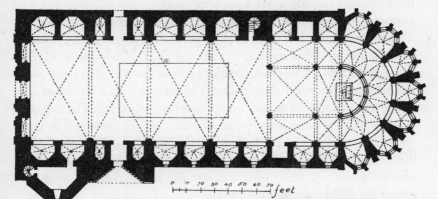

England of the early years of the
14th. The nave of Gerona is plain
and solid, without mystery. So are
at least the exteriors of the Late
Gothic churches of Germany. Their
interiors on the other hand are full
of movement, unrestrained in feeling, romantically rich and romantically vague. They share these
qualities with Bristol and Ely.
Neither Bristol, however, nor Ely
aims at the contrast of square exterior volume and floating interior
space. Nor did Britain, even at
the late date of the Nuremberg
choir of St. Lawrence's, go to such

37. GUILLERMO BOFFIY: GERONA
CATHEDRAL. THE ARCHITECT ADDED
TO A 14TH-CENTURY CHOIR WITH
AMBULATORY A NAVE WITHOUT AISLES
TO THE WIDTH OF CHOIR AND AMBU-
LATORY. BEGUN 1417.

extremes. Nevertheless British architectural style had changed sig-
nally between 1300 and 1450. The change is so obvious that, while
for the Continent the terms High and Late Gothic are sufficient to
indicate the chief stages, English tradition has for more than a hundred years preferred a division into three Gothic phases: Early

English, Decorated and Perpendicular. Early English was at an end when the Angel Choir was growing. Decorated is the style of Bristol and Ely. Perpendicular corresponds to what we have seen of Late Gothic in Germany and Spain, and it is a contribution of equal national vigour. Once it had been created by a few strong-minded, clear-headed architects, it brushed aside all the vagaries of Decorated and settled down to a long, none too adventurous development of a plain-spoken idiom, sober and wideawake. People have tried to connect the coming of this new style with the Black Death of 1349. This is wrong; for it is there in all its perfection as early as 1331 in the south transept and as early as 1337 in the choir of Gloucester Cathedral (pl. xxxvii). The thick circular piers of the Norman choir were left standing but with their galleries hidden behind a screen of lean uprights and horizontals divided up into rows of panels. The east wall was opened into one huge window with, except for the few main partitions, nothing but a system of glazed panels. The number of horizontal divisions invalidates all that might have been left of the upward soar of earlier Gothic architecture. In this the same new tendency is visible as in the double row of windows in German churches. But while on the Continent the walls were made solid too, English Perpendicular walls remained glass screens. And just as thus the wall structure was less drastically changed than in Germany or Spain, so the spatial character of Perpendicular rooms returned—under renewed influence, it seems, of French buildings of about 1240 to 1330—to the clarity of the High Gothic style. Basilican plans were only very rarely given up in favour of the spatially more promising aisled-hall plan of Bristol and Germany. The only fanciful feature in Gloucester and indeed in many other Perpendicular parts of cathedral and abbey churches is the decoration of the vaults (pl. xxxviii). There is as much imagination displayed in them as in the German and Spanish vaults. In fact neither of these two countries, let alone France, has produced anything so complicated as the scheme of Gloucester at so early a date. On the other hand, Perpendicular vault decoration is harsher than that of Continental Late Gothic, just as Perpendicular tracery is harsher than German, Spanish or French tracery of about 1500 (or than English tracery of 1320). The ribs of Gloucester form patterns as abstract and as angular as the matchsticks on the walls of Earl's Barton tower three hundred years before, patterns equally remote from the luxuriance of Ely, the resilience of Lincoln and the structural logicality of classic French rib-vaults.

Of structural logicality especially there is none in Perpendicular vaults. These close-knit patterns of ribs have no longer anything to do with vault construction. The main transverse ribs and cross ribs are no longer distinguishable from the innumerable tiercerons (i.e. ribs connecting the caps of the vault shafts with points on the ridge-rib) and liernes (i.e. ribs neither springing from the vault shafts nor leading to any of the main crossings). The whole is in fact a solidly built tunnel-vault with plenty of decoration applied to it. The use of the term tunnel-vault implies that the effect of Perpendicular vaults is as much an emphasis on the horizontal, as it were, lid character as the star-vaults of Germany and Spain. This interpretation is confirmed by the general substitution in English Perpendicular exteriors of low-pitched, often parapeted roofs for the higher pitch of the 12th and 13th centuries.

Gloucester is the most consistent example of the Perpendicular in English cathedrals. The naves of Winchester and Canterbury (chiefly of the later 14th century) are less uncompromising. In other cathedrals the late Middle Ages did little major work. To find English architecture of 1350 to 1525 at its best, one should not visit cathedrals and abbey churches, one should go to the manor-houses and parish churches for the happiest ensembles and to the royal chapels for the highest architectural standard. This change in the relative importance of buildings is due to social and historical reasons.

Taking domestic architecture first, what had happened between the age of Harlech and that of, e.g., Penshurst in Kent (pl. xxxix) begun, it seems, in 1341, is that half a century of internal peace had made owners of large houses in the country give up thoughts of military defence and allow themselves more domestic comforts. The extremely compact arrangement of rooms in the earlier castles was no longer necessary. Its essentials were kept—the hall as the centre of household life, with the high-table for the lord and his family at one end, the entrance and a screened-off gangway at the other, a parlour or chamber with perhaps a solar above beyond the high-table end of the hall, and kitchen, pantry, larders, buttery etc., on the other side of the screens—but more rooms were added and the hall itself was provided with larger windows of several lights and a bay-window at the high-table end. The grandest of surviving 14th-century halls is John of Gaunt's at Kenilworth, 90 by 45 feet in size. In some houses at that time a separate dining-room must already have existed. That appears from a passage in *Piers Plowman*. It means a first step towards the desertion of the hall as the living-room and dining-room of everybody, master and men. But nearly three centuries had to pass by after Penshurst had been designed, before the hall had finally become a vestibule and nothing else.

It took nearly as long to recover the principle of symmetry for the English house which had governed the plans of Harlech and Beaumaris with such splendid success. In the 14th and 15th centuries a manor-house, or, for that matter, a French *château* and a *Burg* in Germany, were picturesque agglomerations of rooms. Symmetry did not go farther than that sometimes in the 15th and early 16th

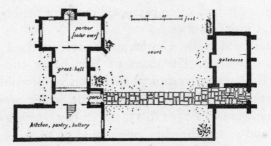

38.   COTHAY MANOR, SOMERSET, LATE 15TH CENTURY.

centuries one straight axis runs from the gate-house to the entrance of the hall. But the hall was not the exact centre of the main block, and its entrance was eccentric anyway. The gate-house, even when it was in the middle of the outer front, did not separate identical halves (fig. 38). The results of this undisturbed growth are in Britain, as well as in France and Germany, extremely charming. But if one enquires about strictly æsthetic qualities, they are certainly not as high as those of Harlech.

A comparison between the English cathedral of the 13th century and the English parish church of the 15th shows the same changes. They are largely due to social developments. A new class had come into its own, the class responsible for the erection of the scores of splendid parish churches in Germany and in the Netherlands, and the class to which in France the business-minded royal administrators of the William of Nogaret type, in Italy the Medici and their friends and competitors and in Northern Germany the leaders of the Hanseatic League belonged. In England Richard the Lion-

Hearted had been on the throne when Lincoln and Wells were designed, and Henry III, the Saintly King as Rome called him, ruled
when Salisbury and the new Westminster Abbey were designed.
Simon de Montfort stood up against Henry III, a hero of the national
English cause against too papal a policy, when the Angel Choir was
added to Lincoln Cathedral. Less than a hundred years later, Edward
III, who was crowned in 1327 and died in 1377, accepted with pleasure the honour of membership in the London Guild of the Merchant
Taylors, i.e. the cloth merchants of the City. This is an eminently
revealing fact, especially if it is viewed in conjunction with commercial and industrial developments in the Netherlands, Germany,
Tuscany and Catalonia. In England the age of Edward III saw a rapid
development of business enterprise. Flemish weavers were called
into the country, trade interests played a considerable part in the
vicissitudes of the Hundred Years War. Vast capitals were accumu-
lated by men such as Dick Whittington and John Poulteney, whose
country seat was Penshurst. In fact more of the manor-houses of the
late Middle Ages were owned by merchants or their descendants
than is usually realised. After the decimation of the old aristocracy
caused by the Wars of the Roses, the proportion of *nouveaux riches*
amongst the peers of the realm grew ever more rapidly, until in the
council of sixteen whom Henry VIII named to reign for his little
son, not one was a peer of twelve years' standing.

Thus by 1500 the most active patrons of art were the king and the
towns. The Crown had, about 1330, built St. Stephen's Chapel in
the Palace of Westminster which was burnt in 1834. Judging from
surviving drawings it must have been a building of great artistic
importance. Then in the 15th century Henry VI and VII built Eton
College Chapel (begun in 1441), King's College Chapel, Cambridge
(begun in 1446), Henry VII and VIII St. George's Chapel, Windsor
Castle (begun in 1481), and Henry VIII the Chapel of Henry VII at
the east end of Westminster Abbey (1503-19). They are buildings
of extremely simple exteriors and plans, but with plenty of master-
fully executed decoration. The contrast is especially poignant at Cambridge. To design this long, tall, narrow box of a college chapel
(pl. XLII), no spatial genius was needed. There is no differentiation
at all between nave and choir. The decoration too is repetitive, the
same window tracery is used twenty-four times, and the same
panelled fan-vaulting motif. They were rationalists, the men who
designed and enjoyed these buildings, proud constructors, of a bold-

ness not inferior to that of the Catalans. Yet they succeeded—and here we are faced with the same problem as in the contemporary German churches—in combining this practical, matter-of-fact spirit with a sense of mystery and an almost oriental effusion of ornament. Standing at the west end of the nave one can hardly think of the supreme economy with which this effect of exuberance has been attained. The fan-vault in particular helps, wherever it is used, to create an atmosphere of heavy luxuriance. Yet it is an eminently rational vault, a technician's invention, one is inclined to surmise. It originated from the vault designs of chapter-houses and their development into the palm-like spread of bunches of ribs towards a heavily bossed ridge-rib in the choir (early 14th century) and then the nave of Exeter. That had been the spatial imagination of the Decorated at its boldest moment. Then the Perpendicular came in and systematised and solidified it all, again first at Gloucester, in the east walk of the cloisters (1357–77). By giving all ribs the same length, the same distance from each other and the same curvature, and by applying the ubiquitous panelling to the spandrels, the palm-vault of Exeter is converted into the fan-vault of Gloucester.

This system the king's masons used at Cambridge, men who, although at this advanced hour in the development of mediæval architecture they are sometimes already mentioned with their names in documents as surveyors of works and directors of works, were still by training and experience in the same category as Villard de Honnecourt and the masters of the English and French cathedrals. But as members of the king's household they now very gradually began to advance into the status of civil servants. This development went on into the 17th century. Not until then were the royal architects in France and also in England primarily civil servants.

In the 14th century a man such as Henry Yevele (died 1400) appears more as the successful London mason and contractor and distinguished member of his city guild than as a royal architect in the modern sense. We find his name coupled in one document with Chaucer's, in another with Dick Whittington's. So we imagine him in his stately fur-lined robes (which incidentally were part of his salary from the king) in his house by St. Magnus, London Bridge, or one of his two manor-houses in Kent. Of work by him, the masonry on Westminster Hall (1394–1402) survives. Such men, dignitaries of their guilds and the fraternities to which they belonged, built the stately town halls of England, the Netherlands and the cities of the Hanseatic League. They also built the halls of the London city companies, and they built the parish churches with their guild chapels. In designing them they felt that they were working for themselves and their equals; that was a more intimate connection between architect and building than had existed before. It gives its own peculiar atmosphere to the Late Gothic parish church. The largest of them are no less lofty than cathedrals and abbey churches. The

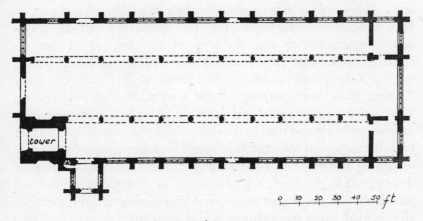

39. ST. NICHOLAS, KING'S LYNN, NORFOLK, 1414–19.

tallest of all mediæval spires in Europe is that of Ulm Minster, which is a parish church. St. Mary Redcliffe in Bristol covers a larger area than many a cathedral. Prosperous small towns such as Lavenham in Suffolk and dozens of others had parish churches in which the whole local population could assemble, and the villagers from the neighbourhood still find accommodation. York has (or had before the Second World War) twenty-one surviving mediæval churches besides the Minster.

Where existing churches were not entirely pulled down, they were enlarged, aisles were widened, naves heightened, new aisles or chapels added to the old, and the result is the picturesque, happy-go-lucky irregularity of plan and elevation of most English parish churches. However, while such churches may reflect most truly the history of their towns from the Anglo-Saxon to the Tudor age, they do not really reflect the æsthetic vision of any one period. What the

71

15th century in England desired the chief parish church of a prosperous town to look like appears in such a building as St. Nicholas,
King's Lynn. The church (fig. 39) was erected as a chapel of ease
from 1414 to 1419. One plan is responsible for the whole building,
and that plan is as uncomplicated as those of the contemporary royal
chapels. It consists of a rectangle of 162 by 70 feet, within which are
comprised nave and aisles as well as aisled chancel. There is no
structural articulation between west and east parts. All that inter-
feres with the uniformity of the outline is the tower taken over
from a previous building, the porch and the slightly projecting
apse. This sturdy plainness is no doubt a reflection of a change of
taste which the friars' architecture had brought about. It is evidently in accordance with the style of the exteriors of German
churches. But inside such churches as St. Nicholas, King's Lynn,
or the two parish churches of Coventry (pl. XL), or Holy
Trinity, Hull, have nothing of the romanticism of Nuremberg.
They stick to the traditional basilican elevation, piers are thin,
mouldings wiry and tracery is of the straightforward Perpendicular
type. There are no corners left in mysterious semi-darkness, nor any
surprising vistas. Where the fantasy of the Late Gothic designer
shows itself in the English parish church is in wooden screens and
wooden roofs. An almost inconceivable profusion of screens originally divided naves from choirs, aisle chapels from nave chapels and
the many guild chapels from the public spaces. The most lavishly
decorated are in Devon on the one hand, in East Anglia on the other.
But the greatest glory of the English parish churches are their timber
roofs (pl. XLI), roofs constructed as boldly by the carpenter as any
Gothic stone vaults by masons, and looking as intricate and technically thrilling as any configuration of flying buttresses around the
east end of a cathedral. There is a variety of types: the tie-beam roof,
the arch-braced roof, the hammerbeam roof (devised for Westminster Hall by Yevele's colleague, the King's master carpenter,
Hugh Herland in 1380), the double hammerbeam roof and others.
The most ingenious of them all is the one of the unaisled church of
Needham Market looking like a whole three-aisled building hover-
ing over our heads without any visible support from below. The
continent has nothing to emulate these achievements of a ship-
building nation. They are, in fact, strongly reminiscent of ships' keels
upside down.

Such roofs add a quality of structural richness to English churches which they would otherwise lack. However even they, looked at in detail, appear with their hard lines of rafters, purlins and braces sinewy, sharp and angular—as English in fact as the ribs of Gloucester choir and the decoration of Earl's Barton tower—directly one compares them with contemporary work in France, Germany or Spain and Portugal.

For even in France the 15th century had brought a belated acceptance of the principles which in England had been incorporated in the Decorated style. Flamboyant is the French term for their Late

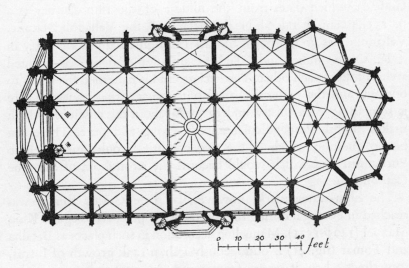

40. ROUEN: ST. MACLOU, BEGUN 1434.

Gothic, and some of the most enchanting examples of it are to be found in Normandy, for instance the main portal, the library court and the Tour de Beurre of Rouen Cathedral, and—in a spatially more interesting way—the church of St. Maclou at Rouen, begun in 1434 (fig. 40).

As for Spain, the briefest comparison between an English parish church or even King's College Chapel and, say, the decoration of the front of the church of St. Paul's at Valladolid (begun shortly after 1486, probably by Simon of Cologne; pl. XLIII) is sufficient to realise the contrast between English restraint and Spanish extremism. Substitute the St. Lawrence portal of Strassburg Cathedral (pl. XLV) for Valladolid, and you would see Anglo-German contrasts as glaringly.

It might be said that German Late Gothic decoration is as extreme as Spanish, which would not be surprising, since Germany and Spain, as against France, England, Italy, are the countries of the extremes in European civilisation. However, there are obvious differences between the Spanish and the German ways of decorating. Ever since Mohammedan days Spain has had a passion for filling large surfaces with close-knit two-dimensional ornament. The Germans share this *horror vacui*, but there is always a marked spatial curiosity in their ornament. That connects German Late Gothic with German Rococo just as the flatness and the frantic movement of the Charterhouse vestry at Granada, which dates from the middle of the 18th century (see p. 133), seems heralded in the details of the Valladolid facade. Valladolid has no dominant motifs. The figure sculpture is petty in scale. Ogee arches and "Tudor" arches (i.e. depressed pointed arches) follow each other. The background is patterned from top to bottom, and the patterns change with every string course. There is something of a thistly undergrowth about this ensemble which makes English Perpendicular appear strong and pure. There can be no question which of the two countries would open itself to Puritanism and which would become the stronghold of Baroque Catholicism.

The high-water mark, however, of Late Gothic frenzy was reached in Portugal during the spectacularly prosperous age of King Manuel (1495–1521). Manueline decoration in such places as Batalha and Tomar (fig. 41) is outrageously rich, a rank growth of forms, sometimes taken, it seems, from crustacean organisms, sometimes from tropical vegetation. Much Portuguese decoration was inspired by Spain and France, but here the architecture of India, Portuguese India, is the only parallel that comes to mind. If this connection is real it is the first instance in Western history of non-European influence on European art.

However, no influence can ever act, unless the one party is ready to receive the message of the other. If the countries of the Pyrenean Peninsula had not already been possessed by a passion for overdone decoration, the art of the colonies would have remained mute to them. When the Indies became Dutch, their style did indeed after a time begin to influence the furniture of Holland and helped to give it its peculiar Baroque opulence, but architects wisely kept away from it. The Dutchmen of the 17th century could never have made of it what the Portuguese could, at that particular moment, the moment just before the ornamental imagination of the late Middle Ages was harnessed into the Renaissance yoke.

The Renaissance on the other hand could never have been conceived in a country which had as recklessly indulged in ornamental vagaries as Spain and Portugal, or as daringly explored spatial mysteries as Germany. In Italy there thus exists no Late Gothic style at all—the most striking illustration of the fact that by the 15th century the present natural divisions of Europe were more or less established. The Romanesque style had been international though regionally subdivided, just as the Holy Roman Empire and the Church of the 11th and 12th centuries had been international forces. Then, in the 13th century, France became a nation and created the Gothic style.

Germany went through the crisis of the Interregnum and decided on a national, as against the previous international policy. The same decision was taken at the same time in England, while in Italy a wholly different development of many small town-states set in. Gothic came into Germany, Spain, England and Italy as a French fashion. Cistercian monasteries first, and then Cologne, Burgos and León, Canterbury and Frederick II's Castel del Monte (see p. 54) followed it closely. But already in Frederick II's Italian buildings there appear purely antique pediments side by side with the novel rib-vaults of France. The appreciative treatment of Roman motifs in Frederick II's Capua Gate is unparalleled anywhere in the North, and in the South only by Nicolò Pisano's pulpits. Nicolò Pisano was the first of the great Italian sculptors, the first in whose work the Italian character dominates over international conventions. His transformation of the current style in sculpture into something more static and more harmonious was paralleled by similar transformations of Gothic architecture. The rôle of the friars in this transformation has been mentioned. There is no *excelsior* in their wide, airy, aisleless halls. The large ones with aisles, such as S. Maria Novella and S. Croce in Florence, have such wide arcades and such shallow aisles that the static nature of the rooms is hardly disturbed. The cathedral of Florence—a cathedral, but due to the financial enterprise of the guild of the wool merchants—belongs to the same family (pl. XLVI). Its piers with their substantial bases and heavy capitals do not point upward. The uninterrupted cornice provides a strong horizontal division. The cross-vaults are dome-shaped, and clearly isolate bay from bay. Clarity is also the expression of the dark structural members against the whitewashed surfaces of walls and vaults. To the traveller coming from the North these Italian interiors of the 14th century appear spacious, restful and serene.

It was only here—this will now be appreciated—that the style of the Renaissance could be conceived, here, in the land of Roman traditions, of sun, blue sea and noble hills, of vineyards and olive plantations, of pine groves, cedars and cypress trees.

41. TOMAR, WINDOW OF CHAPTER-HOUSE, *c.* 1520.

CHAPTER V

Renaissance and Mannerism

c. 1420–c. 1600

THE Gothic style was created for Suger, Abbot of St. Denis, councillor of two kings of France, the Renaissance for the merchants of Florence, bankers to the kings of Europe. It is in the atmosphere of the most prosperous of Southern trading republics that about 1420 the new style emerged. A firm such as that of the Medici had its representatives in London, in Bruges and Ghent, in Lyons and Avignon, in Milan and Venice. A Medici had been Mayor of Florence in 1296, another in 1376, yet another in 1421. In 1429 Cosimo Medici became senior partner of the firm. Just over one hundred years later another Medici was created the first Duke of Tuscany. But Cosimo, whom they called in Florence the Father of the Fatherland, and his grandson Lorenzo the Magnificent, were only citizens, not even, by any official title, the first of their city. To these and to the other princely merchants, the Pitti, the Rucellai, the Strozzi, it is due that the Renaissance was at once wholeheartedly accepted in Florence and developed with a wonderful unanimity of purpose for thirty or forty years, before other cities of Italy, let alone foreign countries, had grown to understand its meaning.

This predisposition of Tuscany cannot be explained by social conditions alone. The cities of Flanders in the 15th century were socially of quite a comparable structure; so up to a point was the City of London. Yet the style in the Netherlands was a flamboyant Late Gothic; in England it was Perpendicular. In Florence what happened was that a particular social situation coincided with a particular nature of country and people, and a particular historical tradition. The geographical and national character of the Tuscans had found its earliest expression in Etruscan art. They were again clearly noticeable in the 11th century in the crisp and graceful facade of S. Miniato (pl. XXIII) and in the 14th in the spacious, happily airy Gothic churches of S. Croce, S. Maria Novella and the cathedral of S. Maria del Fiore (pl. XLVI). Now a flourishing trading republic will tend to worldly ideals, not to the transcendental; to the active, not to meditation; to clarity, not to the obscure. And since the climate was clear, keen and salutary, and the people's minds clear, keen and proud, it was here that the clear, proud and worldly spirit of Roman Antiquity could be rediscovered, that its contrast with Christian faith did not bar its way, that its attitude to physical beauty in the fine arts and beauty of proportion in architecture found an echo, that its grandeur and its humanity were understood. The fragments of the Roman past in art and literature had been there all the time, and had never been entirely forgotten. But only the 14th century reached a point that made a cult of the Antique possible. Petrarch—the first Poet Laureate of modern times, crowned on the Capitol in 1341—was a Tuscan; so was Boccaccio, so was Leonardo Bruni who translated Plato. And as the Medici honoured the philosophers and called them into their innermost circle, as they honoured the poets and wrote poetry themselves, so they regarded the artists in a spirit quite different from that of the Middle Ages. The modern conception of the artist and the respect due to his genius is again of Tuscan origin.

Seven years before Petrarch was crowned in Rome, the civic authorities responsible for the appointment of a new master-mason to the cathedral and city of Florence decided to elect Giotto, the painter, because they were convinced that the city architect should be "a famous man" above all. So for the sole reason that they believed that "in the whole world no one better could be found in this and many other things" than Giotto, they chose him, although he was not a mason at all. Now this marks the beginning of a new period in the professional history of architecture, just as Petrarch's crowning marks a new period in the history of the social status of authors. Henceforth—this is especially characteristic of the Renaissance—great architects were not usually architects by training. And henceforth great artists were honoured and admitted into positions outside their craft simply because they were great artists. Cosimo Medici is probably the first who called a painter, in recognition of his genius, divine. Later this became the attribute universally given to Michelangelo. And he, sculptor, painter and architect, a fanatical worker and a man who never spared himself, was deeply convinced that it was his due. When he felt slighted by some of the pope's servants in an ante-room of the Vatican, he fled from Rome, deserting his post without hesitation and leaving a message that the pope could look for him elsewhere, if he wanted him. Leonardo da Vinci at the time when this happened evolved the theory of the ideal nature of art. He endeavoured to prove that painting and architecture were of the liberal arts, not arts in the trade sense of the Middle Ages. There are two sides to this theory. It demands from the patron a new attitude towards the artist, but also from the artist a new attitude towards his work. Only the artist who approached his art in an academic spirit, that is as a seeker after law, had a right to be regarded as their equal by the scholars and authors of humanism.

Leonardo has not much to say about Antiquity. But the universal fascination of Antiquity was evidently both æsthetic and social, æsthetic in so far as the forms of Roman architecture and decoration appealed to artists and patrons of the 15th century, social in so far as the study of the Roman past was accessible to the educated only. So the artist and architect who until then had been satisfied with learning their craft from their masters and developing it according to tradition and their powers of imagination, now devoted their attention to the art of Antiquity, not only because it enchanted them but also because it conferred social distinction on them. So strongly had this revival impressed the scholars from the 16th to the 19th century that they called the whole period that of rebirth, *rinascita* or Renaissance. Early writers by using this term meant the rebirth of art and letters in quite a general sense. But in the 19th century— a century of unlimited period revival—the emphasis was laid on the imitation of Roman forms and motifs. In re-examining the works of the Renaissance to-day, one must however ask oneself whether the new attitude towards Antiquity is really their essential innovation.

The very first building in Renaissance forms is Brunelleschi's Foundling Hospital, begun in 1419 (pl. XLVIII). Brunelleschi (1377–1446) was a goldsmith by training. Yet he had been chosen to complete the cathedral of Florence by adding the dome over the crossing, a masterpiece of construction and of a shape distinctly Gothic in character. At the same time, however, he designed the Foundling facade, a work of a completely different kind, consisting of a colonnade on the ground floor with delicate Corinthian columns and wide semicircular arches letting enough sun and warmth penetrate into the loggia, and a first floor with generously spaced moderately sized rectangular windows under shallow pediments corresponding exactly to the arches beneath. Medallions in coloured terra-cotta by della Robbia—the famous babes in swaddling clothes sold in cheap copies of all sizes by the souvenir-dealers of Florence—are placed into the

spandrels of the arcade. A subtly scaled architrave divides ground
floor from first floor. Now the pediments over the windows are
certainly a Roman motif. So seem to be the Corinthian columns.
But arches on such slender columns are really in their expression
just as different from those of, say, the Colosseum, as they are from
any Gothic arcades. Their source and that of several other motifs
of the facade is the Tuscan Proto-Renaissance of S. Miniato
(pl. XXIII), i.e. the architecture of Florence in the 11th and 12th

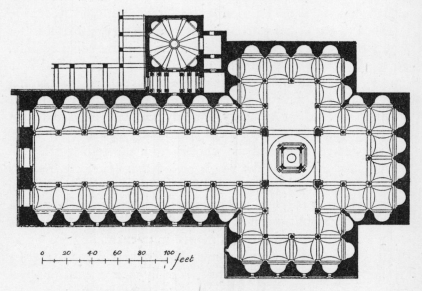

42.   FILIPPO BRUNELLESCHI: STO. SPIRITO, FLORENCE, BEGUN 1435.

centuries, and nothing else. This is an eminently significant fact.
The Tuscans, unconsciously of course, prepared themselves for the
reception of the Roman style by first going back to their own
Romanesque Proto-Renaissance.

The relation of Brunelleschi's churches to the past is very similar.
Sto. Spirito (pl. XLVII and fig. 42), which he designed in 1435, is a
basilica with round-headed arcades and a flat roof; Romanesque,
one can say, in these general characteristics. The bases and capitals of
the Corinthian columns, on the other hand, and the fragments of an
entablature above are Roman, rendered with a correctness and understanding of their vigorous beauty that were beyond the power of
the architects of the Proto-Renaissance. The curious niches of the
aisles are also Roman, though treated in a very original way. But

while the motifs mentioned so far can be traced back to the Middle Ages or Antiquity, the spatial expression created with their aid is wholly new and has all the delicacy and serenity of the Early Renaissance. The nave is just twice as high as it is wide. Ground floor and clerestory are of equal height. The aisles have square bays, again half as wide as they are high. The nave consists of exactly four and a half squares, and the odd half was intended to be disposed of in a special way to be mentioned presently. Walking through the church, one may not at once consciously register all these proportions, but they contribute all the same decisively to the effect of serene order which the interior produces. It is difficult to-day to imagine the enthusiasm of the Early Renaissance for such simple mathematical relations in space. One must remember in order to appreciate it that at that very moment—about 1425—painters in Florence discovered the laws of perspective. Just as they had no longer been satisfied with an arbitrary presentation of the space inside their pictures, so architects were now anxious to find rational proportions for their buildings. The effort of the 15th century to master space is only comparable with that of our own age, although that of the Renaissance concerned an ideal world and ours a material. The invention of printing towards the middle of the century proved a most powerful conquest of space. The discovery of America towards its end produced results nearly as important. Both must be named with the discovery of perspective as aspects of Western space enthusiasm, an attitude utterly alien to Antiquity, and one to which attention has already been drawn more than once in this book.

The feature of Sto. Spirito most important in this connection is the ground plan of its eastern parts. For here Brunelleschi has departed decisively from the normal composition of Romanesque or Gothic churches. The way in which he made the transepts exactly identical with the choir, ran an aisle round all three and placed a dome over the crossing makes us feel, looking eastward, as if we were in a centrally planned building, a type usual in Roman architecture, both religious and secular, but very rare in mediæval Christian churches.

Even the west end was intended to be finished in a way stressing this centralising tendency at the expense of practical advantages. Brunelleschi had originally meant to continue the aisle round the west as round the east, north and south ends. He would then have had to put in four instead of the customary three entrances, to comply with the four bays of aisle along the inner side of the facade. It would all have been exceedingly unusual—a sacrifice to æsthetic consistency and the desire for centralisation. Indeed, during the very year in which Sto. Spirito was begun, Brunelleschi had designed a completely central church, the first of the Renaissance. It is S. Maria degli Angeli (figs. 43 and 44). After three years, in 1437, the building was discontinued, and only ground-floor walls now remain. But we can read the plan and compare it with reliable engravings taken, it seems, from lost original drawings. S. Maria degli Angeli was to be wholly Roman in character and very massive, the outcome no doubt of a long stay of Brunelleschi in Rome to which we can with a good deal of certainty assign the date 1433. The light, slim columns of the other buildings are here replaced by pilasters attached to solid piers at the eight corners of the octagon. Eight chapels surround it, each with niches hollowed out into the thickness of the walls. The dome also was to be of one piece in side and out like a Roman dome and not on the Gothic principle of an outer and a separate inner shell, still applied by Brunelleschi to Florence Cathedral. Of Romanesque or Proto-Renaissance connections there are here none left. What Roman building in particular inspired Brunelleschi we can no longer say. There were plenty of remains still in existence in the 15th century and drawn by architects, which have now disappeared.

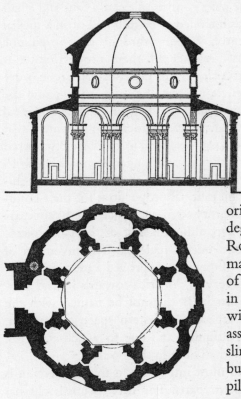

43 AND 44. FILIPPO BRUNELLESCHI: S. MARIA DEGLI ANGELI, FLORENCE, BEGUN 1434.

However, one more central
building, or rather part of a
building, was begun shortly
after S. Maria degli Angeli
and completed, and this is a
direct copy of an existing
Roman monument. Michel-
ozzo (1396–1472) began in
1445 to add to the mediæval
church of the SS. Annunziata
a round east end with eight
chapels or niches exactly as he
had seen it done in the so-called
temple of Minerva Medica

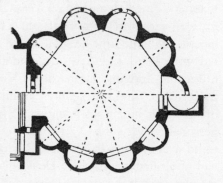

45. UPPER HALF: TEMPLE OF MINERVA MEDICA,
ROME, *c.* A.D. 250. LOWER HALF: MICHEL-
OZZO'S ROTUNDA AT THE EAST END OF THE SS.
ANNUNZIATA, FLORENCE, BEGUN 1444.

in Rome (fig. 45). So while in the early works of Brunelleschi we
cannot too much emphasise the independence of the new forms
from those of Roman antiquity, the discovery of how much could
be learned from Rome to satisfy topical æsthetic needs came as early
as the thirties and forties. That it appears most clearly in centrally
planned buildings is eminently characteristic. For a central plan is
not an other-worldly, but a this-worldly conception. The prime
function of the mediæval church had been to lead the faithful to
the altar. In a completely centralised building (fig. 44) no such
movement is possible. The building has its full effect only when it
is looked at from the one focal point. There the spectator must stand
and, by standing there, he becomes himself "the measure of all
things". Thus the religious meaning of the church is replaced by a
human one. Man is in the church no longer pressing forward to
reach a transcendental goal, but enjoying the beauty that surrounds
him and the glorious sensation of being the centre of this beauty.

No more telling symbol could have been conceived for the new
attitude of the humanists and their patrons to Man and religion.
Pico della Mirandola, one of the most interesting of the philosophers
round Lorenzo the Magnificent, delivered an address in 1486 on *The
Dignity of Man*. Machiavelli, a little later, wrote his book *The Prince*
to glorify the power of Man's will, and set it as the prime moving
force against the powers of religion that had up to his time inter-
fered with practical thought. And again a little later Count Castiglione composed his *Courtier* to show his contemporaries their ideal
of universal man. The courtier, he says, should be agreeable in his

manners, graceful, a good *causeur* and a good dancer, yet strong and fit, well versed in the pursuits of chivalry, riding, fencing and jousting. At the same time he should read poetry and history, be acquainted with Plato and Aristotle, understand all the arts, and practise music and drawing. Leonardo da Vinci was the first amongst artists to live up to this ideal: painter, architect, engineer and musician, one of the most ingenious scientists of his time, and enchanting in his personal ways. Only Christianity apparently did not occupy his mind at all. Lorenzo Valla, a Roman humanist, somewhat earlier had published his dialogue *De voluptate*, in which he openly praised the pleasures of the senses. The same Valla proved with a philological sagacity unknown before the rise of Humanism that the so-called Donation of Constantine, the document on which all papal claims to worldly domination rested, was faked. Yet he died a canon of the Lateran Cathedral in Rome. The philosophers of Florence founded an academy on Plato's model, kept Plato's supposed birthday as a holiday and preached a semi-Greek, semi-Christian religion in which Christ's love is mixed up with Plato's principle of divine love that makes us pine for beauty of soul and body in human beings. On one of the frescoes in the choir of Sta. Maria Novella an inscription can be read stating that the frescoes were completed in 1490, "when this loveliest of lands distinguished in riches, victories, arts and buildings enjoyed plenty, health and peace". About the same time Lorenzo the Magnificent wrote his most famous poem, which begins as follows:

> *Quant'è bella giovinezza.*
> *Che si fugge tuttavia.*
> *Chi vuol esser lieto sia.*
> *Di doman' non c'è certezza.*

The lines are well known, and rightly so. They are here quoted in Italian, because they should be remembered in all their original melodiousness. Literally translated they mean:

> *How lovely is youth.*
> *But it flies from us.*
> *If you want to be happy, be happy now.*
> *There is no certainty of to-morrow.*

Now these men, if they built a church, did not want to be reminded by its appearance of that uncertain to-morrow and of what may come after this life has ended. They wanted architecture to eternalise

the present. So they commissioned
churches as temples to their own
glory. The eastern rotunda of the
Annunziata was intended to be a
memorial in Florence to the Gon-
zaga, rulers of Mantua. At the same
time Francesco Sforza of Milan
seems to have thought of such a
temple. A record of what was intended survives in a medal of about
1460 by the sculptor Sperandio (fig.
46). It seems to represent a building
of perfectly symmetrical plan
though of a type not yet met with:
the Greek cross, that is the cross with
all arms of equal length. It was to
be covered with five domes, just
as Périgueux and St. Mark's in
Venice three or four hundred years
before. The design may be due to
that mysterious Florentine sculptor
and architect Antonio Filarete
(died about 1470), who worked
for Francesco Sforza from 1451 to
1465. His fame now rests mainly
on the Milan hospital, the Ospedale
Maggiore, which was begun in
1457, a vast enterprise not carried
on in elevation to his designs,
though in plan. The plan is remarkable in that it appears the first of
those large symmetrical piles with
many inner courtyards—nine at
Milan—taken up in the 16th and
17th centuries for such royal
schemes as the Escorial, the
Tuileries and Whitehall.

But Filarete's ambitions were for
planning on a yet grander scale. He
wrote a treatise on architecture,

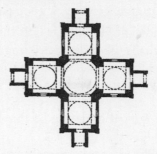

46. PROJECTED SFORZA CHAPEL,
MILAN. PLAN RECONSTRUCTED FROM
SPERANDIO'S MEDAL, c. 1460.

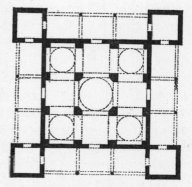

47. ANTONIO FILARETE: PROJECTED
CHAPEL FOR THE HOSPITAL, MILAN.
RECONSTRUCTED FROM THE ORIGINAL
DRAWING, c. 1455.

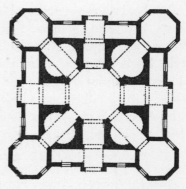

48. ANTONIO FILARETE: CHURCH FOR
ZAGALIA, RECONSTRUCTED FROM THE
ORIGINAL DRAWING, c. 1455-60.

85

dedicated in different copies to Francesco Sforza and one of the Medici of Florence, where the architect returned when he left Milan. Perhaps the most interesting part of the treatise is the description of an ideal town, Sforzinda; for this is the first wholly symmetrical town plan in Western history, a regular octagon with radial streets and with palace and cathedral on the square in the centre—again the central obsession of this first century liberated from the ties of mediæval authority.

Thus it is not surprising to find that the churches of Sforzinda, of Zagalia (another town drawn up in the treatise) and of the hospital —this church was never built either—were meant to be of central plan. They introduce us to yet more varieties. Sforzinda and the Hospital (fig. 47) are square with a central dome and subsidiary little domed chapels in the four corners—a plan for which an Early Christian (or rather 9th century) prototype existed at Milan, the Chapel of the Holy Sepulchre at S. Satiro and a Michelozzo proto-type at S. Maria delle Grazie at Pistoia (begun 1452). Zagalia (fig. 48) has an octagonal central dome and octagonal chapels in the corners. All three churches were to be provided with four fantastically tall minarets over the four corner chapels, or somewhere between them and the centre (for the drawings are ambiguous in this).[1] A chapel actually built at S. Eustorgio in Milan in 1462 to Michelozzo's designs is square and domed and has little turrets on the four corners, but no chapels below. Michelozzo also designed a palace for the Medici Bank at Milan. It was begun in the forms of Florentine Renaissance, but continued with the more irresponsible detail of the North Italian Gothic. The same happened to the hospital.

Lombardy was not yet capable of an understanding of the Renais-sance. Time and again we find that up to the middle of the 15th century and beyond only the Tuscans were at ease with the new style. Michelozzo and Filarete in Milan were Florentine, and of a Florentine family also came the greatest of Quattrocento architects, Leone Battista Alberti, to whose work we must now turn.

In Alberti (1404–72) we have again a new type of architect. Brunelleschi and Michelangelo are sculptor-architects, Giotto and

---

[1] The Warburg Institute kindly arranged for me to have the plan of the Zagalia church and some others specially photographed from Filarete's *Codice Maglia-becchiana* (Biblioteca Nazionale, Florence, II, 1, 140; già XVII, 30). The Zagalia plan is not illustrated in Lazzaroni and Muñoz's book on Filarete and has never been published before. Re-drawing was necessary for reasons of clarity and has been done by Miss Margaret Tallet.

Leonardo da Vinci painter-architects. Alberti is the first of the great dilettante-architects, a man of noble birth who first took an interest in art and architecture in the way Count Castiglione demands it from the educated courtier. He wrote a book on painting and one on the art of building (in Latin), and while working in Rome as a member of the papal civil service, work which left him plenty of free time to travel, he studied intensively the ruins of Antiquity. It is obvious that directly the essence of architecture was considered to be philosophy and mathematics (the divine laws of order and proportion) and archeology (the monuments of Antiquity), the theoretician and dilettante would assume a new significance. Roman architecture, both system and details, must be studied and drawn to be learnt; and the system behind the styles of Antiquity was soon —with the help of Vitruvius, the newly rediscovered Roman writer on architecture—found to lie in the orders, i.e. the proportions belonging to the Doric, Ionic, Corinthian, Composite and Tuscan columns and entablatures. By means of books on the orders foreign countries were taught the rules of classical building.

But Alberti was not a dry theorist. In him the spirit of the scholar lived in a rare and happy union with genuine imaginative and creative powers. The front of S. Francesco in Rimini (pl. L), begun in 1446 but never completed, is the first in Europe to adapt the composition of the Roman triumphal arch to church architecture. So Alberti was much more serious than Brunelleschi in reviving the Antique. And he did not confine himself to motifs. The side of the church, opened in seven round-headed niches with heavy piers dividing them, has perhaps more of the gravity of Flavian Rome than any other building of the 15th century. Now these niches hold sarcophagi, the monuments to the humanists of Sigismondo Malatesta's court. For the east end apparently a large dome was projected, as dominating as that of the Annunziata in Florence, and again as a monument to the glory of Sigismondo and his Isotta. Sigismondo was a typical Renaissance tyrant, unscrupulous and cruel but sincerely fascinated by the new learning and the new art. The church of S. Francesco is in fact known under the name of the Temple of the Malatesta; and on its facade an inscription runs in large letters with Sigismondo's name and the date—nothing else.

Again exactly the same pride is exhibited by Giovanni Rucellai, a merchant of Florence for whom Alberti designed the second of his church fronts. Again his name appears over-conspicuously on the facade of S. Maria Novella, and when in his old age he wrote an account of his life he said of the architectural and decorative work he had commissioned for the churches of his beloved native town: "All these things have given me, and are giving me, the greatest satisfaction and the sweetest feelings. For they do honour to the Lord, to Florence and to my own memory". It is this attitude that made it possible for the donors of the frescoes inside the choir of the same church to appear lifesize in the costumes of the day as if they were actors in the sacred stories. It is this attitude also that made the patricians of Florence—and the cardinals of Rome—build their Renaissance palaces. That of the Medici begun by Michelozzo in 1444 was the first (fig. 49), that of the Pitti, originally, it seems, designed by Alberti about 1458 and considerably enlarged a century later, and that of the Strozzi are the most famous. They are massive yet orderly, faced with heavily rusticated blocks and crowned by bold cornices. Their windows, symmetrically placed, are divided into two by graceful columns (a Romanesque motif again). What one expects of Renaissance delicacy and articulation is to be found chiefly in their inner courtyards. There the ground floors are opened as cloisters with the graceful arcades of the Foundling Hospital and Sto. Spirito, and the upper floors are also enlivened by an open gallery or pilasters dividing the walls into separate bays, or some such feature.

Only in Rome was a severer treatment of courtyards evolved. It appears first in the Palazzo Venezia, a building begun in 1455. It is derived from the classic Roman motif of columns attached to solid piers, the motif of the Colosseum and also of the front of Alberti's S. Francesco in Rimini. Maybe it was he who suggested its resuscitation in Rome, though his name cannot be documentarily connected with the Palazzo Venezia. A most attractive compromise between the Florentine and the Roman systems appears in the Ducal Palace at Urbino (pl. XLIX), another of the architecturally and altogether æsthetically most enterprising smaller courts of Italy. It is known that Luciano Laurana worked at Urbino between 1466 and his death in 1479. Probably we owe the courtyard to him. It preserves the airy lightness of the Florentine arcades, but emphasises the corners by pilasters. The result is the happiest balance, making Michelozzo's courtyard appear flimsy, and the Roman ones clumsy.

Alberti himself designed one palace in Florence, the Palazzo Rucellai (pl. LI), begun in 1446 for the same patron as the facade of S. Maria Novella. The courtyard here has no emphasis, but Alberti

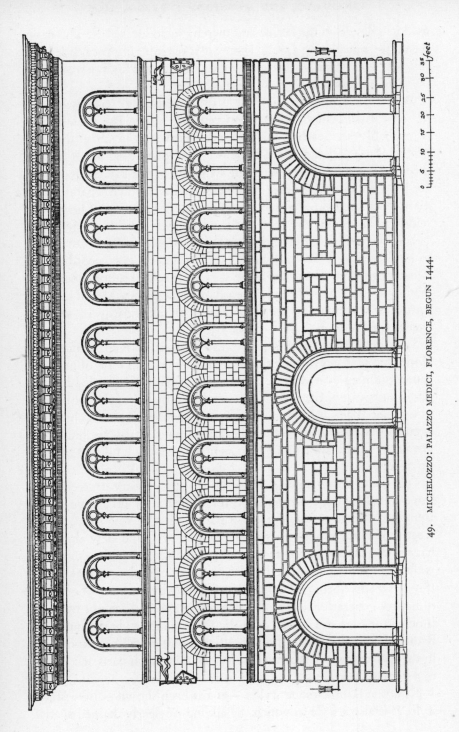

49. MICHELOZZO: PALAZZO MEDICI, FLORENCE, BEGUN 1444.

0 5 10 15 20 25 30 35 feet

used its pilasters in the facade and thereby introduces a splendid new means for articulating a wall. There are three superimposed orders of pilasters with a free Doric treatment on the ground floor, a free Ionic on the first floor and Corinthian on the top.

While these pilasters divide the front vertically, sensitively designed cornices emphasise the horizontal divisions. The top cornice is probably the earliest in Florence, earlier even than that of Michelozzo's Palazzo Medici. Before then projecting eaves in the mediæval way had been used. The windows of the Palazzo Rucellai are bipartite as in the other palaces, but an architrave separates the main rectangle from the two round heads. The relation of height to width in the rectangular parts of the windows is equal to the relation of height to width in the bays. Thus the position of every detail seems to be determined. No shifting is possible. In this lies, according to Alberti's theoretical writings, the very essence of beauty, which he defines as "the harmony and concord of all the parts achieved in such a manner that nothing could be added or taken away or altered except for the worse".

Such definitions make one feel the contrast of Renaissance and Gothic most sharply. In Gothic architecture the sensation of growth is predominant everywhere. The height of piers is not ruled by the width of bays, nor the depth of a capital, or rather a cap, by the height of the pier. The addition of chapels or even aisles to parish churches is much less likely to spoil the whole than in a Renaissance building. For in the Gothic style motif follows motif, as branch follows branch up a tree.

One could not imagine a donor in the 14th century decreeing, as Pope Pius II did when rebuilding the cathedral of his native town (renamed Pienza to perpetuate his name), that no one should ever erect sepulchral monuments in the church or found new altars, or have wall-paintings executed, or add chapels, or alter the colour of walls or piers. For a Gothic building is never complete in that sense. It remains a live being influenced in its destiny by the piety of generation after generation. And as its beginning and end are not fixed in time so they are not in space. In the Renaissance style the building is an æsthetic whole consisting of self-sufficient parts. A composition in the flat or in space is arrived at by grouping such parts according to a static system.

Now the Romanesque style is—as has been shown—also a static style. It is also a style in which the adding of clearly defined spatial

units is essential. How then can the difference in principle be formu-
lated between a Norman and a Renaissance church? Walls are
equally important in both, whereas the Gothic style always endeavours to invalidate them. But a Romanesque wall is primarily
inert. If it is ornamented, the exact place where decoration is applied
seems arbitrary. One hardly ever feels that a little more or a little
less ornament, or ornament shifted to a slightly higher or slightly
lower position, would make a decisive difference. In the Renaissance
building this is not so. The walls appear active, enlivened by the
decorative elements which in their sizes and arrangement follow
laws of human reasoning. It is ultimately this humanising that makes
a Renaissance building what it is. Arcades are airier and more open
than they had been. The graceful columns have the beauty of animate
beings. They keep to a human scale too, and as they lead from part
to part, even when a building is very large, one is never overwhelmed
by its sheer size. This, on the other hand, is just what the Norman
architect wishes to achieve. He conceives a wall as a whole and then
keeps the expression of might and mass to the smallest detail. Hence,
one need scarcely add, Romanesque sculptors could not yet re-
discover the beauty of the human body. This rediscovery, and the
discovery of linear perspective, had to come with the Renaissance.

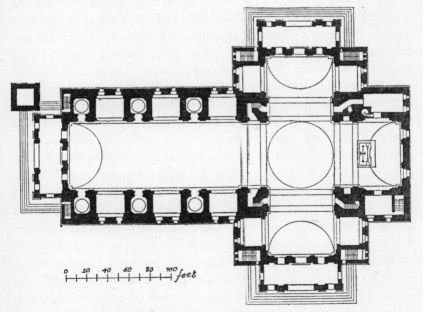

50.   LEONE BATTISTA ALBERTI: S. ANDREA, MANTUA, BEGUN 1470.

Sto. Spirito, or the Palazzo Rucellai, proves this to anyone susceptible to their specific character.

To illustrate the principle of an all-pervading order which Alberti postulates in an interior as well, the plan of S. Andrea in Mantua, Alberti's last work, may be analysed (fig. 50). As in Sto. Spirito the east parts are a central composition. Alberti had in fact also made a contribution to the architects' burning problem of the completely central plan. His S. Sebastiano in Mantua (fig. 51) is a Greek cross. It was designed in 1460, that is just before or just after the Sforza Temple of Sperandio's medal. But Alberti's solution is original whatever its date, austere and aloof, with its curiously pagan facade. No wonder that a cardinal could write of it in 1473: "I don't see if this is meant to turn out a church or a mosque or a synagogue".

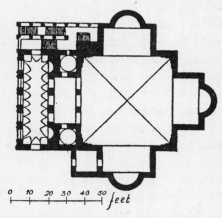

0 10 20 30 40 50 *feet*

51. LEONE BATTISTA ALBERTI: S. SEBASTIANO, MANTUA, BEGUN 1460.

From the point of view of practical church functions such central buildings are conspicuously useless. So we find from the beginning attempts at combining the traditional longitudinal plan with æsthetically more welcome central features. Sto. Spirito was one example. The most influential one, however, is S. Andrea in Mantua which was begun in 1470, two years only before Alberti's death. Here the architect replaces the traditional nave and aisles arrangement by a series of side chapels taking the place of the aisles and connected with the nave alternately by tall and wide and low and narrow openings. The aisles thus cease to be part of the eastward movement and become a series of minor centres accompanying the spacious tunnel-vaulted nave. As to the walls enclosing the nave the same intention is evident in the replacement of the simple basilican sequence of columns following each other without cæsura, by the rhythmical alteration on the *a b a* principle of the closed and the open bays. To what extent the keeping of the same proportions throughout is responsible for the deeply restful harmony of S. Andrea will be appreciated, if one realises that the same *a b a* rhythm, identical even in details, is used

as the chief motif of the facade of the church, and that the proportion of the arches of the crossing repeats that of the side chapels.

Alberti was not the only architect to experiment with such
rhythmical combinations in the longitudinal church building. The
North of Italy proved especially interested in the application of the
principle to the church with nave and aisles, after a Florentine architect had given the first hints at Faenza Cathedral (1474). Ferrara,
Parma and other centres picked them up and soon we see this trend
of thought unite forces with that interested in central plans on the
Milanese scheme of a central dome with four smaller and lower domes
in the corners. Venice and the Veneto had begun to build central
churches of this type shortly before 1500, and in 1506 an otherwise
little-known architect, Spavento, found the classic solution for its
application to the basilica. S. Salvatore in Venice (fig. 52) consists of
a nave of two of the Milano-Venetian units plus an exactly identical
crossing. Only the transepts and apses are tacked on a little incon-
gruously.

S. Salvatore stands in a similar relation to Alberti's S. Andrea in
Mantua as, in the field of domestic architecture, stands the Cancelleria
in Rome (fig. 53) to Alberti's Palazzo Rucellai. The Cancelleria was
built in 1486–98 as the private residence of Cardinal Riario, nephew
of Sixtus IV, one of the most formidable of the Renaissance popes.
These popes considered themselves worldly rulers almost more than
priests. Julius II, another nephew of Sixtus IV, under whom the new
St. Peter's was begun, and for whom Michelangelo painted the

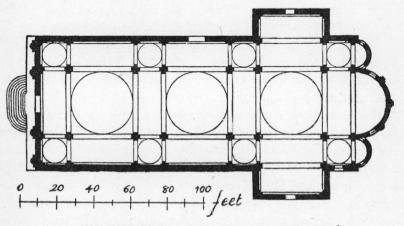

0   20   40   60   80   100   feet

52.   GIORGIO SPAVENTO: S. SALVATORE, VENICE, BEGUN 1506.

53. THE CHANCERY PALACE (PALAZZO DELLA CANCELLERIA) IN ROME, 1486–98.

Sistine Chapel and Raphael the *Stanze* of the Vatican, asked Michelangelo to portray him in a statue for Bologna with a sword instead of a book; for, he said: "I am a soldier, not a scholar". Of Alexander VI, and his nephew Cesare Borgia, it is sufficient to mention the names in this connection. The Palazzo Riario has a ground floor without pilasters, because it seemed more reasonable, to preserve the integrity of the rustication, where only small windows were required. On the first and second floors there are pilasters, but not in the simple sequence of the Palazzo Rucellai. Again the *a b a* rhythm is used to give life and rule to the facade. It will also be noticed that, whereas Alberti's horizontal divisions had to serve as cornices and at the same time window sills, the unknown architect of the Cancelleria gives each function its clearly visible architectural expression. Moreover the corner bays of the building are slightly projected, so that to the right and the left there is no vagueness about the composition either.

The Cancelleria is the first Renaissance building of more than local importance in Rome. About the time, however, when it was completed, Rome took the leadership in architecture and art out of the hands of Florence. This moment marks the beginning of the High Renaissance. The Early Renaissance was essentially Tuscan. The High Renaissance is Roman, because Rome was at that time the only international centre of civilisation, and the High Renaissance has an ideal classicity which made it internationally acceptable and in fact internationally canonic for centuries. Rome's place in the history of the Renaissance style corresponds exactly to that of Paris and the cathedrals around Paris in the history of the Gothic style. We do not know to what part of France the architects of Notre Dame, Chartres, Rheims and Amiens belonged by birth and upbringing, but we do know that Donato Bramante came from Lombardy, Raphael from Umbria and Michelangelo from Tuscany. These are the three greatest architects of the High Renaissance, and none of them—again the case we have met before—was an architect by training. Bramante was originally a painter, Raphael too, and Michelangelo a sculptor.

Bramante was the oldest of them. He was born in 1444 near Urbino. There he grew up while Laurana's palace rose, and the great Piero della Francesca painted for the duke. Bramante as a youth must have been greatly impressed by Piero's figures and his Albertesque architectural backgrounds. In 1472 he went to Milan. His first building there, the church of S. Satiro, begun in 1479, presupposes a knowledge of Alberti's S. Andrea in Mantua, a building only started a few years before. It looks as if Bramante had carefully studied the plans. His own church had no space for a chancel, and so—delighted to make a daring show of his knowledge of linear perspective—he feigned one in flat relief. If you stand in the right position, the trick comes off to perfection.

The same church, S. Satiro, has a sacristy, centrally planned; and S. Maria delle Grazie, Bramante's next architectural work in Milan, has an east end also on a central plan, very similar incidentally to Alberti's S. Sebastiano in Mantua. But when S. Maria delle Grazie was begun in 1492, another artist had already lived at Milan for nine years, the most universal that ever was, and one considerably to influence the slightly older Bramante: Leonardo da Vinci. Leonardo had gone to Milan in 1483

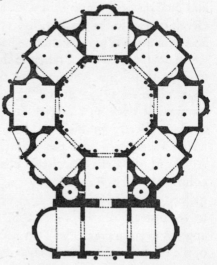

54. LEONARDO DA VINCI: DESIGN FOR A CHURCH. REDRAWN FROM THE MS. PARIS, INSTITUT DE FRANCE, BN 2037, FOLIO 56.

as an engineer, a painter, a sculptor, a musician—as anything and everything, but not as an architect. Yet in his fertile mind architectural problems moved all the time. In Florence he had already sketched the plans of Brunelleschi's Sto. Spirito and S. Maria degli Angeli, and in Milan he looked carefully at the specifically Milanese solutions proposed by Filarete. The out-

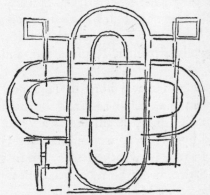

55. LEONARDO DA VINCI: SKETCH FOR A CHURCH. FROM THE MS. PARIS, INSTITUT DE FRANCE, B, FOLIO 57 *v.*

come were drawings in his sketch-books showing several kinds of complex central structures, for instance one with a central octagon and eight chapels, each of the Milanese plan with centre dome and little square corner bays (fig. 54). So here we find as against the central schemes worked out by Renaissance architects before Leonardo not a major contrasted with a number of radiating minor members, but a system of three grades each subordinate to the one above. Another project was to prove even more important for the future. It appears in Leonardo's Paris Manuscript B and consists of a combination of a major Greek cross with minor Greek crosses in the corners (fig. 55). Bramante must have seen this, and remembered it years after he had left Milan and moved to Rome.

Apart from what Bramante had learnt from Leonardo, the change from the Milanese to the Roman atmosphere, which took place in 1499, altered his style decisively. His architecture assumed at once an austerity far beyond anything in Milan. This appears already in his first Roman designs, the cloister for S. Maria della Pace and the Tempietto of S. Pietro in Montorio. At S. Maria della Pace the courtyard has piers and attached columns in the Roman way on the ground floor, and an open gallery on the first whose slim columns support a straight archi-trave instead of arches. At S. Pietro in Montorio Bramante appears even graver. The Tempietto of 1502 is the first monument of the High as against the Early Renaissance—truly a monument, i.e. more a sculptural than a strictly architectural achievement (pl. LIII). It was built to mark the spot on which St. Peter was supposed to have been crucified. One can thus call it an enlarged reliquary. In fact the intention had been to alter the courtyard in which it stood into a circular cloister to house the little temple. The first impression of the Tempietto after the churches and palaces of the 15th century is almost forbidding. The order of the colonnade is Tuscan Doric, the earliest modern use of this severe, unadorned order. It supports a correct classical entablature, again a feature that adds weight and strictness. There is, moreover, except for the metopes and the shells in the niches, not a square inch of decoration on the whole of the exterior. This in conjunction with the less novel but equally telling simplicity of the proportions—the ratio between width and height of the ground floor is repeated in the upper floor—gives the Tempietto a dignity far beyond its size. Here for once the classic Renaissance has achieved its conscious aim to emulate classic Antiquity. For here is—beyond motifs and even beyond formal expression—a building that appears as nearly pure volume as a Greek temple. Space—that all-important ingredient of Western architecture—seems here defeated.

But Bramante did not stop there. Only four years after he had accomplished the ideal Renaissance expression of architectural volume, he set out to reconcile it with the ideal Renaissance expression of space, as it had been evolved by the 15th-century architects from Brunelleschi to Leonardo da Vinci. In 1503 Julius II commissioned him to rebuild St. Peter's, the holiest of Western churches. It was to be a building on a strictly central plan, an amazing decision, considering the strength of the tradition in favour of longitudinal churches on the one side and the immense religious significance of St. Peter's on the other. With the pope adopting this symbol of worldliness for his own church, the spirit of Humanism had indeed penetrated into the innermost fortress of Christian resistance.

Bramante was over sixty when in 1506 the foundation stone was laid of the new St. Peter's (fig. 56). It is a Greek cross, with four apses, so extremely symmetrical that on the plan nothing indicates which of the apses was to hold the high altar. The main dome was to be accompanied by minor domes over corner chapels. And just as in the Leonardo sketch of fig. 55 the rhythm is amplified by enlarging the corner chapels into Greek crosses so that each of them has two apses of its own, the other two being cut off by the arms of the major Greek cross. Thus a square ambulatory is created framing a huge central dome, designed to be semispherical like the dome over the Tempietto. Four corner turrets (of Milanese origin) are added to finish the diagonal axes and complete the exterior into a square with projections only for the main apses. So far Bramante's scheme was not more than a magnificent development of 15th-century ideas. What is new and entirely of the 16th century

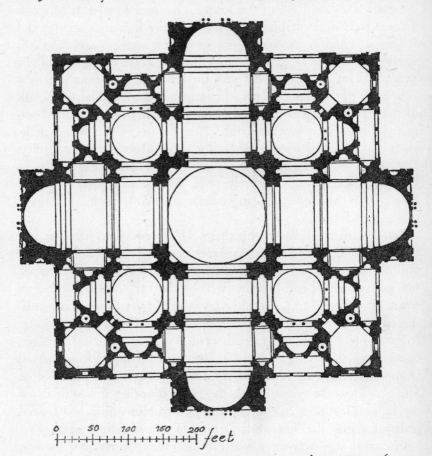

56. DONATO BRAMANTE: ORIGINAL PLAN FOR ST. PETER'S IN ROME, 1506.

is the modelling of the walls and above all the piers supporting the central dome, the only parts of Bramante's plan that were executed and still stand. In them nothing is left of the human scale and gentle modelling of Early Renaissance members. They are massive pieces of masonry, boldly hollowed out as if by the sculptor's moulding hand. This conception of the plastic potentialities of a wall, in its origin Late Roman, and first rediscovered (though less massively used) by the late Brunelleschi of S. Maria degli Angeli, was to be of the greatest importance for the future development of Italian architecture.

The immediate future however belonged to Bramante, the master of classic harmony and greatness, not to Bramante, the herald of the Baroque. Raphael (1483–1520) was the architect to follow most closely the Bramante of the Tempietto, and the new courts of the Vatican (1503 seqq.), Bramante's other Roman masterpiece. Of Raphael's architectural works few are actually documented. Amongst the buildings attributed to him on good evidence is the Palazzo Vidoni Caffarelli in Rome (pl. LII), a very near descendant of the Palazzo Caprini which Bramante had designed just before he died in 1514 and which Raphael had bought in 1517. It is now altered out of recognition. The Palazzo Caffarelli is also no longer as Raphael intended it to be. It was at a later date considerably enlarged in width and height. Here again the change of scale is noticeable which marks the High Renaissance. Balance and harmony are still the aims, but they are now combined with a solemnity and greatness unknown to the 15th century. Tuscan Doric columns replace the pilasters of the Palazzo Rucellai and the Cancelleria, and the happy *a b a* rhythm is contracted into a weightier *a b* with a new accent on the *a* by the duplication of the columns, and on the *b* by the straight architraves over the windows. The design of the rustication on the ground floor also emphasises the horizontality, i.e. the gravity of the composition.

The development from the Early to the High Renaissance, from delicacy to greatness and from a subtle planning of surfaces to a bold high relief in the modelling of walls encouraged an intensified study of the remains of Imperial Rome. Only now their drama was fully understood. Only now humanists and artists endeavoured to visualise and perhaps recreate the Rome of the ruins as a whole. It is thus more than a coincidence that Raphael was appointed by Leo X, the Medici pope, in 1515 to be Superintendent of Roman Antiquities, that he had Vitruvius translated by a humanist friend for his private use, and that he (or in all probability he) drew up a memorandum to the pope advocating the exact measuring of Roman remains, with ground plans, elevations and sections separate, and the restoration of such buildings as could be "*infallibilmente*" restored.

Here precisely archæology in the academic sense begins, an attitude quite different from that of the 15th-century admirers of Roman architecture. It produced scholars of ever wider knowledge and ever deeper appreciation of Antiquity, but artists of weakened self-confidence, classicists where Bramante and Raphael had been classics.

At this point a warning must be sounded against confusion between the three terms classic, classical and classicist. The difference between classic and classical has been pointed out on p. 26. If classic is the term denoting that rare balance of conflicting forces which marks the summit of any movement in art, and if classical is the term for anything belonging to or derived from Antiquity, what then is classicist? A definition is far from easy. In our context it can be arrived at only in a somewhat roundabout way.

Neither classic nor classicist are terms which signify historic styles such as Romanesque, Gothic and Renaissance. They coincide rather with æsthetic attitudes. However, in so far as æsthetic attitudes as a rule change with historic styles, the two sets of terms can often be co-ordinated. In England the position until a relatively short time ago was that the term Renaissance was used to cover the art from the 15th right to the early 19th century. But there had been so many fundamental changes of styles during these more than three hundred years, that the term covering such a long period could not stand for any distinct æsthetic characteristics. Thus, on the example of the Continent, it was gradually divided up into Renaissance and Baroque, the Baroque to cover the work of such artists as Bernini, Rembrandt, Velasquez. However, since our knowledge of, and susceptibility to, distinctions in æsthetic expression has grown considerably within the last fifty years or so, it is becoming more and more patent that Renaissance and Baroque do not really define the qualities of all art of importance in the 15th, 16th and 17th centuries. The contrast between Raphael and Bernini or Rembrandt is evident, but art of the period between roughly 1520 or 1530 and 1600 or 1620 does not fit into the categories of the Renaissance or the Baroque. So a new name was introduced about twenty or twenty-five years ago: Mannerism, a name which was not specially coined, but which in a derogatory sense had already been used to characterise certain schools of 16th-century painting. The name in its new sense is only now becoming known in this country. It has much to recommend it. It certainly helps to make one see the important differences between art of the High Renaissance and art of the later 16th century.

If balance and harmony are the chief characteristics of the High Renaissance, Mannerism is its very reverse; for it is an unbalanced, discordant art—now emotional to distortion (Tintoretto, El Greco), now disciplined to self-effacement (Bronzino). The High Renaissance is full, Mannerism is meagre. There is luxuriant beauty in Titian, stately gravity in Raphael and gigantic strength in Michelangelo, but Mannerist types are slim, elegant and of a stiff and highly self-conscious deportment. Self-consciousness to this extent was a new experience to the West. The Middle Ages, and the Renaissance too, had been much more naïve. Reformation and counter-Reformation broke up that state of innocence, and this is why Mannerism is indeed full of mannerisms. For the artist now for the first time was aware of the virtues of eclecticism. Raphael and Michelangelo were recognised as the masters of a Golden Age equal to the Ancients. Imitation became a necessity in quite a new sense. The mediæval artist had imitated his masters as a matter of course, but he had not doubted his own (or his time's) ability to surpass them. This confidence had now gone. The first academies were founded, and a literature on the history and theory of art sprang up. Vasari is its most famous representative. Deviation from the canons of Michelangelo and Raphael was not ostracised, but it assumed a new air of the capricious, or the demonstrative, or the daring: forbidden pleasures. No wonder that the 16th century has seen the sternest ascetics and the first writers and draughtsmen to indulge in the hidden sins of pornography (Aretino and Giulio Romano).

So far only names of painters have been mentioned because the qualities of 16th-century painting are at least a little more familiar than those of architecture. The application of the principles of Mannerism to architecture is only in its very tentative stages on the Continent and in America; in England it has not even been attempted. Yet if we now turn to buildings and compare the Palazzo Farnese (fig. 57 and pl. LIV) with the Palazzo Massimi alle Colonne (pl. LV) as the most perfect examples of High Renaissance and Mannerist palace architecture in Rome, the contrast between their emotional qualities will at once be visible. The Palazzo Farnese was designed in 1530 by Antonio da San Gallo the Younger (1485–1546). It is the most monumental of Roman Renaissance palaces, an isolated rectangle of about 150-feet frontage, facing a square. The facade has strongly emphasised quoins, but no rustication. The ground-floor windows are provided with straight cornices, those on the first floor with alternating triangular and segmental pediments, supported by columns (i.e. so-called *ædiculæ*), a Roman motif revived during the High Renaissance. The top floor and the overpowering top cornice were added later and in a different spirit (see p. 114). The symmetry and spaciousness of the interior is worth

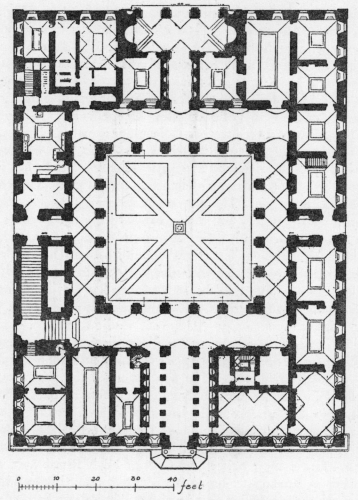

0   10   20   30   40 feet

57.   ANTONIO DA SAN GALLO: PALAZZO FARNESE, ROME, BEGUN 1530.

noting, especially the magnificent central entrance with the tunnel-vaulted passage leading into the courtyard. This (pl. LIV) possesses the cloistered ground floor of all Renaissance palaces, now, in accordance with the Bramante tradition, with Tuscan Doric columns and a correct frieze of metopes and triglyphs instead of the light columns of the Tuscan 15th century. The first floor has no gallery, but noble, pedimented windows set into blank arcades, and an Ionic order. This is correct according to Roman usage (Theatre of Marcellus): the sturdier Tuscan Doric must be on the ground floor, the elegant Ionic on the first and the rich Corinthian on the second. In this (but only in this) the later second floor of the Palazzo Farnese follows the archeological example.

The Palazzo Massimi by Baldassare Peruzzi of Siena (1481–1536), a member of the Bramante-Raphael circle in Rome, begun in 1535, disregards all canons of the Ancients. Nor does it really show much regard for the achievements of Bramante and Raphael. Both the Palazzi Vidoni and Farnese were logical structures in which the knowledge of any one part gives a clue to the whole. The entrance loggia of the Palazzo Massimi with its coupled Tuscan Doric columns and its heavy cornice is in no way a preparation for the upper floors. Both the Palazzi Vidoni and Farnese are modelled into a generous though not overcharged relief. In the Palazzo Massimi there is a poignant contrast between the deep darkness of the ground-floor loggia and the papery thinness and flatness of the upper parts. The first-floor windows are shallow in relief compared with what the High Renaissance regarded as appropriate, the second- and third-floor windows are small and have curious leathery surrounds. They are in no way differentiated in size or importance, as the Renaissance would have done. Moreover a slight curve of the whole facade gives it a swaying delicacy, whereas the squareness of the Renaissance front seemed to express powerful solidity. The Palazzo Massimi is no doubt inferior to the Palazzi Vidoni and Farnese in dignity and grandeur; but it has a sophisticated elegance instead which appeals to the over-civilised and intellectual connoisseur.

Now this brings us back to the fact that classicism is an æsthetic attitude first appreciated during this phase of Mannerism. The Early Renaissance had rediscovered Antiquity and enjoyed a mixture of detail copying and a naïve licence in the reconstruction of more than details. The High Renaissance was in their use of Roman forms hardly more accurate, but the Antique spirit was for a brief moment truly revived in the gravity of mature Bramante and Raphael. After their death imitation began to freeze up initiative. Classicism is imitation of Antiquity and even more the classic moment of the Renaissance, at the expense of direct expression. The attitude culminated, needless to say, during the late 18th and early 19th centuries, in that phase of classicism *par excellence* which is on the

Continent often called Classicism pure and simple, but which in England goes under the name of Classic Revival. The idea of copying a whole Antique temple exterior (or a whole temple front) for Western use is the quintessence of classicism. The 16th century did not go quite so far. But it did conceive that blend of academic rigidity with distrust of emotional freedom which made the latter-day all-out revival possible.

A pupil of Raphael, Giulio Romano (1494–1546), artist-in-chief to the Duke of Mantua, designed a house for himself about 1544 (pl. LVI). It is a striking example of Mannerist classicism—apart from being one of the earliest architect's houses on such an ambitious scale. The facade is again flatter than would have pleased the High Renaissance. Detail, e.g. in the window surrounds and the top frieze, is hard and crisp. There is a proud aloofness, an almost arrogant taciturnity and a stiff formality about the building that reminds one at once of the Spanish etiquette accepted everywhere in the later 16th century. Yet the apparent general correctness is broken by an occasional, as it were, surreptitious licence here and there (one such licence in Giulio Romano's work as a draughtsman has been mentioned before). The smooth band above the windows of the rusticated ground floor seems to disappear behind the keystones of the windows. The entrance has a most illicit depressed arch, and the pediment on top with no base to it is nothing but the main string course at sill height of the first-floor windows lifted up by the effort of the arch. These windows themselves are recessed in blank arcades like those of the Palazzo Farnese, but as against the logical and structurally satisfying surrounds and pediments there, one flat ornamental motif runs without hiatus along sides, top and pediments. It is exquisite, but very self-conscious, just like the contemporary sculpture of Benvenuto Cellini.

This style, first conceived in Rome and Florence, appealed almost at once to North Italy and the transalpine countries. Giulio Romano was the first to show it north of the Apennines. Sammicheli, though fifteen years older, followed, partly under direct Roman influence, partly under the influence of Giulio's early Mantuan masterpiece, the Palazzo del Té of 1525–35, and reshaped the appearance of Verona in this spirit of Mannerist classicism. At Bologna Sebastiano Serlio, a pupil of Peruzzi, though six years his senior, and twenty-four years older than Giulio, preached it. In 1537 he began to publish a first part of a treatise on architecture which proved a source of lasting inspiration to classicist minds the other side of the Alps. Serlio himself went to France in 1540 and was almost at once made "peintre et architecteur du roi". The so-called school of Fontaine-bleau, where Serlio and the Italians Primaticcio and Niccolò dell' Abbate worked, is the transalpine centre of Mannerism. Spain accepted the new style even earlier—a violent reaction against the violence of her Late Gothic. Charles V's new and never finished palace on the Alhambra at Granada (begun in 1526 by Pedro Machuca) looks, with its vast circular colonnaded inner court and the motifs of its 207 foot-long facade, as though it were based on Giulio, somewhat provincially interpreted. England and Germany were slower in succumbing to the dictatorship of classicism. The style was not in all its implications appreciated before the second decade of the 17th century (Inigo Jones and Elias Holl, see pp. 157–60), and then not so much in its problematical Giulio Romano-Serlio form as in that created by the happiest and most serene of all later 16th-century artists, by Andrea Palladio (1508–80).

Palladio's style, though it first followed Giulio, Sammicheli and Serlio, and as far as possible Vitruvius, the obscure and freely mis-interpreted Roman authority on architecture, is highly personal. His work must be seen at and around Vicenza. He designed no churches there (though his San Giorgio Maggiore and Il Redentore in Venice are amongst the few really relevant churches in the Mannerist style, as will be shown later). What he was called upon to do was almost exclusively the designing of town and country houses, *palazzi* and *ville*, and it is significant that the far-reaching effect of his style can quite adequately be demonstrated without any analyses of his churches. For from the Renaissance onwards secular architecture became as important for visual self-expression as religious architecture, until during the 18th century the ascendancy of domestic and public buildings over churches was established. For the Middle Ages, in a book such as the present, it was sufficient to describe one Norman castle, one Gothic castle and one Gothic manor-house. As to the Renaissance examples discussed, half of them were secular. This will remain the proportion for the next two hundred years in the Roman Catholic countries. In those converted to Protestantism secular architecture was dominant at an even earlier date.

Palladio's buildings, despite their elegant serenity, would hardly have had such a universal success, if it had not been for the book in which he published them and his theory of architecture. Palladio's *Architettura* superseded Serlio's, especially after its revival in England early in the 18th century. His style appealed to the civilised taste and the polite learning of the Georgian gentry more than that of any other architect. Palladio is never dry or demonstratively scholarly. He combines the gravity of Rome with the sunny breadth of Northern Italy and an entirely personal ease not achieved by any of his contemporaries. In his Palazzo Chiericati (pl. LVII), begun in 1550, the Tuscan Doric and correct Ionic order of the Bramante tradition with their straight entablatures are unmistakable. But the freedom in placing what had been confined to the courtyards of Roman palaces into the facade, thus opening up most of the facade and retaining only one solid piece in the centre of the first floor surrounded on all sides by air, is all Palladio's. He was especially fond of colonnades in his country houses, where he used them to connect a square main block with far out-reaching wings (fig. 58).

The contrast between solid and diffused had a great fascination for him. In one of his most complete schemes, the Villa Trissino at Meledo on the Venetian mainland (fig. 58), the house is almost completely symmetrical. The most extreme case, still existent and well preserved, of such extreme symmetry is the Villa Capra, or Rotonda, just outside Vicenza (pl. LVIII, begun *c.* 1567), an academic achievement of high perfection and one specially admired by Pope's England. As a house to live in it has nothing of the informal snugness of the Northern manor-house, but it has nobility and, with its slender Ionic porticoes, its pediments, its carefully placed few pedimented windows and its central dome, it appears stately without being pompous. Now to get the totality of a Palladian countryside composition one has to add to such a nucleus the curved colonnades and low outbuildings by which the villa takes in the land around. This embracing attitude proved of the greatest historical consequence. For here for the first time in Western architecture landscape and building were conceived as belonging to each other, as dependent on each other. Here for the first time the chief axes of a house are continued into nature; or, alternatively, the spectator standing outside sees the house spread out like a picture closing his vista. It is worth mentioning that in Rome at about the same time Michelangelo planned a comparable vista for the Palazzo Farnese which he had been commissioned to finish, across the Tiber with the Farnese gardens on the other side of the river.

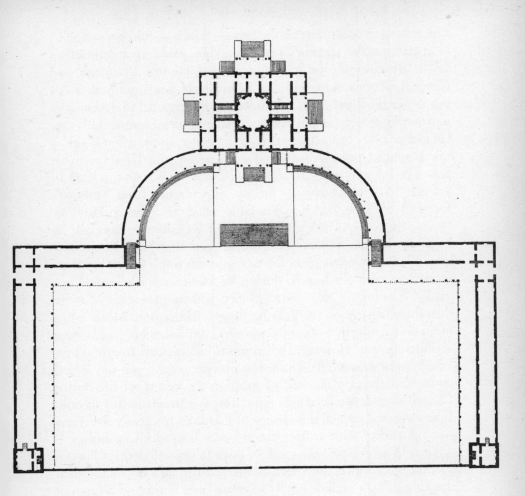

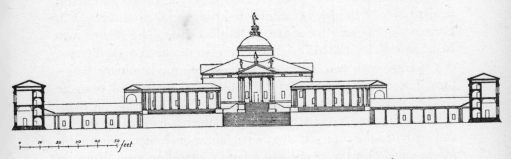

58. ANDREA PALLADIO: VILLA TRISSINO AT MELEDO, c. 1560.

It may seem odd to us that the Farnese family should have gone to Michelangelo the sculptor to complete their palace after San Gallo's death. But it must be remembered that Giotto, Bramante and Raphael were painters, and that Brunelleschi was a goldsmith. All the same, the story of how Michelangelo became an architect is worth telling, because it is equally characteristic of him and his age. He had as a boy been apprenticed to a painter, until, when Lorenzo the Magnificent had discovered him, given him lodgings in his palace and drawn him into his private circle, he was sent to learn in a freer, less mediæval way the art of sculpture from Lorenzo's favourite sculptor, Bertoldo. His fame rested on sculpture. His huge David, the symbol of the civic pride of Renaissance Florence, he began at the age of twenty-six. A few years later Julius II commissioned him to prepare plans for an enormous tomb which the Pope wanted to erect for himself during his lifetime. Michelangelo regarded it as his *magnum opus.* The first scheme provided for more than forty life-size or over life-size figures. The famous Moses is one of them. Architecture of course was also involved, though only as an accompaniment. However, when Julius had decided to rebuild St. Peter's to Bramante's design, he lost interest in the tomb and forced upon Michelangelo the task of painting the ceiling of the Sistine Chapel instead. Michelangelo never forgave Bramante for having, as he suspected, caused this change of mind. So for nearly five years —as he worked without an assistant—he had to stick to painting.

Then he returned to the tomb of Pope Julius, and perhaps in connection with conceptions that had passed through his mind when thinking of how architecturally to relate large figures with the wall against which they were going to stand, he began to take an interest in the plans of the Medici family to complete their church of S. Lorenzo in Florence by at last adding a facade. The church was Brunelleschi's work. Michelangelo in 1516 designed a facade two stories high, with two orders and ample accommodation for sculpture. The commission was given to him, and for several years he worked in the quarries—a work he loved. Then however, in 1520, the Medicis found too many difficulties in the transport of the marble and cancelled the contract. But they made at once another one with Michelangelo for the erection of a family chapel or mausoleum by S. Lorenzo. This was in fact begun in 1521 and completed, though less ambitiously than originally planned, in 1534. The Medici Chapel is thus Michelangelo's first architectural work, and the work, it must be added, of one never initiated into the secrets of building technique and architectural drawing. It has already—though again chiefly conceived as background for sculpture—all the characteristics of his personal style. Architecture without any support from sculpture is to be found in his work for the first time in another job for the Medicis at S. Lorenzo, the library and the anteroom to the library (pl. LIX). The library was designed in 1524, the anteroom (with the exception of the staircase for which the model was supplied as late as 1557) in 1526.

The anteroom is high and narrow. This alone gives an uncomfortable feeling. Michelangelo wanted to emphasise the contrast to the long, comparatively low and more restful library itself. The walls are divided into panels by coupled columns. At the ground-floor height of the library itself the panels have blank windows and framed blank niches above. The colour scheme of the room is austere, a dead white against the sombre dark grey of columns, window niches, architraves and other structural or decorative members. As for the chief structural members, the columns, one would expect them to project and carry the architraves, as had always been the function of columns. Michelangelo reversed the relations. He recessed his columns and projected his panels so that they painfully encase the columns. Even the architraves go forward over the panels and backward over the columns. This seems arbitrary, just like the relations between ground-floor loggia and flat facade above or between second- and third-floor windows, in the Palazzo Massimi. It is certainly illogical, because it makes the carrying strength of the columns appear wasted. Moreover they have slender corbels at their feet which do not look substantial enough to support them and in fact do not support them at all. The thinness of the Massimi front characterises the blank windows with their tapering pilasters, fluted without any intelligible reason in one part only. The pediment over the entrance to the library is held only by the thin line around the door, raised into two square ears. The staircase tells of the same wilful originality; but the sharpness of detail which Michelangelo developed in the twenties is now replaced by a heavy, weary flow as of lava.

It has often been said that the motifs of the walls show Michelangelo as the father of the Baroque, because they express the superhuman struggle of active forces against overpowering matter. I do not think that anybody who examines without prejudice his sensations in the room itself would subscribe to this statement. There seems to me no expression of struggle anywhere, though there is conscious discordance all the way through. This austere animosity against the happy and harmonious we have seen already, although hidden under a polished formalism, in Giulio Romano. What Michelangelo's Laurenziana reveals is indeed Mannerism in its most sublime architectural form and not Baroque—a world of frustration much more tragic than the Baroque world of struggles between mind and matter. In Michelangelo's architecture every force seems paralysed. The load does not weigh, the support does not carry, natural reactions play no part—a highly artificial system upheld by the severest discipline.[1]

In its spatial treatment the Laurenziana is just as novel and characteristic. Michelangelo has exchanged the balanced proportions of Renaissance rooms for an anteroom as tall and narrow as the shaft of a pit, and a library proper, reached by a staircase, as long and narrow as a corridor. They both force us, even against our wills, to follow their pull, upward first and then forward. This tendency to enforce movement through space within rigid boundaries is the chief spatial quality of Mannerism. It is well enough known in painting, for instance in Correggio's late Madonnas, or Tintoretto's Last Suppers with the figure of Christ at the far, far end. The most moving of all examples is Tintoretto's painting of the Finding of the Body of St. Mark (Brera, Milan, *c.* 1565). Nowhere else is Mannerist space so irresistible. In architecture this magic suction effect is introduced into Giulio Romano's extremely severe Cathedral at Mantua with its double aisles, the inner one with tunnel-vaults, the outer one and the nave flat. The uninterrupted rhythm of its monotonous columns is as irresistible as that of an Early Christian basilica. In secular architecture its most familiar and easily accessible example is no doubt Vasari's Uffizi Palace in Florence (pl. LX). It was begun in 1560 to house Grand Ducal offices. It consists of two tall wings along a long narrow courtyard. The formal elements are familiar to us: lack of a clear gradation of stories, uniformity coupled with heretical detail, long, elegant and fragile brackets below double pilasters which are no pilasters at all, and so on. What must be emphasised is the finishing

---

[1] But to Jacob Burckhardt, the Swiss historian of the 19th century and the discoverer of the Renaissance in the sense in which we understand the style to-day, the anteroom of the Laurenziana is but "an incomprehensible joke of the great master" (*Geschichte der Renaissance in Italien*, 7th edition, 1924, p. 208; written in 1867).

accent of the composition towards the River Arno. Here a loggia, open
in a spacious Venetian window on the ground floor and originally also
in a colonnade on the upper floor, replaces the solid wall. This is a
favourite Mannerist way of linking room with room, a way in which
both a clear Renaissance separation of units and a free Baroque flow
through the whole and beyond are avoided. Thus, Palladio's two
Venetian churches terminate in the east, not in closed apses, but in
arcades—straight in S. Giorgio Maggiore (1565), semicircular in the
Redentore (1577)—behind which back rooms of indistinguishable
dimensions appear. And thus Vasari, together with Vignola (1507–73)
designed the Villa Giulia, the country *casino* of Pope Julius III (1550–
55), as a sequence of buildings with loggias towards semicircular courts

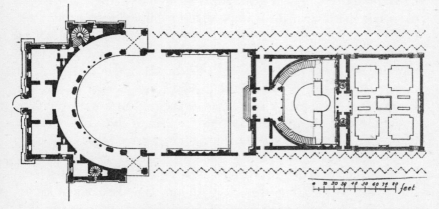

59. GIORGIO VASARI, GIACOMO VIGNOLA AND BARTOLOMMEO AMMANATI: THE VILLA OF
POPE JULIUS III, ROME, BEGUN 1552.

and with vistas across from the entrance through the first loggia
towards the second, through it towards the third and through that
into a walled back garden (fig. 59).

For the garden of the 16th century is still walled in. It may have
long and varied vistas, as you also find them at the Villa Este in
Tivoli or at Caprarola, but they do not stretch out into infinity as in
the Baroque at Versailles. Neither do the low colonnades on the
ground floors of Mannerist buildings, such as the Palazzo Massimi
and the Uffizi, indicate infinity—that is, a dark, unsurveyable background of space, as a Rembrandt background. Back walls are too
near. The continuity of the facade is broken by such colonnades—
that is what the Renaissance would have disliked—but the layer of
opened-up space is shallow and clearly confined in depth. Palladio's

Palazzo Chierigati is the most perfect example of this screen technique in palace architecture, although, in its serenity, different from Florentine and Roman Mannerism and particularly from Michelangelo. Palladio's palace may have a certain coolness too, but it is not icy as the Laurenziana.

This frozen self-discipline is not usually connected with the genius of Michelangelo and therefore needs special emphasis, emphasis above all because textbooks in Britain very often still treat Michelangelo as a master of the Renaissance. The truth is that he belonged to the Renaissance only for a very few years of his early career. His Pietà of 1499 may be a work of the High Renaissance. His David may be in the spirit of the Renaissance too. Of his Sistine Ceiling this can be said only to a limited extent; and of his work after 1515 hardly ever. His character made it impossible for him to accept the ideals of the Renaissance for long. He was the very opposite of Castiglione's *Courtier* and Leonardo da Vinci: unsociable, distrustful, a fanatical worker, negligent in his personal appearance, deeply religious and uncompromisingly proud. Hence his dislike for Leonardo, and for Bramante and Raphael, a dislike made up of contempt and envy. We know more of his character and his life than of those of any artist before. The unprecedented adoration for him caused the publication of two biographies while he was still alive. Both are based on a systematic collecting of material. It is good that it should be so; for we feel we must know much about him to understand his art. In the Middle Ages the personality of an architect could never to that degree have influenced his style. Brunelleschi, though clearer to us as a character than the architects of the Gothic cathedrals, is still surprisingly objective in his forms. Michelangelo was the first to turn architecture into an instrument of individual expression. The *terribilità* that frightened those who met him fills us with awe immediately we are faced with any work of his, a room, a drawing, a piece of sculpture or a sonnet.

For Michelangelo was a consummate poet too, one of the profoundest of his age; and in his poems he gives to posterity a reckoning of his struggles. The fiercest of them was that between a platonic ideal of beauty and a fervent faith in Christ. It is in the most concentrated form the struggle between the age of the Renaissance in which he lived when he was young, and that of the Counter-Reformation and Mannerism that began when he was about fifty years old, just before the sack of Rome in 1527. Now new stricter religious orders were founded, the Capuchins, the Oratorians and above all the Jesuits (1534). Now new saints arose, St. Ignatius Loyola, St. Teresa, St. Philip Neri, St. Charles Borromeo. In 1542 the Inquisition was reintroduced, in 1543 literary censorship. In 1555 the Emperor Charles V abdicated and retired to the silence of a Spanish monastery. A few years later his son, Philip II, began his bleak and enormous palace of the Escorial, more a monastery than a palace. Spanish etiquette stood for a discipline as rigid as that of the early Jesuits and the Papal court of the same decades. In Rome nothing seemed left of the Renaissance gaiety. The Venetian ambassadors wrote home that even the carnivals were cold and lean. Paul V, the strictest of the popes, had meat on his table only twice a week.

Michelangelo too had always been exemplarily sober and self-denying. He trained himself to need little sleep, and used to sleep with his boots on. While at work he sometimes fed on dry bread, eaten without putting his tools aside. He felt his duties to his genius more heavily than the light-hearted architects of the Renaissance—and he could therefore venture to reply to a critic who objected to his having represented Giuliano de Medici on his tomb beardless, though he wore a beard in life: "Who in a thousand years will care for what he looked like?" a saying utterly impossible before the Renaissance had freed artists. For while the Middle Ages did not demand portrait likeness, because it is part of what is merely accidental in human nature, and while the early Renaissance had enjoyed portrait likeness, because it had only just discovered the artistic means for attaining it, Michelangelo refused to comply with it, because it would have hemmed in his æsthetic freedom. Yet his religious experience was of the most exacting, and it grew more so as he grew older and the century grew older, until he, the greatest sculptor of the West, and the most admired artist of his age, gave up painting and sculpture almost entirely. Architecture alone he still carried on, and he refused to accept a salary for his work at St. Peter's.

The final break seems to have come after he had passed his seventieth year. Between the Medici buildings of the mid-twenties and 1547 he seems to have designed and built only the fortifications of Florence in 1529—an engineering job, we would say, but a type of job in which Leonardo da Vinci and San Gallo, his predecessor in most of his Roman works, also excelled. In 1534 he had left Florence for good and gone to Rome In 1535 Paul III appointed him Superintendent of the Vatican Buildings, an all but nominal appointment at first. In 1537 he was consulted about a more stately rebuilding of the municipal palaces on the Capitol; but nothing materialised. Then in 1546 San Gallo died, and now Michelangelo was called upon almost at once to complete the Palazzo Farnese, redesign St. Peter's and replan the Capitol. At the Palazzo Farnese we shall now easily discover his Mannerism in the second-floor details (pl. LIV). The triplicating of the pilasters and especially the odd discordant framing of the windows with corbels on the sides not supporting anything and special corbels immediately above, on which the segmental pediments rest, are Michelangelo's personal expression, individual to an unprecedented extent and impossible before the breaking up first of the transcendentally ordered world of the Middle Ages and then of the æsthetically ordered world of the Renaissance.

Michelangelo's architectural masterpiece, the back and the dome of St. Peter's, are also an expression of revolt against Bramante and the spirit of the Renaissance, although they are not to the same extent Mannerist. When Michelangelo was appointed by Paul III, the Farnese Pope, to be architect of St. Peter's, he found the church essentially left as it had been at Bramante's death. Raphael and San Gallo had designed naves to comply with the religious demands of the first post-Renaissance generation. But they were not begun. Michelangelo returned to the central plan, but he deprived it of its all-governing balance (fig. 60). He kept the arms of the Greek cross, but where Bramante (fig. 56) had intended sub-centres repeating on a smaller scale the motif of the main centre, Michelangelo cut off the arms of the sub-centres, thus condensing the composition into one central dome resting on piers of a dimension that Bramante would have refused as colossal, i.e. inhuman, and a square ambulatory round. As for the exterior, he altered Bramante's plans in exactly the same spirit, replacing a happily balanced variety of noble and serene motifs by a huge order of Corinthian pilasters supporting a massive attic and by strangely incongruous windows and niches surrounded by *ædiculæ* and smaller niches of several sizes—a mighty yet somewhat discordant *ensemble*. At the west end, Michelangelo wanted to add a portico of ten columns with four columns in front of the middle ones. This—it was never built, because Maderna after 1600 added a nave—would have destroyed Bramante's ideal symmetry, and in fact the classic ideal of symmetry altogether;

for the duplication of the centre columns is of course an utterly un-antique conception. Bramante's cupola was to be a perfect semi-sphere, Michelangelo's (pl. LXII)—if we can take it (in spite of the emphatic denial by some scholars) that its present shape is Michel-angelo's and not della Porta's who completed it in 1588-90—is elongated and with the projecting coupled columns of the drum,

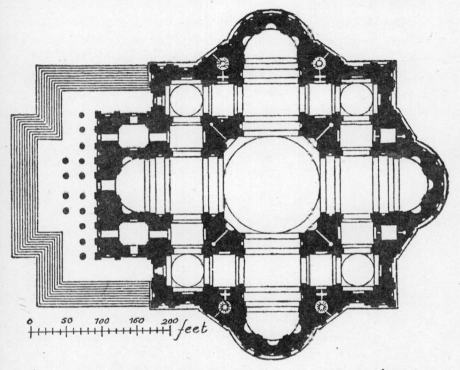

0   50   100   150   200 feet

60.   MICHELANGELO BUONARROTI: PLAN FOR THE COMPLETION OF ST. PETER'S IN ROME, 1546.

the ribs up the dome and the coupled columns and concave top of the lantern a revision in very personal Renaissance forms of the essentially Gothic design of Brunelleschi's Florentine dome. Now the triumphant soar of this dome is not Mannerist. This superhuman victory of gigantic forces against huge masses points towards the Baroque. To admit that does not mean invalidating the thesis that Mannerism was the predominant tendency of later 16th-century architecture. It merely means admitting the vastness of Michel-angelo's genius. He—and the same is true of the other greatest masters of his generation, of Raphael and Titian—in growing out of, and beyond, the Renaissance conceived both the styles of the 16th and the 17th centuries. The 16th followed his manner and turned it into Mannerism, the 17th appreciated the *terribilità* of his conflicts and made Baroque out of it. So the eternal city is crowned not by a symbol of Renaissance worldliness, as Julius II has visualised it, but by an overwhelming synthesis of Mannerism and Baroque, and at the same time of Antiquity and Christianity.

It was Michelangelo's last three-dimensional work of such violence. He was seventy-two when he designed it. The eighteen years that were left to him he spent in meditation on life after death. "Let there be no more painting, no more carving," he says in one of his late sonnets, "to soothe the soul turned towards that Divine Love which opened His arms from the cross to receive us."

> *"Nè pinger nè scolpir fia più che quieti*
> *L'anima volta a quell' Amor Divino*
> *C'aperse, a prender noi, 'n croce le braccia."*

He carved after this only three more groups, all three Entombments of Christ. One of them was for his own tomb, one he left unfinished, or rather sublimated to so immaterial a form that it can no longer be regarded as sculpture in the Renaissance sense. His late drawings too are spiritualised to a degree almost unbearable in an artist who had done more than any before him to glorify the beauty and vigour of body and movement. And one of his last architectural plans—a fact not widely enough known—was to design the Roman church of the newly founded, severely counter-reformatory order of the Jesuits. He offered to take charge of the building without any fee, just as he had refused to accept a salary as architect to St. Peter's.

The Gesù was not begun until four years after Michelangelo's death. It has perhaps exerted a wider influence than any other church of the last four hundred years (fig. 61). Giacomo Vignola (1507–73), the architect, following probably Michelangelo's ideas, combines in his ground plan the central scheme of the Renaissance with the longitudinal scheme of the Middle Ages—an eminently characteristic fact. The combination as such is not new. Alberti had done the same a hundred years before at S. Andrea in Mantua (fig. 50). The facade too (fig. 62) seems to take up a theme that Alberti had conceived. The problem for architects of the Renaissance, and since the Renaissance, was how to project the dimensions of tall nave and lower aisles on to the exterior without abandoning the orders of classical architecture. Alberti's solution was to have a ground floor on the triumphal arch system and a top floor the width of the nave only but with volutes, i.e. scrolls, rising towards it from the entablature in front of the lean-to roofs of the aisles. This method was adopted by Vignola in his design for the Gesù facade (though with the fuller and less harmonious orchestration of his age), and then by della Porta who substituted a new design for Vignola's. It has been

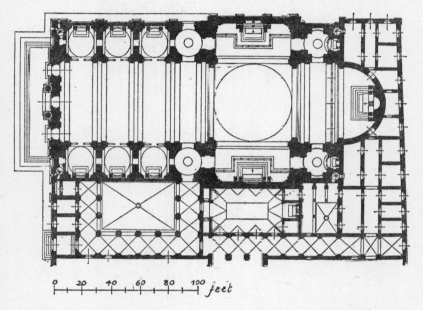

61.   GIACOMO VIGNOLA: CHURCH OF JESUS (GESÙ), ROME, BEGUN 1568.

repeated innumerable times and with many variations in the Baroque churches of Italy and the other Roman Catholic countries.

As for the interior (pl. LXI) Vignola keeps Alberti's interpretation of the aisles as series of chapels opening into the nave. He does not however concede them as much independence as the Renaissance architect considered necessary, always anxious as he was to let every part of a building be a whole. The extreme width of the nave under its powerful tunnel-vault degrades the chapels into mere niches accompanying a vast hall, and it has been suggested (Weise) that this motif was chosen by the Jesuits themselves to whom it was familiar from the late Gothic churches of Spain with their chapels between the buttresses and sometimes a passage connecting them (see p. 63). If the suggestion is accepted, there is here

62. GIACOMO VIGNOLA'S DESIGN FOR THE FRONT OF THE GESÙ.

yet another instance of the post-Renaissance return to mediæval
ideals—another, after the revival of Catholic faith which showed
itself in the new Saints and the new Orders, after the Gothic curve
of the dome of St. Peter's and the reintroduction of a longitudinal

emphasis in the Gesù plan. In the Gesù this emphasis on the eastward drive is obviously deliberate. The tunnel-vault and above all the main cornice, running all the way through without a break, take it up most eloquently in the elevation. There is however one element in Vignola's design that it would be impossible to find in the same sense in any mediæval church: the light. In the cathedral of the 13th century the stained-glass windows glow by means of light penetrating, but light itself is not a positive factor. Later on, in the Decorated style, light begins to model walls with their ogee-arched niches and play over filigree decoration, but it is never a major consideration of architectural design. In the Gesù, on the other hand, certain important features are introduced into the composition exclusively in order to make light-effects possible. The nave is lit from windows above the chapels—an even, subdued light. Then the last bay before the dome is shorter, less open and darker than the others. This contraction in space and lightness prepares dramatically for the majestic crossing with its mighty cupola. The floods of light streaming down from the windows of the drum create that sensation of fulfilment that Gothic architects achieved in so much less sensuous a way.

The decoration of the Gesù appears sensuous too, luxurious though sombre. However, it is not of Vignola's day. He would have been more moderate, with smaller motifs and a shallower relief; this is certain from what we know of late 16th-century decoration. Thus the effect of the mediæval movement towards the east would have been much stronger, with less to deflect attention from the cornice and the mighty tunnel-vault. The redecoration was done in 1668–83. It belongs to the High Baroque, whereas the building is, to say it again, Mannerist, neither of the equanimity of all High Renaissance, nor of the expansive vigour of all Baroque.

CHAPTER VI

The Baroque in the Roman Catholic Countries

c. 1600–c. 1760

MANNERISM, it has been pointed out, was originally, and in this country still is, a noun connected with "mannered" and nothing else. In Continental and American terminology however, some twenty years ago, it changed its meaning and became the term for a specific historic style in art, the post-Renaissance style of the 16th century, particularly in Italy. The same process had taken place about fifty years earlier with regard to Baroque. Baroque had originally signified odd, especially of odd shape. It was therefore adopted to descibe an architectural style which to the classicist appeared to revel in odd, extravagant shapes, that is, the style of Italy during the 17th century. Then, chiefly in the 'eighties of the last century and chiefly in Germany, it lost its derogatory flavour and became a neutral term to designate the works of art of that century in general. It is now fairly familiar as such in Britain too.[1]

We have seen the Baroque style first heralded in the massive forms and the gigantic *excelsior* of the dome of Michelangelo's St. Peter's. We have then seen that these efforts of Michelangelo towards the Baroque remained exceptional and that he himself in other works of architecture gave way to the pressure of Mannerism. It was only after Mannerism had completed its course that a new generation at the beginning of the 17th century, especially in Rome, tired of the forced austerity of the late 16th, rediscovered Michelangelo as the father of the Baroque. The style thus introduced culminated in Rome between 1630 and 1670, and then left Rome, first for the north of Italy (Guarini and Juvara in Piedmont) and then for Spain and Portugal and Germany and Austria. Rome, since the late 17th century, turned back to its classical tradition,

---

[1] But as late as 1927 it was printed in an accepted English textbook of the history of architecture that Baroque signifies "a heavy and clumsy treatment of Renaissance architecture, with coarse and florid detail", and that it is "improperly used to denote a supposed 'style' which has no existence as the style of any period".

partly under the influence of Paris. For the Paris of Richelieu, Colbert and Louis XIV had become the centre of European art, a position which until then Rome had held unchallenged for well over 150 years.

The popes and cardinals of the 17th century were enthusiastic patrons, eager to commemorate their names by magnificent churches, palaces and tombs. Of the severity of fifty years before, when the Counter-Reformation had been a militant force, nothing was left. The Jesuits became more and more lenient, the most popular saints were of a lovable, gentle, accommodating kind (such as St. François de Sales), and the new experimental science was promoted under the very eyes of the popes, until in the 18th century Benedict XIV could accept books which Voltaire and Montesquieu sent him as presents.

However, a general decline in the religious fervour of the people can hardly be noticed before 1660 or even later. Not the intensity of religious feelings, only their nature changed. Art and architecture prove that unmistakably. We can here analyse but a few examples, and it is therefore advisable not to choose the most magnificent, say the nave and facade of St. Peter's, as Carlo Maderna designed them in 1606, and as they were completed in 1626, but the most significant.

Maderna was the leading architect of his generation in Rome. He died in 1629. His successors in fame were Gianlorenzo Bernini (1598–1680), Francesco Borromini (1599–1667) and Pietro da Cortona (1596–1669). Bernini came from Naples, Maderna and Borromini from the north of Italy, the country round the lakes, and Cortona, as his name shows, from the south of Tuscany. As in the 16th century, so there were in the 17th only very few Romans amongst the great men of Rome. In architecture the influx from Lombardy had a considerable effect on the appearance of the city. A breadth and freedom were introduced in distinct contrast to Roman gravity. Thus Maderna's ground plan of the Palazzo Barberini (fig. 63)— its facade is by Bernini and a good deal of its decorative detail by Borromini—is of a kind wholly new in Rome, but to a certain extent developing what Northern Italian palaces and villas (especially those of Genoa and its surroundings) had done in the later 16th century. As against the austere blocks of the Florentine and Roman palaces (cf. the Palazzo Farnese, fig. 57), the Barberini Palace has a front opened in a wide loggia and with short wings jutting forward on the right and the left. The Roman plan with colonnaded inner courtyard is, one might say, cut into two, and only one half remains. The colonnades are now part of the facade. This exposing to the public of what had until then been kept private is eminently characteristic of the Baroque, as will be seen presently. The main staircase of the Barberini Palace also is wider and more open than those of

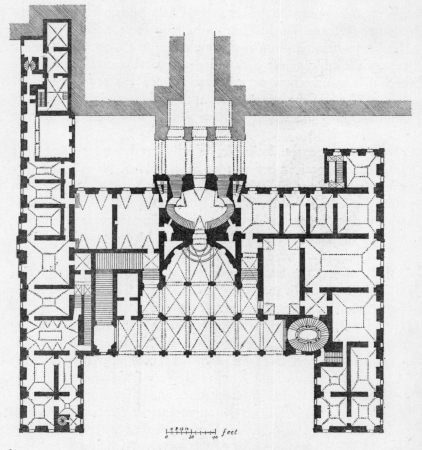

63. CARLO MADERNA (AND GIANLORENZO BERNINI?): PALAZZO BARBERINI, ROME, BEGUN 1628.

the 16th century, the oval second staircase is a typical Serlio-Palladio motif, and the semicircular niche to the entrance hall in the centre, as well as the oval saloon to which it leads, are forms that the architect might have found in Roman churches and in the ruins of Imperial Rome, but that in domestic architecture are also distinctly in the spirit of Palladio (and the Lombards too).

It is important to remember that when Bernini with his South Italian impetuosity won the first place in Roman sculpture and architecture, this infiltration of North Italian elegance had already done its work. His noble colonnades in front of St. Peter's (pl. LXIII) have something of the happy openness of Palladian villa architecture, in spite of their Roman weight and their Berninesque sculptural vigour. For Bernini was the son of a sculptor and himself the greatest sculptor of the Baroque. He incidentally also painted, and as for his reputation as an architect, it was so great that Louis XIV invited him to Paris to design plans for an enlargement of the Louvre Palace. Bernini was as universal as Michelangelo, and nearly as famous. Borromini, on the other hand, was trained as a mason, and, since he was distantly related to Maderna, found work in a small way at St. Peter's when he went to Rome at the age of fifteen. There he worked on, humble and unknown, while Bernini created his first masterpiece of Baroque decoration, the bronze canopy under Michelangelo's dome, in the centre of St. Peter's, a huge monument, nearly 100 feet high, and with its four gigantic twisted columns the very symbol of the changed age, of a grandeur without restraint, a wild extravagance, and a luxury of detail that would have been distasteful to Michelangelo.

The same vehemence of approach and the same revolutionary disregard of conventions characterise Borromini's first important work, the church of S. Carlo alle Quattro Fontane (pl. LXIV), begun in 1633. The interior is so small that it would fit into one of the piers which support the dome of St. Peter's. But in spite of its miniature size it is one of the most ingenious spatial compositions of the century. It has been said before that the normal plan for longitudinal churches of the Baroque was that of the Gesù: nave with side chapels, short transepts and dome over the crossing. It was broadened and enriched by the following generations (S. Ignazio, Rome, 1626 seqq.). But the centralised ground plan was not given up either. It was only the predominance of the circle in central churches which the Baroque discarded in Rome. Instead of the circle the oval was introduced, already in Vignola's S. Anna dei Palafrenieri (fig. 64), a less finite form, and a form that endows the centralised plan with longitudinal elements, i.e. elements suggestive of movement in space. An infinite number of variations on the theme of the oval was developed first by the architects of Italy and then by those of other countries. They constitute the most interesting development of

Baroque church architecture, a development belonging in Italy chiefly to the second half of the 17th century. In Vignola's S. Anna the longer axis of the oval is placed at right angles to the facade. This is repeated by most of the others, but S. Agnese in Piazza Navona (fig. 65), begun in 1652 (by Carlo Rainaldi and provided by Borromini with its North Italian two-tower

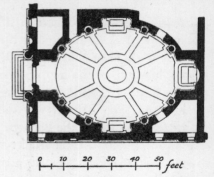

64. GIACOMO VIGNOLA: S. ANNA DEI PALA-
FRENIERI, ROME, BEGUN *c.* 1570.

facade), consists of an octagon in a square, with little niches in the corners, and extended by identical entrance and choir chapels in west and east, and by considerably deeper north and south transeptal chapels so as to produce an effect of a broad oval parallel to the facade, with masonry fragments sticking into its outline. Bernini placed a real oval with eight niches into the same position in his late church of S. Andrea al Quirinale, 1678 (fig. 66). Vignola's composition was taken up by Maderna at S. Giacomo al Corso, 1594, and by Rainaldi at S. Maria di Monte Santo, 1662. This, incidentally, is one of the two identical churches by the Porta del Popolo, marking the start of three radiating streets towards the centre of Rome.

The oval even captured France, especially by the efforts of Louis Levau, as we shall see later. Meanwhile by far the most brilliant paraphrase on the oval theme is Borromini's S. Carlo. The church can serve better than any other to analyse what tremendous advantages the Baroque architect could derive from composing in ovals instead of rectangles or circles. Whereas all through the Renaissance spatial clarity had been the governing idea, and the eye of the spectator had been able to run unimpeded from one part to another and read the meaning of the whole and the parts without effort, nobody, standing in S. Carlo, can at once understand of what elements it is made, and how they are intertwined to produce such a rolling, rocking effect. To analyse the ground plan (fig. 67) it will be best not to set out from the oval at right angles to the facade which, broadly speaking, the church seems to be, but from the domed Greek cross of the Renaissance. Borromini has given the dome absolute supremacy over the arms. Their corners are bevelled off so that the walls under the oval dome read like an elongated lozenge

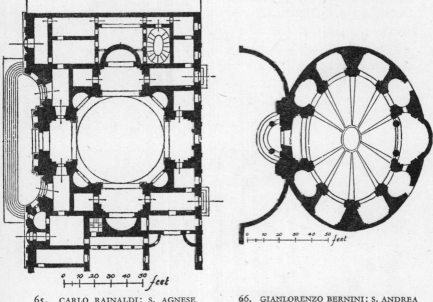

65. CARLO RAINALDI: S. AGNESE,
ROME, BEGUN 1652.

66. GIANLORENZO BERNINI: S. ANDREA
AL QUIRINALE, ROME, BEGUN 1678.

opening out into shallow chapels, the dwarfed arms of the original
Greek cross. The chapels on the right and the left are fragments of
ovals. If completed, they would meet in the centre of the building.
The entrance chapel and the apsidal chapel are also fragments of
ovals. They just touch the side ovals. Thus five compound spatial
shapes merge into each other. We can stand nowhere without
taking part in the swaying rhythm of several of them. The Late
Gothic churches of Germany had achieved a similar wealth of
spatial relations, but by means of forms that seem wiry when compared with the undulating walls of S. Carlo. Michelangelo is responsible for this turn of architecture towards the plastic. Space
now seems hollowed out by the hand of a sculptor, walls are
moulded as if made of wax or clay.

Borromini's most daring enterprise in setting whole walls into
motion is the facade of S. Carlo which was added in 1667, the year
of his death (pl. LXV). The ground floor and its cornice give the
main theme: concave—convex—concave. But the first floor answers
by a concave—concave—concave flow, complicated by the insertion
of a kind of flattened-out miniature oval temple set into the centre
concavity so that this bay seems convex as long as one does not look
up to its top part. Such relations in volume and space sound dry

when described; when seen, however, there is *brio* and passion in them, and also something distinctly voluptuous, a swaying and swerving as of the naked human form. Watch how the two west towers of S. Agnese stand away from the main front of the church, separated by the convex curves of the two sides of the facade centre, or how in Pietro da Cortona's—S. Maria della Pace (1656–57) the front is spread out—with straight wings on the ground floor, but a sweeping convex curve on the first floor out of which the centre of the facade reaches forward, ending in a semicircular portico on the ground floor and a slightly set back shallower convex curve on the first floor (pl. LXVI). Columns and pilasters crowd together on it in a way that makes the composition of Vignola's Gesù front seem restrained in the extreme.

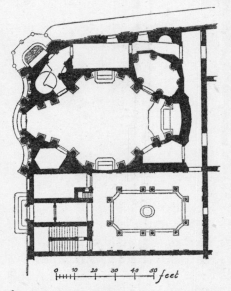

67. FRANCESCO BORROMINI: S. CARLO ALLE QUATTRO FONTANE, BEGUN 1633. FRONT, 1667.

In fact the majority of Roman Baroque facades kept to the basic composition of Vignola and only endowed it with a new meaning by way of an excessive abundance of columns jostling against each other, and the most unconventional use and motives of decoration (fig. 68). None however was more daring in his detail than Borromini. In the facade of S. Carlo the curious oval windows on the ground floor should be observed with the palm leaves that surround them, and with a crown above, and some sort of a Roman altar in relief beneath, and so, motif for motif, up the facade until the ogee arch at the top is reached, and the polygons of odd shapes and diminishing sizes that decorate the cupola inside. Every one of these details is senseless, unless they are seen together and as parts of a super-ordinate decorative whole.

To understand the Baroque it is essential to see it in this per-spective. We are too much used—especially in this country—to looking at decoration as something that may or may not be added to architecture. In fact all architecture is both structure and decoration, decoration for which the architect himself, or the sculptor, the painter, the glass-painter may be responsible. But the relation of decoration to structure varies in different ages and with different nations. In the Gothic style of the cathedrals all decoration served the mason's work. Then ornamental sculpture, late in the 13th and early in the 14th century, seemed to overgrow sculpture. Then, again somewhat later, figure sculpture and painting freed

68. MARTINO LUNGHI THE YOUNGER: SS. VINCENZO ED ANASTASIO, ROME, 1650.

themselves from the supremacy of architecture altogether. A monument like Verrocchio's Colleoni in Venice, standing free in a square without any architectural support, would have been inadmissible in the Middle Ages. Just as novel was the conception of easel painting as such, painting independent of the wall against which it was going to be placed. The Renaissance accepted the independence of the fine arts, but was able to hold them together within a building, because of the principle of relatively independent parts that governed all Renaissance composition. Now however, in the Baroque, that principle had been abandoned. Again, as in Gothic architecture, parts cannot be isolated. We have seen that at S. Carlo. But the Baroque, although believing in the unity of all art, could not restore the supremacy of structure. Architects of the 17th century had to accept the claims of the sculptor and painter, and in fact often were sculptors and painters. Instead of the Gothic relation of superordinate and subordinate, there is now a co-operation of all the arts. The result was still that "*Gesamtkunstwerk*" (total art) which Wagner, in his operas, after it had been wilfully destroyed at the end of the Baroque, endeavoured in vain to recover for the 19th century. In the works of Bernini and Borromini, what binds architectural, ornamental, sculptural and pictorial effects into indivisible unity is the decorative principle common to all.

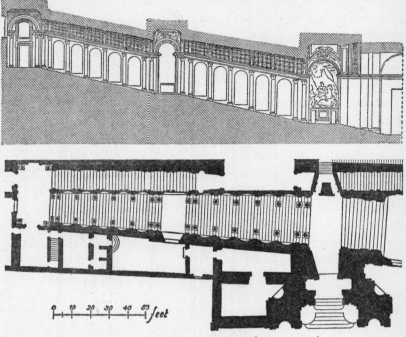

69.   GIANLORENZO BERNINI: THE ROYAL STAIRCASE (SCALA REGIA) IN THE VATICAN
PALACE, ROME, *c.* 1665.

Now this decorative creed could leave no room in the minds of
patrons and artists of the Baroque to be squeamish about honesty
in the use of materials. As long as the effect was attained, what could
it matter whether you attained it with marble or with stucco, with
gold or with tin, with a real bridge or a sham bridge such as we find
sometimes in English parks? Optical illusion is in fact (to Ruskin's
grave displeasure) amongst the most characteristic devices of Baroque
architecture. Bernini's Royal Staircase, the *Scala Regia* in the
Vatican Palace (pl. LXVII and fig. 69), illustrates this at its most
suggestive. It was built during the same sixties which saw Borromini's facade of S. Carlo rise from the ground and the colonnades
in front of St. Peter's (pl. LXIII). As they are a masterpiece of stage
setting, seemingly raising the height and weight of Maderna's
facade, and at the same time making the loggia of the Papal bene-
dictions and the *Porta Santa* visible to everybody amongst the tens
of thousands who would stand in the forecourt on the occasion
of great celebrations, so is the Scala Regia designed with a supreme
knowledge of scenic effects. It is the main entrance to the palace.

Coming from the colonnades, one reaches it along a corridor. The corridor ends in about fifteen or twenty steps, and then there is a slight break just at the point where one enters at right angles from the galilee porch of St. Peter's. So here two main directions meet. They had to be joined and connected up. It was a master-stroke of Bernini to place opposite the entrance from the church an equestrian monument to the Emperor Constantine. Coming up from the corridor it appears on the right and forces us to halt, before we enter the Royal Staircase itself. The sudden appearance of the white prancing horse against a storm-swept drapery lit by windows above serves to conceal the otherwise unpleasant change of direction.

The *Scala Regia* had to be fitted into an awkwardly shaped area between church and palace. It is long, comparatively narrow and has irregularly converging walls. Bernini turned all this to advantage by means of an ingenious tunnel-vaulted colonnade of diminishing size. The principle is that of vistas on the Baroque stage. Streets there were made to appear long by the use of exaggerated perspective. In the same way Borromini treated the niches at S. Carlo (pl. LXIV) and the windows on the top floor of the Palazzo Barberini. Such scenic illusions were not entirely new. They are to be found in Bramante's early works in Milan. Michelangelo too in his design for the Capitol in Rome had placed the palaces on the sides at such an angle as to increase the apparent height of the Senate House. Light is another means for dramatising the ascent up the Royal Staircase. On the first landing halfway up it falls in from the left, on the second in the far distance a window faces the staircase and dissolves the contours of the room. Finally there is the decoration, the splendid angels, e.g. with their trumpets holding up the Pope's arms, to complete this gorgeous overture to the Vatican Palace.

Angels, genii and such-like figures, preferably in realistic colouring, are an essential part of Baroque settings. Not only do they serve to cover up structural joints and to hide the contraptions "behind the scenes" which make these illusions work, but they also act as intermediaries between the real space in which we move and the space created by the artist. The Baroque does not want to keep the border line visible between audience and stage. Such terms from the world of the theatre—or should one rather say: the world of the opera, which was an Italian invention of the 17th century—come into one's mind with good reason. However, there is more than a mere theatrical trick in this flow from reality into illusion and from illusion into reality. Bernini's famous chapel of St. Teresa in the church of S. Maria della Vittoria in Rome proves that (pl. LXVIII). The chapel, which dates from 1646, is faced with dark marbles, their gleaming surfaces of amber, gold and pink reflecting the light in ever-changing patterns. In the middle of the wall in front of the entrance is the altar of the saint. It is flanked by heavy coupled columns and pilasters with a broken pediment, placed on the slant so that they come forward towards us and then recede to focus our attention on the centre of the altar, where one would expect to find a painting, but where there is a niche with a sculptural group, treated like a picture and giving an illusion of reality that is as startling to-day as it was three hundred years ago. Everything in the chapel contributes to this *peinture vivante* illusion. Along the walls on the right and the left there are also niches opened into the chapel walls, and there Bernini has portrayed in marble, behind balconies, members of the Cornaro family, the donors of the chapel, watching with us the miraculous scene, precisely as though they were in the boxes, and we in the stalls of a theatre.

The boundary line between our world and the world of art is in this most ingeniously effaced. As our own attention and that of the marble figures is directed towards the same goal, we cannot help giving the same degree of reality first to them as to ourselves, and then to the figures on the altar too. And Bernini has used all his mastery in the modelling of St. Teresa and the angel to help in that deception. The heavy cloak of the nun, the fluffiness of the clouds, the light drapery of the youthful angel and his soft flesh are all rendered with an exquisite realism. The expression of the saint in the miracle of the union with Christ is of an unforgettable voluptuous ecstasy. She faints as though overwhelmed by a physical penetration. At the same time she is raised into the air, and the diagonal sweep of the group makes us believe the impossible. Beams of gold—they are gilt metal shafts—conceal the back wall of the niche, and an opening high up behind the entablature glazed with a yellow pane models the scene with a magical light.

The chapel of St. Teresa is the most daring example of such illusionism in Rome. It is in fact an exception. Rome has never really believed in extremes. Bernini was a Neapolitan; and Naples was Spanish. To experience the thrills of extremes and excesses one must indeed go to Spain, or else to Portugal, or of course Germany. To these countries the Baroque came late, but it was taken up with tremendous fervour. Italy has no examples of such orgiastic inter-penetration of reality and fiction as can be seen in some few Spanish and many more South German churches of the early 18th century.

The most outstanding example on Spanish soil is Narciso Tomé's *Trasparente* in Toledo Cathedral (pl. LXIX and fig. 70). The cathedral is a 13th-century building in the style of classic French Gothic. It has a high altar with a vast Late Gothic reredos. Catholic orthodoxy objected to people walking along the ambulatory behind the Blessed Sacra-ment. So an ingenious plan was worked out by which the Sacrament could be seen and would be respected from the ambulatory as well. It was placed in a glass-fronted receptacle—hence the name *Tras-parente*—and an altar scenery was built up around it of unheard-of pomp. The work was completed in 1732. Attention was focused on to the Sacrament by richly decorated columns. They are linked up with large outer columns by cornices curved upwards. These curves and the relief scenes in perspective on the panels below give the illusion—in the same way as Bernini's colonnade in the *Scala Regia* —as though the distance from front to back of the altar was far deeper than it really is. Moreover, the glass-fronted opening is surrounded by angels to cover all structural props. By the clouds of angels our eyes are led up to where the last Supper is acted—at a fantastic height—by figures of polychromatic marble. Higher up still is the Virgin soaring up to Heaven. To enhance the effect of a miraculous apparition, the whole scene is floodlit from behind where we stand while we stare at it, lit that is in the way special stage lighting is operated to-day. What the ingenious architect has done is to take out the masonry between the ribs of half a Gothic vault of the ambulatory—the engineering skill of the 13th century allowed him to do so without weakening the construction—spread groups of angels around the opening, and then erect above it a dormer with a window, invisible from below, which lets in a flood of golden light past the angels and the bay of the ambulatory in which we stand, on to the altar with its figures and the Sacrament. And when, to discover this source of magic light, we turn round, away from the altar, we see in the dazzling light beyond the angels Christ himself seated on clouds, and prophets and the Heavenly Host surrounding Him.

Such spatial extremism, the pulling of a whole room into one vast stupefying ornament, is, it has been said before, exceptional in Spain. What Spain and Portugal excelled in was this same extremism

70. NARCISO TOMÉ: "TRASPARENTE" IN THE CATHEDRAL OF TOLEDO, COMPLETED 1732.

expressing itself in the piling of ornament on to surfaces. This ornamental mania had been a Spanish heritage ever since Mohammedan times, the Alhambra, and the Late Gothic of such works as the front of St. Paul's at Valladolid (pl. XLIII), but never yet had it taken quite such fantastic shapes as it now did in the so-called Churrigueresque style, named after its chief exponent José de Churriguéra (1650–1725). The immediate inspiration of the barbaric scrolls and thick mouldings of, e.g., the Sacristy of the Charterhouse at Granada (1727–64; pl. LXX; by Luis de Arévalo and F. Manuel Vasquez) must have been native art of Central or South America, as the immediate inspiration of the Manueline style in Portugal has been found in the East Indies. It is in fact in Mexico that the Spanish architects celebrated the wildest orgies of decoration.

The *Trasparente* stands on a higher æsthetic level no doubt than the incrustations of the Churrigueresque, though morally, especially to the Ruskinian morality of Late Victorian England, they may both be equally objectionable. Southern Germany in the 18th century was almost as fond of ornament for ornament's sake as Spain. There again the tradition leads back to the Middle Ages. But as it has been shown that German Late Gothic was fonder of spatial complexity than the late Gothic of any other country, so the exploitation of space became now the central problem of German Late Baroque, a problem occasionally solved with the knock-out technique of the *Trasparente*, but more often by purer strictly architectural means.

Two architects only out of the many working between 1720 and 1760 can here be introduced: Cosmas Damian Asam (1686–1739) and Johann Balthasar Neumann (1687–1753).

Cosmas Damian Asam was a painter and decorator, his brother Egid Quirin (1692–1750) a sculptor. The two as a rule worked together, not considered as anything but competent craftsmen and not apparently considering themselves as anything else either. They, and in common with them the majority of the German 18th-century architects, were not really architects in the Renaissance or modern sense. They were brought up in villages to know something about building, and that was enough. No big ideas about professional status entered their heads. In fact the sociological position of architecture in Germany before the 19th century was still mediæval, and most of the patrons were still princes, bishops, abbots, just as they had been three hundred years earlier. Neumann belongs to another category, one that had not existed in the Middle Ages or the Renaissance. Its source is the France of Louis XIV, as will be shown later (see p. 168). He had started in the artillery force of the Prince-Bishop of Würzburg. There he had shown a keen interest in mathematics and fortification. Michelangelo too, it will be remembered, had worked on the defence engineering, and some of the other leading 16th-century architects in Italy, e.g. Sammicheli, had been distinguished military engineers. The Prince-Bishop singled out young Neumann for architectural work, made him his surveyor of works and sent him to Paris and Vienna to discuss the plans for his new palace at Würzburg with his opposite numbers there, the French king's and the Emperor's architects, and to learn from them. Thus his most famous work, the palace at Würzburg, is only partly his; but his experience grew, and the Bishop appreciated him more and more. He was made a captain, then a major, then a colonel, but he had no longer any duties of active service and could devote all his time to architecture. He did all the designing and supervising for the Bishop that had to be done, and was soon also asked to design palaces and churches for other clients.

Thus churches of the 18th century in Germany may originate from very different *milieus*: the workshop of the mediæval craftsman or the drawing-board of the technically skilled courtier. Differences in architectural character may often be explained in this way. Asam churches are naïve, Neumann's are of an intellectual complexity equal to Bach's. Spatial effects, however, are as important in the Asams' as in Neumann's work. But the Asams stick to the more ostentatious devices of optical illusion (raising them, it is true, to a high emotional pitch), while Neumann composes his configurations of space scorning easy deceptions.

At Rohr near Ratisbon the Asams, instead of a High Altar, placed in the chancel of the church a showpiece, cruder than Bernini's St. Teresa, and twice as melodramatic: the Apostles, life-size figures standing around a life-size Baroque sarcophagus, and the Virgin rising to Heaven supported by angels to be received into a glory of clouds and cherubs high above. Wild gesticulation and dark glowing colour all help to inflame the passions of faith. The chancel at Weltenburg, another church near Ratisbon, is the stage for a more mysterious apparition: a silver St. George on horseback wielding a flame-shaped sword and riding straight towards us out of a background of dazzling light which is let in from concealed windows. The dragon and the princess stand out as dark golden silhouettes against all this glitter. Rohr was built in 1718–25, Weltenberg in 1717–21. They are early works of the Asams.

In their best later work they endeavoured to achieve more than a *Trasparente* effect. Egid Quirin owned a house at Munich; when he approached the age of forty he began to think of a monument that he might proudly leave behind after his death. So he decided in 1731 to build on a site adjoining his house a church as his private offering. The church was built from 1733 to about 1750 and dedicated to St. John Nepomuk. It is a tiny church (pl. LXXI) less than thirty feet wide, relatively tall and narrow with a narrow gallery all the way round, a ground-floor altar and a gallery altar. The gallery balancing on the fingers of pirouetting termini or caryatid angels sways forward and backward, the top cornice surges up and droops down, the colour scheme is of sombre gold, browns and dark reds, glistening in sudden flashes where light falls on it, light which comes only from the entrance, that is from behind our backs, and from concealed windows above the cornice. The top east window is placed in such a way that a group of the Trinity appears against it; God holding the Crucifix, and the Holy Ghost above, the whole again surrounded by angels—wildly fantastic, yet of a superb magic reality. What raises St. John Nepomuk above the level of Rohr, Weltenberg and the *Trasparente* is the co-operation of strictly architectural composition with the merely optical deceptions to achieve an intense sensation of surprise which may turn easily into religious fervour.

But sensational it is all the same, sensational in a literal sense: no artists before Bernini, the Asams and Tomé have aimed at such violent effects. And are they therefore debauched, unscrupulous and pagan as our Pugins and Ruskins have made them out? We should not accept their verdicts uncritically, lest we might deprive ourselves of a good deal of legitimate pleasure. We may indeed, up here in the North, where we live, find it hard to connect Christ and the Church with this obtruding physical closeness of presentation. To the Southerner, in Bavaria, in Austria, in Italy, in Spain, where people live so much more with all their senses, it is a genuine form of religious experience. While in the North during the lifetime of Bernini, the Asams and Tomé, Spinoza visualised a pantheism, with God pervading all beings and all things, Rembrandt discovered the infinite for painting in his treatment of light and his merging of action into undefined but live background, and Newton and Leibniz discovered it for mathematics in their conception of the calculus, the South had its more concrete realisation of an all-embracing oneness and a presence of the infinite in the architects' and decorators' unification of real and fictitious worlds, and in their spatial effects stepping beyond the bounds of what the beholder can rationally explain to himself. And Neumann's work proves conclusively what architectural purity and subtlety can be achieved by such spatial magic, provided the visitor to his buildings is able to follow his guidance. We of the 20th century do not usually find it easy to concentrate on spatial counterpoint just as our audiences in church and concert no doubt hear musical counterpoint less distinctly than those for whom Bach wrote. The parallelism is in fact striking in quality too. The best German 18th-century architecture is up to the standard of the best German 18th-century music.

Take Neumann's pilgrimage church of Vierzehnheiligen in Franconia, built from 1743 to 1772 (pl. LXXII and figs. 71–73). The first impression on entering this vast, solitary pilgrimage church is one of bliss and elation. All is light: white, gold, pink. In this the church testifies to its later date than that of St. John Nepomuk. Asam's work is still Baroque in the 17th-century sense, Neumann's belongs to that last phase of the Baroque which goes under the name Rococo. For the Rococo is not a separate style. It is part of the Baroque, as Decorated is part of the Gothic style. The difference of Baroque and Rococo is only one of sublimation. The later phase is light, where the earlier was sombre; delicate, where the earlier was forceful; playful, where the earlier was passionate. But it is just as *mouvementé*, as vivacious, as voluptuous as the Baroque. One connects the term Rococo chiefly with France and the age of Casanova on the one hand, Voltaire on the other. In Germany it is not intellectually or sensually sophisticated—it is as direct an expression of the people's æsthetic instinct as late Gothic architecture and decoration had been, and one can see from the devotion to-day of the peasants in these German Baroque—and the Italian Baroque—churches that their style is not a style of interest only to a privileged set of virtuosi.

Yet the style of Vierzehnheiligen is not an easy style. It is not enough to be overwhelmed by it, as anyone may be in Asam churches; it asks for an exact understanding—which is a job for the expert: architects' architecture, as the fugue is musicians' music. The oval central altar in the middle of the nave may well please the rustic worshippers who kneel round this gorgeous object, half a coral reef and half a fairy sedan chair. Having taken in this glory of confectionery, the layman will then look up and see on all sides glittering decoration, surf and froth and rocket, and like it immensely. But if he starts walking round, he will soon find himself in utter confusion. What he has learned and so often seen of nave and aisle and chancel seems of no value here. This confusion of the lay mind, a keen thrill of the trained, is due to the ground plan, one of the most ingenious pieces of architectural design ever conceived (figs. 71–73). The church, if one looks at it from outside, has apparently a nave and aisles, and a centrally planned east end with polygonal ends to transepts and choir. In fact the choir is an oval, the transepts are circular, and the nave consists of two ovals following each other so that the first, into which one enters immediately one has passed the Borrominesque undulating front, is of the size of the choir oval and the second considerably larger. It is here that the altar of the fourteen saints stands. Here then is the spiritual centre of the church. So there arises an antagonism of great poignancy between what the exterior promises as the centre and what the interior reveals to be the centre—namely between the crossing where nave and transepts meet, and the centre of the principal oval. As for the aisles they are nothing but spatial residues. Walking along them, one feels painfully behind the scenes. What matters alone is the interaction of the ovals. At vault height they are separated by transverse arches. These however are not simple bands across from one arcade column to the one opposite. They are three-dimensional, bowing to each other, as the nodding arches had done on a small scale in the 14th century. This has the most exciting and baffling effect at the crossing. Here in a church of the Gesù type—and Vierzehnheiligen appears from outside to belong to this type—one would expect a dome, the summit of the composition. Instead of that, there lies, as has been said before, just at the centre of the crossing, the point where choir oval and central oval meet. The two transverse arches struck from the piers of the crossing bend, the western one eastward, the eastern westward until they touch each other in exactly the same place as the ovals, purposely emphasising the fact that, where a normal Baroque church would have had the crest of the undulating movement of the vaults, Vierzehnheiligen has a trough—a most effective spatial counterpoint. Yet another spatial complication is incidentally provided by the insertion of a second minor transept farther west than the main one. Side altars are placed in it, just as altars stand against the east end of the church and against the east piers of the

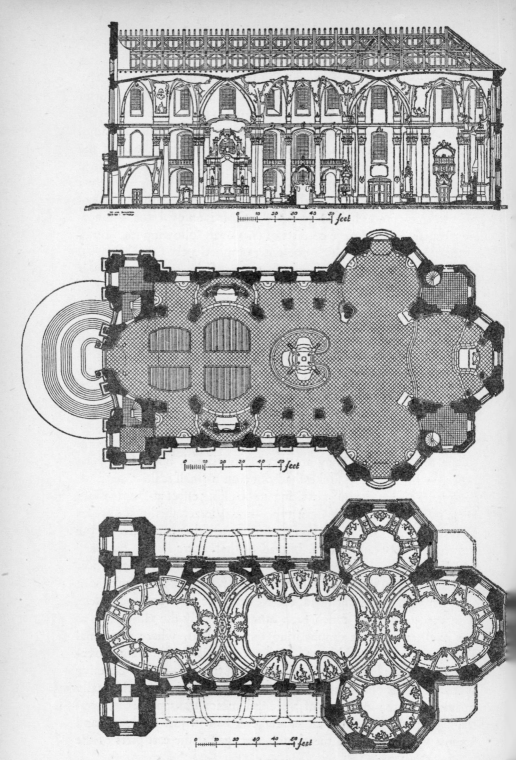

71, 72 AND 73. BALTHASAR NEUMANN: VIERZEHNHEILIGEN IN FRANÇONIA, BEGUN 1743. SECTIC
(NOT SHOWING THE WEST TOWERS), PLAN ON GROUND-FLOOR LEVEL, PLAN OF VAULTS.

crossing. The latter are set diagonally so as to guide the eye towards the splendid high altar—a decidedly theatrical effect.

This is one of the chief objections against such churches. Its validity has already been queried. Besides, why did architects and artists so fervently strive to deceive and create such intense illusion of reality? What reality was the Church concerned with? Surely that of the Divine Presence. It is the zeal of an age in which Roman Catholic dogmas, mysteries and miracles, were no longer, as they had been in the Middle Ages, accepted as truth by all. There were heretics, and there were sceptics. To restore the first to the fold, to convince the others, religious architecture had both to inflame and to mesmerise. But, it is brought forward as another argument against Baroque churches, that they seem worldly as compared with the churches of the Middle Ages. Now it is true that the character of Baroque decoration in a church and a palace is identical. But is not exactly the same true of the Middle Ages? The idea behind the identity is perfectly sane. By the splendour of the arts we honour a king; is not supreme splendour due to the King of Kings? In our churches to-day and in those churches of the Middle Ages which the 19th century restored, there is nothing of this. They are halls with an atmosphere to concentrate the thoughts of a congregation on worship and prayer. A church of the Baroque was literally the house of the Lord.

Still, there is no denying the fact that we, observers or believers, never feel quite sure where in a church such as Vierzehnheiligen the spiritual ends and the worldly begins. The ecstatic *élan* of the architectural forms at large is irresistible, but it is not necessarily a religious *élan*. There was, it is true, a real mania in Southern Germany and Austria between 1700 and 1760 for building vast churches and monasteries. However, not all this building was done entirely *ad majorem Die gloriam*. Did a monastery like Weingarten near the lake of Constance really need these far-stretched, elegantly curved outbuildings which appear in a rebuilding scheme of 1723 (fig. 74)? This scheme was never carried out; but others—e.g. at Klosterneuburg, St. Florian and Melk, all three on the Danube—were. Melk was begun in 1702 by Jakob Prandtauer (died 1726); it is in many ways the most remarkable of the three (pl. LXXIII), shooting up out of the rocks, steep above the river. The church with its undulating front, its two many-pinnacled towers and its bulbous spires is set back. Two pavilions of the monastery buildings, housing the marble hall and the library, jut forward to its right and left converging as they approach the front bastion. They are here connected by lower roughly semicircular wings. Between these, exactly in line with the church, is an oddly Palladian arch to keep the vista open from the west portal towards the river. It is an exquisite piece of visual calculation—a late and subtle development of Palladio's so much simpler connecting of villa and landscape, and

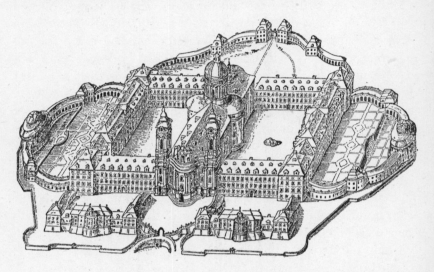

74. PLAN FOR THE REBUILDING OF THE MONASTERY OF WEINGARTEN, 1723.

evidently the work of the century which discovered landscape gardening (see p. 184).

But, to return to our question, while the towering church on the cliff—a Durham of the Baroque—may be rightly considered a monument of militant catholicism, the palaces for abbot and monks with their richly ornamented saloons and their terraces are amenities of this world, on exactly the same level, and planned and executed in exactly the same lavish manner, as the contemporary palaces of the secular and clerical rulers of the innumerable states of the Holy Roman Empire or the country palaces of the English aristocracy, or Caserta, the palace of the King of Naples, or Stupinigi, the palace of the Duke of Savoy and King of Sardinia.

One of the most irresponsible of these schemes is the Zwinger in Dresden, built by Mathäus Daniel Pöppelmann (1662–1736) for the Elector Augustus the Strong, athlete, glutton and lecher. The

Zwinger—very badly damaged in 1944 and in course of restoration now—(pl. LXXIV) is a combined orangery and electoral grandstand for tournaments and pageants. It was not supposed to stand on its own, as it does now, attached only to the 19th-century picture gallery; it was meant to form part of a palace stretching across to the River Elbe. It consists of one-storied galleries with two-storied pavilions between. The galleries are comparatively restrained in design, but the most exuberant decoration is lavished over the pavilions. Especially the gate pavilion is a fantasy unchecked by any consideration of use. The ground-floor archway has instead of a proper pediment two bits of a broken pediment swinging away from each other. The first-floor pediment is broken too, but nodding inward instead of outward. The whole first floor is open on all sides —a kiosk or gazebo, as it were, and above its attic swarming with figures of putti is a bulbous cupola with the royal and electoral emblems on top.

If those who can admire a Gothic Devon screen feel repelled by the Zwinger, they either do not really look at the object before them, or they look at it with the blinkers of puritanism. What an exultation in these rocking curves, and yet what a grace. It is joyful, but never vulgar; vigorous, boisterous perhaps, but never crude. It is of an inexhaustible creative power, with ever new combinations and variations of Italian Baroque forms placed against each other and piled above each other. The forward and backward motion never stops. Borromini appears massive against this swiftness of movement through space.

As in every original style, the same formal intention seems, in the German Rococo, to model space and volume. The three-dimensional curve is the *leitmotif* of the period. It appears at Vierzehnheiligen as it appears in the Zwinger, and it pervades buildings from their main theme of composition down to the smallest ornamental details. Nowhere else perhaps can this be seen as convincingly as in one of Neumann's secular masterpieces, the staircase of the Bishop's Palace at Bruchsal (pls. LXXV, LXXVI a & b and fig. 76). The palace itself is not by Neumann. It was in quite an advanced state when, in 1730, Neumann was called in to redesign the staircase.

The palace, one of the most deplorable of all war casualties, consisted of a rectangular centre block or *corps de logis* and lower projecting wings, i.e. the Palladian scheme which had from Northern Italy spread to England and also to France, where it

75. ENRIQUE DE EGAS: STAIRCASE IN THE HOLY CROSS HOSPITAL, TOLEDO, 1504–14.

has been modified and then, in its revised shape with the space between the wings treated as a formal *cour d'honneur*, taken over by Germany. In the centre of the *corps de logis* is the staircase, an oval room, larger than any other in the palace. This alone is a most significant fact.

In the Middle Ages staircases had mattered little. They were nearly always tucked away—a purely utilitarian part of the building. Newel staircases taking up as little space as possible were the rule.

The very latest phase of the Gothic style with its new appreciation of space had sometimes tried to endow them with spatial expression. A proper show however was only made of staircases when Italian splendour had revealed to the peoples of the West the crabbed tightness of mediæval forms. Then the French of Francis I's time could enjoy the exterior newel staircase of Blois (pl. LXXIX) and the splendid interior double newel staircase—two parallel spirals within the same well—in the centre of the symmetrical palace of Chambord, and the Spanish, bolder still, could create shortly after 1500 a new type of staircase to be of the greatest influence in the centuries to come: the squared-up newel staircase, with three straight flights of steps around a spacious open well and the landing on the fourth side. This type occurs for the first time in Enrique de Egas's Hospital of the Holy Cross at Toledo (1504–14 ; fig. 75) and in Michele Carlone's castle of Lacalahorra (1508–12). Now Michele Carlone came from Genoa, and it has often been said that the Genoese, who made wide and airy staircases open towards courtyards the happy rule in the later 16th century, were the inventors of this influential type. No case has however yet been pointed out quite as early as the first Spanish examples. Moreover, Spanish architects also seem to have conceived the other most spectacular Baroque type of staircase, and conceived it as early as the 1560's (fig. 91). This type, which runs in a large oblong cage, starting with two straight arms and then, after turning by 180 degrees at the landing, leads up to the upper floor in one arm between the two below (or starting with one and continuing with two), appears to my knowledge for the very first time in Juan Bautista de Toledo's and Francisco de Herrera's Escorial (1563–84). It is eminently characteristic that these staircases, in which space is experienced most vividly by those who ascend them or descend them, originated outside Italy. The Italian Renaissance had no use for them, no use for this flow of spatial strata or compartments into one another. The best Italian Renaissance staircases, such as the one in the Palazzo Farnese (fig. 57), were comfortably wide, but led up between solid walls. Bramante's most interesting staircase, in the Vatican Palace, was of the traditional newel type, though with a wide open well and of gentle rise and generous measurements. Serlio and Palladio followed Bramante in this, although they knew and used the Spanish square three-flight type. However their hearts were not in staircase design. The only innovation in their books which is worth noting because it is so characteristically Mannerist

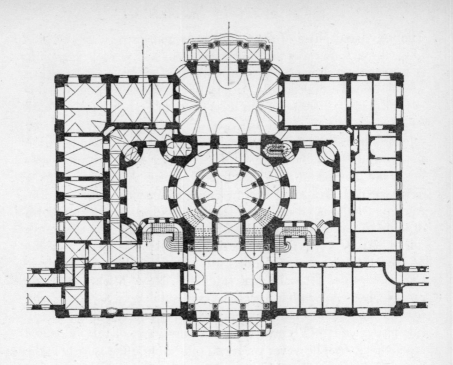

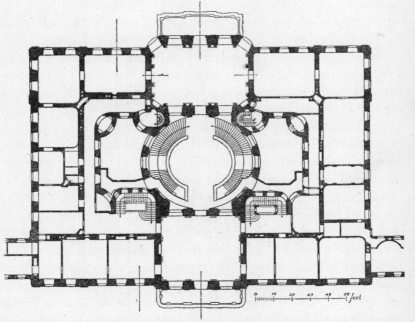

76. BRUCHSAL: EPISCOPAL PALACE. THE CENTRAL STAIRCASE BY BALTHASAR NEUMANN, 1732. TOP; GROUND FLOOR; BOTTOM: FIRST FLOOR.

is the newel staircase elongated into an oval shape (Maderna incidentally kept to this in the Barberini Palace (fig. 63)). The Baroque of the 17th century, especially in France, enriched the current types (see p. 177). That of the Escorial became in many variations the hall-mark of princely magnificence. Neumann's Würzburg staircase with its Tiepolo paintings belongs to it.

But the staircase at Bruchsal is unique. Words can hardly re-evoke the enchanting sensation that one experiences in walking up one of its two arms. They start in the rectangular vestibule. After about ten steps one enters the oval. On the ground floor it is a sombre room, painted with rocks in the rustic manner of Italian grotto imitations. The staircase itself then unfolds between two curved walls, the outside wall solid, that on the inside opened in arcades through which one looks down into the semi-darkness of the oval grotto. The height of the arcade openings of course diminishes as the staircase ascends. And while we walk up, it grows lighter and lighter around us, until we reach the main floor and a platform the size of the oval room beneath. But the vault above covers the larger oval formed by the outer walls of the staircase. Thus the platform with its balustrade separating it from the two staircase arms seems to rise in mid-air, connected only by bridges with the two principal saloons. And the vast vault above is lit by many windows, painted with the gayest of frescoes and decorated with a splendid fireworks of stucco. The spatial rapture of the staircase is in this decoration transformed into ornamental rapture. It culminates in the cartouche over the door leading into the Grand Saloon (pl. LXXVII). The cartouche is not Neumann's design. It is by a Bavarian stuccoist, Johann Michael Feichtmayr. The contract was made in 1752. These Bavarian stuccoists nearly all came from the same village of Wessobrunn, where boys were as a matter of course trained to become proficient in stucco work, just as the decorators of Romanesque churches so often came from certain villages round the North Italian lakes, the makers and vendors of plaster-of-Paris statuettes in the 19th century from Savoy, and the onion-men of to-day from Brittany. Feichtmayr travelled about from job to job, and, when he worked for a monastery, still received wages and board just as the workmen did seven hundred years ago. Neumann must have met him on some job and have recognised his immense wealth of ornamental inventiveness. He appears at Vierzehnheiligen as well as at Bruchsal. In his stucco ornament not one part is symmetrical. The main composition is a zig-zag, from the alluring young angel on the right, up to the cupid or cherub higher up on the left, and up again to the cherub at the top. The forms in detail seem to be incessantly changing, splashing up and sinking back. What are they? Do they represent anything? Sometimes they look like shells, sometimes like froth, sometimes like gristle, sometimes like flames. This kind of ornament is called *rocaille* in France, where it was invented in the 1720's by Meissonier, Oppenord and a few others of provincial or semi-Italian background. It has given the Rococo style its name, and rightly so; for it is a completely original creation, not dependent on anything of the past, as the ornament of the Renaissance had been. It is abstract art of as high an expressional value as any that we are offered to-day so much more pretentiously.

Bruchsal with its perfect unity of space and decoration was the high-water mark of the Baroque style. It was also its end. For only a few years after it had been completed and Neumann had died, Winckelmann published his first books, initiating the Classical Revival in Germany. Between Neumann's world and that of Goethe there is no link. The men of the new world no longer thought in terms of churches and palaces. No church designed anywhere after 1760 is amongst the historically leading examples of architecture. Napoleon built no palaces.

The English nobility, it must be admitted, did; right into the Victorian age. But they had nothing of the unreflecting attitude of the Baroque. This change from a style binding for all and understood by all to a style for the educated only, did not take place in Germany and Italy until 1760. In France and Britain it had come about earlier. But then neither France nor Britain (nor the north of Germany, Holland, Denmark and Scandinavia) had ever accepted the Baroque with all its implications. Their world—it is in many respects *the* modern world—is that of Protestantism. In Roman Catholic countries mediæval traditions lived and flourished down to the 18th century. In the North the Reformation had broken that happy unity. But it had also opened the way for independent thinking and feeling. The Protestant countries (and one should include here the France of the Gallicans, Jansenists and Encyclopædists) had created Puritanism, Enlightenment, the modern predominance of experimental science, and finally the Industrial Revolution in the material and the symphony in the spiritual world. What the cathedral had been to the Middle Ages, the symphony was to the 19th century.

CHAPTER VII

Britain and France from the 16th to the 18th Century

A T THE time of Bruchsal and the *Trasparente*, large houses of Palladian or Neo-Classical style appeared all over England, houses such as Prior Park, near Bath, Holkham Hall, Stowe and Kenwood. In France meanwhile the classic grandeur of Versailles had given way to the Neo-Classical delicacy of the Place de la Concorde and the Petit Trianon. Evidently the development of architecture after the end of the Gothic syle had been very different in Western Europe from that in Central Europe.

Yet in Britain, France, the Netherlands, Spain and Germany, the position had been virtually the same early in the 16th century. In all these countries artists almost at the same moment turned their backs on their Gothic past, attracted by the same new style, the Italian Renaissance. Everywhere during the 15th century, the fascination of Humanism, of Roman literature and the clarity and suppleness of the classic Latin style had been experienced by scholars. The invention of printing helped to spread the new ideals, and many patrons arose among princes, noblemen and merchants. A few of these, when for some reason or other they found themselves in Italy, were converted to Italian art as well, as soon as they had understood its humanistic character. How forceful the sensation must have been it is hardly possible for us to appreciate. One keeps forgetting that it was still a time of scanty and slow communications. Perpendicular to the English, Flamboyant to the French and their national versions of Late Gothic to the Spaniards and Germans were the only architecture they knew. Now all of a sudden, when Charles VIII of France set out on his campaign against Italy in 1494, marched right across the country and captured Naples, or when Dürer, the greatest of German painters, went to Venice in the same year as a young man of twenty-three, they were faced with a style that made all they had known appear confused, crabbed and petty. At the same time, however, these airy, spacious halls, these bold square palaces, these columns, balusters and round-headed arches, these garlands and

Again the contrast between the only slightly older chapel itself and this addition from abroad is striking. And as the one was in the idiom with which everybody had grown up, while the other seemed to speak a foreign language, it is understandable that English patrons wavered between admiration and bewilderment. Very few were prepared to go the whole way (more in fact in France, where there was less of a racial contrast than in England), and those who did, had to rely on craftsmen from Italy, because the English or even the French mason could not at once get into a manner so novel both technically and spiritually.

Now of Italians there were more and more who found their way into France and were welcomed by Francis I, but few who travelled on to Britain. Leonardo da Vinci died in France. Primaticcio came in 1532, Serlio in 1540. They were all painters and not trained for building in the mediæval sense. They only designed, and for the execution of their designs had to rely on the native master masons. A deep antagonism developed at once between the Italians and the competent traditional craftsmen of France to whom these Italian intruders were mountebanks and jacks-of-all-trades. So the new ideal of the artist-architect entered France in this interesting form of a struggle between the builder and the decorator.

However, the contrast does not often appear in actual buildings. For—again probably thanks to racial affinity—the French master masons very soon adopted the Italian vocabulary and used it to produce an essentially original style neither Gothic nor Renaissance. Two stages can be distinguished: the first that of the Loire school, the second that of Lescot's work at the Louvre. The wing of Francis I at Blois (pl. LXXIX) was built between 1515 and about 1525. Every motif used in its decoration is of the North Italian Early Renaissance. On the other hand, the very existence of a newel staircase, and also the fact that its vertical supports are scarcely disguised buttresses, are mediæval. Yet the emphasis on horizontal divisions, the even stronger emphasis on the top cornice, and the arcaded galleries along the whole garden front prove that the designer of Blois, a Frenchman for all we know, had a feeling for what the Renaissance meant.

The attitude of English architects was characteristically different. Hampton Court had been begun in 1515 for Cardinal Wolsey. A little later Henry VIII asked Wolsey to make him a present of the palace in its unfinished state. He added to it, amongst other parts, the Great Hall (fig. 78). Now the palace with its courtyard and gate towers is just as completely in the Gothic tradition as the hall with its hammerbeam roof. Of the Italian Renaissance there is nothing but a limited number of ornamental details, the medallions with the heads of Roman emperors on the gate towers and the putti and foliage in the spandrels of the hall roof. They are competently done, but no attempt is made to bridge the gulf between English construction and Italian decoration.

78.   HAMPTON COURT: GREAT HALL, DETAIL FROM THE HAMMERBEAM ROOF, 1533. PROBABLY BY JAMES NEEDHAM.

So while the first stage in the process of assimilation had been identical in Britain and France, their ways separated at the second already. The distance widened at the third. In the thirties two or three of the most talented French architects of the younger generation, Philibert Delorme (c. 1515–70), Jean Bullant (c. 1515–80) and perhaps Pierre Lescot (c. 1510–78), had gone to Rome where they had devoted their time to the study of Antiquity and the Renaissance, and in 1545 Serlio had begun to publish parts of his treatise on architecture in French at Lyons. Thus the facade of the Louvre towards the court designed by Lescot in 1546 is both classical and French (pl. LXXX). Italian forms are handled with ease and at the same time with a freedom which proves that they had become the architect's natural idiom. The central motif especially is beyond a doubt of Italian origin: the triumphal arch motif with coupled columns in superimposed orders and niches between each pair. The motif goes back to Bramante if not further, and was also used by Bullant at Ecouen (c. 1550) and by Delorme at Anet (also c. 1550). The pediments on brackets above windows and the garlands held by cupids are also of Italian stock, but there is an agility in the presentation, a polish and a graceful splendour, that are French in the extreme. The segmental pediment especially, so sharply drawn and yet so smooth, with the two female figures holding with an inimitable rhetorical ostentation the shield with Henri II's crowned initial, would be impossible in Rome, where at that time Michelangelo placed his mighty cornice on the Farnese palace; impossible also in Northern Italy, where Palladio built the first of his serene villas and palaces, and utterly impossible in both Spain and England.

For Spain after her early welcome of the severest Italian 16th-century classicism (see p. 105) had almost at once relapsed into the ornamental vagaries of her past. The austerity of the Escorial, Philip II's vast castle-monastery, with its seventeen courts and its 670 feet of frontage without any decoration, is exceptional. What meets the traveller everywhere is the Plateresque, a wildly mixed style of Gothic, Mohammedan and Early Renaissance ingredients, spread over facades and inner walls as irresponsibly as ever. The Renaissance had evidently not yet been grasped in its meaning (fig. 79).

Almost the same happened in the Netherlands and Germany. An international centre such as Antwerp might put up a town hall (1561–65, by Cornelis Floris, fig. 80), tall, proud, square, of considered proportions and with a three-bay centre of proud Italian display. The motif of the coupled columns with Ionic correctly placed on top of Tuscan and Corinthian on top of Ionic and the niches in between may have been seen by the architect in France rather than Italy, or else it may come from Serlio. The date of the Antwerp Town Hall is too early to make it probable or even possible that another of the popular and soon apparently indispensable Books of Orders or general Books of Architecture served as a model: Hans Blum's *Five Orders* of 1550, Ducerceau's *Livre d'Architecture* of 1559, Vignola's *Rule of the Five Orders* of 1562, Bullant's *Règle Generale des Cinque Manières* of 1564, Delorme's *Architecture* of 1568 or Palladio's *Architecture* of 1570. How characteristic of the ruling style of Mannerism this sudden outcrop of books on theory is has been pointed out before. It must however here be emphasised to what extent France shared in the new zest for publication. Germany, in the person of the humble Blum, made her voice heard, and England took part too, in a somewhat homespun way, with John Shute's *Chief Groundes of Architecture*, published in 1563, and with John Thorpe's drawings at the Soane Museum in London, done no doubt with an eye to publication but never printed. They were worked on

79.   SALAMANCA: PORTAL OF THE UNIVERSITY, c. 1525–30.

late in the 16th and even in the first years of the 17th century, and Thorpe derived as much inspiration from French and Italian books as he did from the fantastic ornamental pattern books of the Netherlands, especially those by Vredeman de Vries which came out in 1565 and 1568.

These pattern books summed up what is the most remarkable contribution of Flanders and Holland to the style of Mannerism, a

80. CORNELIS FLORIS: ANTWERP TOWN HALL, 1561–65.

novel language of ornament known as bandwork or strapwork. Floris in his town hall handles it with discretion. It hardly appears in the towering gable with its obelisks, scrolls and caryatid pilasters, the finishing flourish to this ponderous building, and a motif entirely in the Northern mediæval tradition. But in the smaller town halls, guild halls and market halls, and the private houses of the Netherlands these gables, the *leitmotif* of the 16th and early 17th centuries, are overcrowded with strapwork. The provincial decorator-architects were not prepared to give up any of the exuberance to which the Flamboyant of the 15th century had accustomed them. And instead of making up an *olla podrida* of Gothic and Renaissance, such as the Spanish did in their Plateresque, they were headstrong and imaginative enough to invent something for themselves. For invention these forms must be called, even if they can be traced back to such Mannerist detail as that round the top windows of the Palazzo Massimi (pl. LV), and to the work of the Italian decorators at Fontainebleau. They consist chiefly of somewhat stocky thick-set curves of fretwork or leather-strap appearance (fig. 81), sometimes flat, but more often three-dimensional and contrasted with naturalistic garlands and caryatids. The popularity of the strapwork style soon spread into the adjacent countries— not to France of course, but to Germany as well as England.

81. TYPICAL FLEMISH AND DUTCH STRAPWORK ORNAMENT OF THE LATER 16TH CENTURY (FROM THE RHINELAND COUNTY HALL, LEIDEN, 1596–98).

To understand Elizabethan and Jacobean architecture in England one has to be familiar with the three sources just mentioned: the Italian Early Renaissance, the Loire style in France and the strapwork decoration of Flanders. This wide-awake interest in so many foreign developments is the æsthetic equivalent of England's new international outlook since Queen Elizabeth, Gresham and Burghley. However, one has also to remember all the time that a strong Perpendicular tradition, the tradition of the picturesque, asymmetrical.

stone-gabled manor-house with its mullioned windows and its extreme ornamental restraint, was still alive. Thus English architecture between 1530 and 1620 is a composite phenomenon with French and Flemish elements prevailing, where we are near the court, and English traditions, as soon as we get away from it. Much of it is derivative, both in the sense of imitation and of conservatism, but occasionally a new expression is developed as original and as nationally characteristic as Lescot's Louvre.

Burghley House, near Stamford, is the work of William Cecil, Lord Burghley, Queen Elizabeth's trusted adviser and friend. It is a mighty rectangle of about 160 by 200 feet with an inner courtyard. The central feature of this courtyard is a three-storied pavilion, dated 1585 (pl. LXXXI). It is again designed on the French triumphal arch motif with the typically French niches between the coupled columns. It has three orders, correctly applied; but on the third floor between the Corinthian columns there sits an utterly incongruous English mullioned and transomed bay window (the English have at no time been happy without bay windows) and above that the pavilion shoots out bits of strapwork and obelisks—a crop of Flemish decoration. The analysis of style is confirmed by documentary evidence. We know that no architect in a modern sense was wholly responsible for the building. Lord Burghley himself must have made a good many of the suggestions embodied in the design. He represents a coming type: the architectural dilettante. In 1568 he wrote to Paris for a book on architecture, and some years later he wrote again specifying one particular French book which he desired. On the other hand it is also certain that workmen for Burghley came from the Netherlands and that a certain amount of work was actually done at Antwerp and then shipped to England. Thus Flemish as well as French motifs are easily accounted for. What is harder to understand is why this happy-go-lucky mixing up of foreign phrases with the English vernacular (the chimney stacks are coupled Tuscan Doric columns complete with entablature) does not appear disjointed. The England of Queen Elizabeth—this is all that can be said by way of an explanation—possessed such an overflowing vitality and was so eager to take in all that was sufficiently adventurous and picturesque and in some cases mannered that it could digest what would have caused serious trouble to a weaker age.

However, while Burghley (and Wollaton Hall of 1580 and the entrance side of Hatfield of 1605–12) are spectacular and stimulating enough, the real strength of English building lay in less out-landish designs. One of the earliest, if not the earliest, in an unmis-takable Elizabethan style is Longleat in Wiltshire, begun in 1567 (pl. LXXXII). Here you find strapwork only very inconspicu-ously on the top balustrade. The portal is small and in the Italian style; with its Tuscan Doric columns it appears surprisingly re-strained. Ornament is sparingly used. The effect is one of sturdy squareness. The roof is flat, the hundreds of many-mullioned, many-transomed windows are straight-headed, and the bay windows project only slightly and have straight sides. This English squareness and the predominance of large expanses of window creates some-times, for instance at Hardwick Hall and even more in the garden side of Hatfield House, a curiously modern, that is 20th-century, effect. More often these large windows, the windows of Perpendic-ular tradition, are combined with the plain customary English tri-angular gables. Small houses of this type are still as asymmetrical as of old, larger houses are symmetrical at least in plan, of L or E shape or, if larger, still developed round courtyards. There is a great deal of difference between Longleat and Burghley, but it took a William Cecil and a Raleigh, a Shakespeare and a Spenser, and many clear-minded, hard-headed and strong-bodied businessmen to make up the England of Elizabeth. Yet it is one England, of one spirit and one style in building, vigorous, prolific, somewhat boast-ful, of a healthy and hearty soundness which, it is true, is sometimes coarse and sometimes dull—but never effeminate and never hysterical.

Compared with the gulf that separates buildings like Burghley House (or Audley End of 1603-16, or Hatfield House) from Inigo Jones's supreme achievements, the Queen's House at Greenwich, designed in 1616, though not completed until immediately before the Civil War, and the Banqueting House in Whitehall of 1619-22, the change in English architecture between 1500 and 1530 seems almost negligible. Only now England experienced what France had experienced before the middle of the 16th century, and experienced it far more startlingly, because Inigo Jones transplanted whole buildings of purely Italian character into England, where such men as Lescot, Delorme and Bullant had only transplanted features and—up to a point—the spirit that stood behind them.

Inigo Jones (1573-1652) began, it seems, as a painter. At the age of thirty-one he appears as a designer of costumes and stage-settings for one of the masques which were a favourite entertainment of the court at that period. He became soon the accepted theatrical designer to the royal family. Plenty of drawings for masques exist. They are brilliantly done, the costumes of that fantastic kind which the Baroque connected with ancient history and mythology, the stage-settings nearly all in the classical Italian style. Jones had, perhaps, been in Italy about 1600, interested probably more in painting and architectural decoration than in architecture proper. Then, however, the Prince of Wales made him his surveyor, i.e. architect, as did a short time later the Queen, and, in 1613, the King. So he went back to Italy, this time, we know from his sketch-books, to study Italian buildings seriously. His ideal was Palladio: an edition of Palladio annotated by Jones is preserved.

Looking back from the Queen's House (pl. LXXXIII)—a villa in the Italian sense, out at Greenwich—to Palladio's Palazzo Chierigati (pl. LVII), the close connection of style is evident, though nothing is copied. In fact we find nowhere in Jones's work mere imitation. What he had learned from Palladio and the Roman architects of the early 16th century, is to regard a building as a whole, organised throughout—in plan and elevation—according to rational rules. But the Queen's House has not the weight of the Roman Renaissance or Baroque palace. It was originally even less compact than Palladio's country houses, for it was not a complete block, as it is now, but consisted of two rectangles standing to the right and the left of the main Dover Road and only connected with each other by a bridge (the present centre room on the first floor), across the road— a curious, if not unique, composition of a spatially most effective openness. In contrast to this freedom in general plan, the strictest symmetry governs the grouping of the rooms. Now in Elizabethan country houses we find the decision already taken to tidy up facades into more or less complete symmetry. One may even come across blocked windows and similar contrivances to force into outward symmetry what could not be made to match inside. For wholly symmetrical plans were still rare by 1610, although the trend towards them is unmistakable. In this Inigo Jones is the logical successor to the Jacobeans. But if one takes his elevations, their dignified plainness is in the strongest contrast to the Jacobean animation by windows of varying sizes, bay windows, rounded and polygonal, dormer windows, gables and high-pitched roofs. The centre portion of the Queen's House with the loggia projects slightly: that is the only movement of the wall surface. The ground

floor is rusticated, the top floor smooth. A balustrade sets the
facade off against the sky. The windows are thoughtfully proportioned. There is no ornament anywhere but the delicately
moulded cornices above the first-floor windows.

This was a principle with Inigo Jones. He wrote on Jan. 20, 1614:
"Ye outward ornaments oft to be sollid, proporsionable according
to the rulles, masculine and unaffected". The character of the Queen's
House could not be better described. And Jones knew that in building
thus he was holding up an ideal not only in opposition to contemporary Britain but also to contemporary Rome, i.e. the Baroque.
"All thes composed ornaments", he added, "the which Proceed
out of ye aboundance of dessigners and wear brought in by Michill
Angell and his followers in my oppignion do not well in solid
Architecture." Yet he did not despise ornament altogether. He uses
it inside the Queen's House and, with luxurious exuberance, in the
so-called double-cube room at Wilton House. Even there however
there is nothing crowded. The form of his wreaths and garlands of
flowers and fruit is compact. They fit into clear-cut panels, and
never overgrow the structural divisions of a room. Again, Jones was
fully aware of the contrast between his simple exteriors and his
rich interiors. He wrote: "Outwardly every wyse man carrieth a
graviti in Publicke Places, yet inwardly hath his imaginacy set on
fire, and sumtimes licenciously flying out, as nature hirself doeth
often times stravagantly", and demands the same attitude in a good
building. And once more the way in which he puts his observation
is personal to a degree inconceivable in an architect in England in
Elizabethan and Jacobean days. For Inigo Jones is the first English
architect in the modern sense. He achieved in this country what the
earliest artist-architects had achieved in Italy at the beginning of the
Renaissance. And as one is interested in Alberti or Leonardo da
Vinci as individuals, so the genius of Inigo Jones makes one deplore
over and over again how little is known of his personality.

Of Jones's other works—and those attributed to him with
some degree of certainty—only two more can be mentioned.
One is Lindsay House in Lincoln's Inn Fields, because with its rusticated ground floor and its giant order of pilasters above, supporting
entablature and top balustrade, it is the prototype for a whole series
of representational English town houses down to the Royal Crescent
at Bath (p. 186) and Nash's Regent's Park terraces. The other is
the layout of Covent Garden with its tall houses, dignified and un-

adorned, open in galleries on the ground floor, which Jones had taken from a *piazza* at Leghorn (in fact Covent Garden was known in Evelyn's and Pepys's time as the Piazza), because it is the first of the regularly planned London squares. Its west side was centred on the small church of St. Paul's with its low, very grave, Antique portico, a design inspired by the Italian 16th-century books on architecture and the earliest classical portico of detached columns erected in the North.

Now here, though only for a moment, a church had to be mentioned. For about one hundred years church architecture had all but stopped in Britain. And in France, although there are a number of interesting 16th-century churches with curious mixtures in varying proportion of Gothic conceptions with Southern detail (for instance St. Eustache and St. Etienne du Mont, both in Paris), they are not amongst the historically leading works. The same might also be said of the 17th century, or at least its beginning. Paris now took over the Gesù scheme of facade and interior (see pp. 116–118), the scheme which, as has been said before, became more widely popular than any other during the period between 1600 and 1750 (Jesuit Novitiate Church begun 1612, now destroyed; St. Gervais begun 1616 by de Brosse; Church of the Feuillants begun 1624? by François Mansart).

The parallelism between this French development based on Vignola and the English one based on Palladio need not be specially stressed. It was part of the universal tendency of the north of Europe early in the 17th century. In Germany at exactly the same time Elias Holl (1573–1646) built his Palladian Augsburg Town Hall (1610–20). And in palace architecture in France Salomon de Brosse (*c.* 1550/60–1626) at the request of Maria de' Medici incorporated into his monumental plan for the Luxembourg Palace, begun in 1615, motifs of the Mannerist parts of the Pitti Palace in Florence. The plan of the Luxembourg consists of an H-shaped *corps de logis* with lower wings along a *cour d'honneur* and a screen wall on the front side. The central axis is strongly marked by the entrance pavilion in the screen wall and the centre pavilion of the *corps de logis*.

Such grand symmetrical schemes, more rigidly formal as a rule than Elizabethan and Jacobean compositions, are characteristic of France. They were originally (that is early in the 16th century, at the time when the Loire *château* of Chambord was designed in perfect symmetry with thick round towers) a fusion of symmetrical discipline in mediæval castles and in Italian Renaissance palaces. With Delorme's plan of 1564 for the Tuileries (devised no doubt under the influence of the Escorial) the grand scale was reached. The Tuileries were to have a 200-foot front and five courts. A little later, under Charles IX, a yet bigger project was drawn up by Jacques Androuet Ducerceau (c. 1510–85) who has so far only been mentioned as a writer on architecture. Charleval in Normandy was intended to be a large square with a square inner courtyard and a *cour d'honneur* in front, possessing on the right and left service wings each again with two courts. The size intended was over 1000 by 1000 feet, far more that is than the Escorial. From such schemes Charles I's and Charles II's ideas for a gigantic Whitehall palace were derived, the ideas which were first put on paper by Inigo Jones and then in exactly as Italian a style by John Webb, his pupil.

But before 1650 or 1660 Jones and Webb were almost alone in pursuing such Southern ideas. The popular style in England after the Jacobean and often still side by side with the Jacobean was a homely Dutch style with curved and pedimented gables (Kew Palace, etc.). To this corresponds in France the style of Henri IV still lingering on into the thirties of the 17th century, a style of brick buildings with stone quoins and window dressings, best illustrated by the architecture of the Place des Vosges in Paris (1605–12) and by Richelieu's little town of Richelieu, founded in 1631 and designed with his palace by Lemercier (c. 1585–1654). The palace, long since destroyed, was modelled on the Luxembourg pattern and thus already a conservative work when it was completed.

For in monumental French architecture Richelieu's period and even more that of Mazarin are characterised by a broad new influx of Italian ideas—and that now meant ideas of the Baroque—and by the way they were developed in the hands of a few leading architects into a classic French style which corresponds in terms of building to that of Poussin in painting, of Corneille in drama and of Descartes in philosophy. There is no parallel in England to this phase, though from 1660 onwards parallelism, if in very different national idioms, is again patent.

François Mansart (1598–1664) is the first great protagonist, Louis Levau (1612–70) the second. Mansart's two *magna opera* were built between 1635 and 1650: the Orléans wing at Blois and the country house of Maisons-Lafitte. The *cour d'honneur* at Blois especially (pl. LXXXIV; on the extreme right a corner of Francis I's wing is just visible) is a masterpiece of civilised reticence, elegant, not very warm-hearted, yet far from pedantically correct with its two-storied triumphal arch and the remarkably original little semicircular third-storied pediment above. The links backward with Lescot's age are as evident as the links forward with the subtle perfection of the Rococo *hôtel*. The curved colonnades especially convey that distinct feeling of Rococo. The way in which they smooth over the angular break at the corners is very French and very accomplished. A similar interior effect is achieved at Maisons-Lafitte by the oval rooms in the wings. These were new to France; an Italian motif introduced, it appears, by Mansart and Levau. Of its Italian use in churches and palaces (Palazzo Barberini) enough has been said. Its most prominent occurrence in France is in the mighty, very Italian and very Baroque fancy palaces published in Antoine Lepautre's (1621–91) *Desseins de plusieurs palais* in 1652—the parallel to Puget's sculpture—in Louis Levau's church of the Collège des Quatre Nations (now Institut de France) of 1661 and in his country house of Vaux-le-Vicomte, begun in 1657. The church of the Collège des Quatre Nations (fig. 83) is, broadly speaking, a Greek cross, but the arms and the corners between the arms are designed with considerable freedom and differ widely from each other. The dominant features of the church are the oval centre with its dome and an oval atrium. Oval also is the effect of the earlier Sorbonne Church (fig. 82) by Jacques Lemercier (1635–42), where a Greek cross is combined with a circular centre but with a great deal of deliberate stress on one axis of the cross as against the other. There is just as much spatial ingenuity in these plans as in those of contemporary Italy, although their detail appears cold and restrained against the Baroque of Rome.

Vaux-le-Vicomte (figs. 84 and 85) is in many ways the most important French building of the mid-17th century. It was begun by Levau for Colbert's predecessor Fouquet, and is surrounded by gardens in which the great Lenôtre first experimented with ideas later to be developed so spectacularly at Versailles. Lebrun, Louis's *Premier Peintre*, also worked at Vaux before he started at Versailles.

In the house itself (as at Maisons and some others before) the traditional plan of the Luxembourg is given up for that of the Palazzo Barberini with very much shorter projecting wings, and the centre pavilion is occupied by a domed oval saloon, again on the pattern of the Barberini Palace. In the wings the roofs have still the

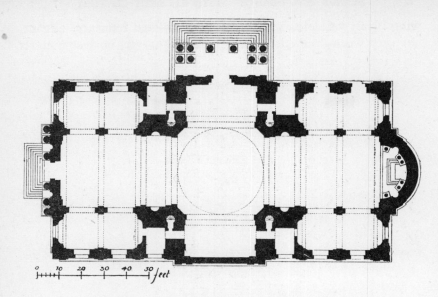

82.   JACQUES LEMERCIER : CHURCH OF THE SORBONNE, PARIS, 1635–42.

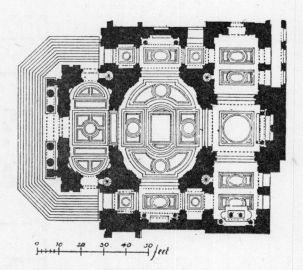

83.   LOUIS LEVAU: CHURCH OF THE COLLÈGE DES QUATRE NATIONS (NOW INSTITUT DE FRANCE), PARIS, 1661.

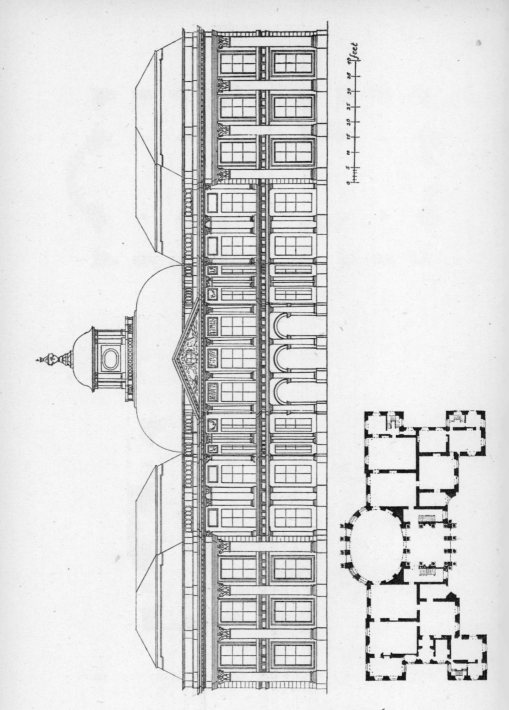

84 AND 85.   LOUIS LEVAU: VAUX-LE-VICOMTE, BEGUN 1657.

high pitch characteristic of the French 16th and early 17th centuries, but slender Ionic pilasters appear in one giant order for both stories. Giant orders were nothing new. We have found them in Inigo Jones and before. Palladio had had them and France herself occasionally too (Bullant at Ecouen, Ducerceau at Charleval, etc.). But in this particularly light and elegant manner they are curiously similar to those which since about 1630 Holland had favoured.

Holland just at that time attained the leadership of Western commerce, and she was much envied and imitated by both Colbert and the English. She also led in science and could boast more men of artistic genius than at any other period in her national existence. In architecture her development had led her from a gay and jolly style of 1600, parallel to Henri IV's style and the Jacobean, to a new classicism, parallel to Mansart's in France and Inigo Jones's in England. The Mauritshuis at The Hague, built by Jacob van Campen in 1633–35 (pl. LXXXV), has a correct pediment on correct giant pilasters, and giant pilasters also along its sides. In this it may well have influenced France and Vaux in particular, but its intimate size for a princely residence, its unpretentious plain brick walls and its all-pervading feeling of solid comfort are very Dutch and quite different from anything French of that period.

England, on the other hand, could sympathise with these North-Western qualities of the Dutch. And her architecture since 1660 was indeed greatly influenced by the buildings of van Campen and Vingboons, and by Vingboons's engraved publications of 1648, 1674 and 1688. However, architects, amateurs and scholars, and especially the Stuart court, were not blind either to the glamour and the real achievements of the Paris of Colbert and Louis XIV. There was trading success on the one hand, the grandeur of absolute monarchy on the other. Hence representational architecture tended towards the Parisian, domestic architecture towards the Dutch. In Sir Christopher Wren's work inspiration from both sources can be traced. He must have studied engravings of Dutch architecture with great care, and he went to Paris personally, when he had realised that the designing and supervising of buildings was to be his main job in life. For Wren (1632–1723)—this is again characteristic of Renaissance and Baroque—had not been trained as an architect or a mason. Nor was he a painter or sculptor or engineer. He represents yet another type, a type not so far met in this book.

Wren's father had been Dean of Windsor, his father's brother Bishop of Ely. He was sent to Westminster School. At the age of fifteen, after he had finished school, he was made an assistant demonstrator in anatomy at the College of Surgeons. Then he went up to Oxford. His main interest was science, in that curious mixed and vague sense which science still had in the mid-17th century. During the time he was at college, "that miracle of a youth", as John Evelyn called him, put before the authorities fifty-three inventions, theories, experiments and mechanical improvements. Some of them seem trifling now, others aimed right at the central problems of astronomy, physics and engineering. In 1657 he was made professor of astronomy in London, in 1661 in Oxford. It was the moment when experimental science was just coming to the fore everywhere in Europe. In Paris the Royal Academy of Science was established. The Royal Society in London started its activities even earlier. Wren was one of its founders and most distinguished members. Newton calls him together with Huygens and Wallis "huius ætatis geometrarum facile principes". His most important scientific work is on cycloids, the barometer and Pascal's problem. In his inaugural lecture in London he revealed a prophetic vision of nebulæ as the firmaments of other worlds like ours. In 1664 he illustrated Willis's *Anatomy of the Brain*. And in 1663 he presented to the Royal Society a model for a building which he had designed at the request of Oxford University, the Sheldonian Theatre, completed in 1669. Its roof is an ingenious piece of timber engineering, but its architecture is awkward, evidently the work of a man with little designing experience. The same can be said of his second work, Pembroke Chapel, Cambridge, of 1663–66. An even earlier connection with building construction is indicated by Charles II's request to him to fortify Tangier. So architecture, engineering, physics and mathematics go hand in hand in the development of Wren's mind. The resolution to specialise in architecture may have been brought about by the Fire of London in 1666. Wren found himself a member of the Royal Commission for the rebuilding of the city, and very soon also the elected designer of the many new churches to be built in the city, including St. Paul's. In 1669 the King made him Surveyor-General. His only important journey abroad took him not to Italy but to Paris. That is a very significant fact. At the time of Inigo Jones's *Wanderjahre*, Paris could not have been more than a station on the way to Rome. Now Wren, in a letter, called Paris "a School of Architecture, the best probably at this Day in Europe". The most important it certainly was. While Wren was in Paris, Louis XIV, who intended to rebuild the east parts of the Louvre, had invited Bernini to come and contribute designs. He did so, but his plans, a colossal square on the Roman pattern with giant orders of detached columns on the outer and the courtyard fronts and with a vigorous top cornice crowned by a balustrade, plans which Wren only succeeded in examining for a short, precious few minutes, were dropped as soon as the great man left. They were replaced by the famous east front with the colonnades which Claude Perrault (1613–88) designed in 1665.

The choice of Perrault was characteristic. He was an amateur, a distinguished doctor, his brother was a lawyer and courtier, author of a mediocre poem on *Le Siècle de Louis le Grand*, and had in 1664 been made Inspector-General of the King's buildings. In the history of French literature he is chiefly known as one of the leaders in the *Querelle des Anciens et des Modernes*. Boileau defended Antiquity, Perrault a contemporary style—which of course did not really mean more than a certain amount of freedom in applying the rules of the ancients.

Claude Perrault's Louvre front (pl. LXXXVI) goes beyond Mansart and Levau in several ways. It represents the change from Mazarin to Colbert, or from early to mature Louis XIV. It has a disciplined formality to which Perrault's knowledge of Bernini's project contributed two important motifs. Bernini as well as Perrault have flat balustraded roofs, and Bernini as well as Perrault model their fronts without any marked projections or recesses of wings. Both these features were new in France. Otherwise, however, Perrault is wholly national. French in feeling, though very original and so un-academic that his less adventurous contemporaries never forgave him, are the slim coupled giant columns of the main story raised up on the tall smooth podium-like ground floor. French are the segment-headed windows, and French (of direct Lescot derivation) the oval shields with garlands hanging down from them.

The whole is a of grandeur and yet a precise elegance that the 17th century, in spite of Blois and Maisons, had never before achieved, and that the architects of Louis XIV's later years never surpassed. Perrault has summed up to perfection the various, sometimes seemingly contradictory tendencies of the *siècle de Louis XIV*, the gravity and *raison* of late Poussin, Corneille and Boileau, the restrained fire of Racine, the lucid grace of Molière, the powerful sense of organisation of Colbert.

It is necessary for an appreciation of this style to remember the atmosphere in which it grew, the struggles first between Protestantism and Catholicism in the 16th century, Henri IV's decision to return to the Roman Church, because, as he put it, "Paris is worth a mass", then the spreading of religious indifference, until it became all-powerful in the policy of Richelieu, the cardinal, and Father Joseph, the Capuchin, who fought Protestants in France but favoured them abroad, in both cases purely for reasons of national expediency. For the centre of their thoughts and ambitions was France, and a strong and prosperous France could only be created by first building up a rigorously centralised administration. Now the only visible symbol of the might of the state could be the person of the king. Absolutism was therefore the appropriate form of government for whoever was in favour of a national policy. Thus Richelieu prepared the ground for absolutism, Mazarin followed, and Colbert, the indefatigable, competent and tenacious bourgeois, made a system of it. He organised France with an unheard-of thoroughness: mercantilism in industry and commerce, royal workshops, royal trading companies, close supervision of roads, of canals, of afforestation—of everything.

Art and architecture were an integral part of the system. A flourishing school of painting, sculpture and the applied arts stimulated export and at the same time enhanced the glory of the court. Architecture was useful to create work and again to celebrate the greatness of king and state. But there should be no licence; style had to conform to standards set by the prince and his minister. Thus academies were founded, one for painting and sculpture, another for architecture, the earliest of a modern type, both educational and representational, and the most powerful that have ever existed. And when artists had gone through these schools and gained distinction, they were made royal sculptors or royal architects, drawn nearer and nearer to the court, honoured and paid accordingly, but made more and more dependent on the will of Louis and Colbert. It was in Paris at that time that the principle of architecture as a department of the civil service was established. The French and English kings had had their royal master-masons ever since the 13th century. But they were craftsmen, not civil servants. Also the competencies of the various surveyors, inspectors and whatever they

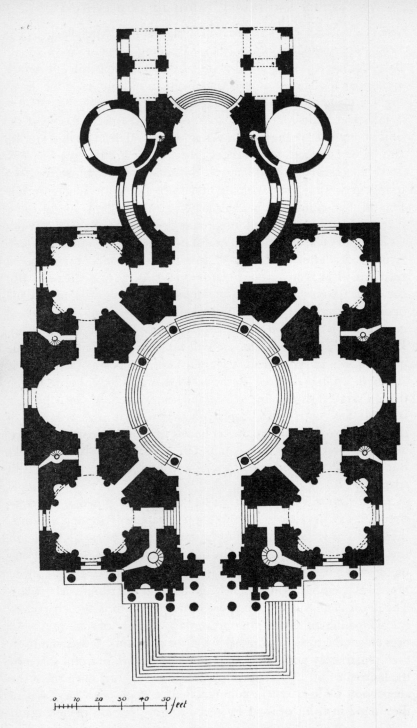

JULES HARDOUIN-MANSART: ST. LOUIS DES INVALIDES, PARIS.

were called later on, were never clearly defined. Michelangelo had been Superintendent of the Papal Buildings; but nobody would have considered such an appointment a full-time job. Now the architectural office developed, and a system of training at the drawing board and on the jobs.

Jules Hardouin-Mansart (1646–1708) was the perfect type of the official French architect, competent, quick and adaptable. In his church of St. Louis des Invalides (pl. LXXXVII and fig. 86) of 1675–1706 he achieved, just as Perrault did, that specific combination of grandeur and elegance which is not to be found anywhere outside France. The composition, externally and internally, is meant to be taken as an improvement on Lemercier's Sorbonne and Levau's Collège des Quatre Nations. The interior, except for the oval chancel, is more academically balanced, that is less dynamic in its spatial relations, than the works of Hardouin-Mansart's predecessors. But the dome is constructed so that in looking up one sees through a wide opening in the inner cupola on to the painted surface of a second cupola, lit by concealed windows—a wholly Baroque spatial effect. Examining now the facade one will become aware of its Baroque qualities too, in spite of its seemingly correct portico with Doric and Ionic orders. The free rhythmical spacing of the columns (taken from Perrault) should be noted, and the graded advance in plan towards the centre: first step from the walls to the columns of the wings, second step to the columns on the sides of the portico and third step to the four middle columns. Not only the Greeks but also Palladio and even Vignola would have deprecated this strongly.

Sir Christopher Wren did not. His St. Paul's Cathedral of 1675–1710 (pl. LXXXVIII and fig. 87) though apparently so much a monument to Classicism is in fact just as much a blend of the classical and the Baroque as the Dôme des Invalides. The dome of St. Paul's, one of the most perfect in the world, is classical indeed. It has a more reposeful outline than Michelangelo's and Hardouin-Mansart's. The decoration with a colonnade round the drum is also characteristically different from the projecting groups of columns and broken entablatures of St. Peter's and the segment-headed windows —so remarkably domestic-looking—and the slim, graceful shape of the lantern of St. Louis's. But looking more closely, even there the alternation of bays where columns flank niches, with bays where they stand in front of loggias, introduces an element of unclassical variety. The lantern, too, is at least as bizarre as Mansart's. And as for the facade of St. Paul's, begun in 1685, it is, with the coupled columns which Wren (just as Hardouin-Mansart) took over from Perrault's Louvre facade, and the two fantastic turrets on the sides (designed after 1700), a decidedly Baroque composition. The side elevations are dramatic, though of a secular, palace-like effect. The windows

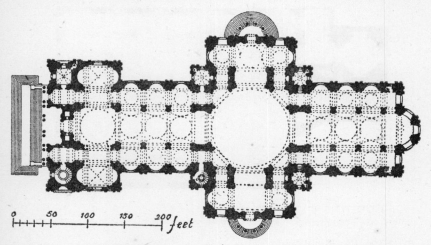

87.   SIR CHRISTOPHER WREN: ST. PAUL'S CATHEDRAL, LONDON, 1675–1710.

have even a framing of sham-perspective niches of the S. Carlo and Palazzo Barberini type (see pl. LXIV). Inside there is a poignant contrast between the firmness of every part and the spatial dynamics of the whole. The dome rests on diagonally placed piers with colossal niches hollowed out. Niches also set the outer walls of the aisles and choir aisles into an undulating motion. With a similar effect windows are cut into the tunnel-vaults and saucer domes of choir and nave. Wren's style in churches and palaces is Palladian, no doubt, but it is a Baroque version of Classicism. Such city churches as the ingeniously multiform St. Stephens, Walbrook (1672–87, pl. LXXXIX and fig. 88), show this especially clearly.

To analyse its ground plan is almost as hard as to analyse Vierzehnheiligen. Yet its expression is of cool clarity. Outside it is a plain rectangle as silent about the interior surprises as Vierzehnheiligen. Inside its centre is a spacious gently rising saucer dome resting on eight arches supported by nothing but twelve slender columns. The technical achievement is as remarkable as the effortless lightness of appearance. The twelve columns form a square, and four arches connect the two central columns of each side of the square, while fragmentary vaults curve up from the three columns of each corner of the square to form four more arches in the corners. Now, these three corner columns on each side are also tied together by straight entablatures, so that each of the four sides has a rhythm of straight and low—arched and tall—straight and low. Here is a first ingenious

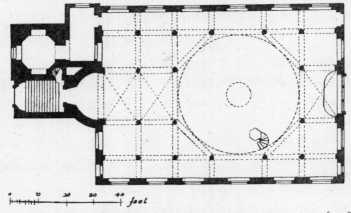

88. SIR CHRISTOPHER WREN: ST. STEPHENS, WALBROOK, LONDON, 1672-87.

interlocking of effects. Looking up the dome we perceive eight arches of identical height, but looking straight in front of us towards any one side of the square there is differentiation of the bays. However, that is not all. The arched centres of the sides can also be regarded as the entrances to four arms of a cross, a Latin cross, since the tunnel-vaults of the south and north arms are very shallow, whereas the east arm with the altar has a somewhat longer cross-vault, and the west arm one double the length of the altar arm. To achieve that, the western arm consists of two bays separated by columns in the normal manner of longitudinal churches. As these columns are exactly identical with all the other columns, the first impression one receives on entering the church is one of a short nave with aisles leading towards a dome of unaccountable width. To finish the story, this seeming nave has narrow flat-ceilinged outer aisles as well, and these outer aisles run right through to the east wall. Only we cannot call them aisles all the way through, because at one point they rise into being the north and south arms of the cross and then sink again to become chancel aisles. The inner aisles of course, one discovers later, run into the wide crossing just as the nave. The whole rectangle of the church is set out with sixteen columns altogether, noble columns of almost academical neutrality. Yet they are used to create a spatial polyphony which only the Baroque could appreciate —architecture of Purcell's age.

It is in connection with the spatial qualities of his ground plans that one should consider Wren's plan for the rebuilding of London after the fire of 1666. He suggested sweeping alterations in the pattern of the city, new long, wide and straight streets meeting in star-shaped squares. Now this principle of the *rond-point* with radiating streets originated from the Italy of the Renaissance (see p. 86), was put into practice by the Mannerists—the most famous example is Scamozzi's nonagonal town and fortress of Palmanova in the Veneto (1593), a Baroque example of about 1660 is the Piazza del Popolo in Rome with the Corso and the two other straight streets (see p. 124) —and taken over late in the 16th century by the French. Under Louis XIV. France (where the radiating chapels of the church plan · had been conceived six hundred years before) became the second home of the *rond-point*. From Louis's reign dates the Place de l'Étoile, although it was then in the country and became part of the city of Paris only after 1800. The grandest example of such planning on an enormous scale is, of course, Versailles (fig. 89). The garden front of the palace, 1,800 feet long, faces Le Nôtre's magnificent park with its vast parterres of flowers, its cross-shaped sheet of water, fountains, seemingly endless parallel or radiating avenues, and walks between tall trimmed hedges—Nature subdued by the hand of Man to serve the greatness of the king, whose bedroom was placed right in the centre of the whole composition. On the town side the *cour d'honneur* receives three wide converging roads coming from the direction of Paris. Town-planning was strongly influenced by these principles everywhere. Of the 18th century the most notable examples are perhaps Karlsruhe in South-West Germany, a whole town designed in 1715 as one huge star with the Ducal Palace as its centre, and L'Enfant's plan of 1791 for Washington, D.C.

As for Britain, Wren's plan fell through after having been considered by the king for only a few days. Was it too daring? Could it have been carried out only in an absolute monarchy, where expropriation for schemes of civic grandeur was easier than in the City of London? Or was this logical, uncompromising programme to organise the background for future London life simply too un-English ever to be taken seriously? The fact remains that the contribution of London to town-planning of the 17th and 18th centuries

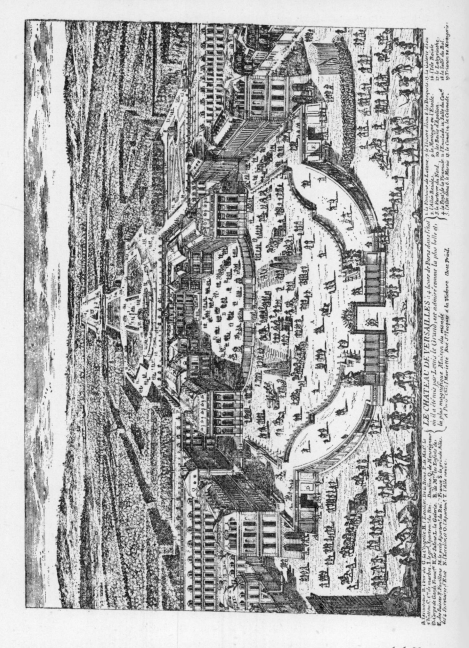

89. VERSAILLES. THE GARDEN FRONT BY JULES HARDOUIN-MANSART, 1676–88, THE
GARDENS BY ANDRÉ LE NÔTRE, BEGUN 1667.

is the square—introduced, as has been said, by Inigo Jones—i.e. an isolated, privately owned area with houses of, as a rule, similar but not identical design, examples of good manners and not of regimentation. It might be worth adding that the sensation in walking through the West End of London from square to square is clearly a modern and secular version of the typically English sensation of the visitor passing from isolated compartment to isolated compartment in a Saxon or Early English church.

Regarding the individual town house, there is the same contrast between London and Paris. In London, but for a few exceptions, the nobleman and the wealthy merchant lived in terrace houses, in Paris in detached *hôtels*. In London a ground plan had been evolved for these houses that was convenient enough to become standardised before the end of the 17th century. With its entrance on one side, leading straight to the staircase, one large front room and one large back room on each floor, and the service rooms in the basement, it remained practically unaltered for the largest and the smallest house until the end of the Victorian era. Of spatially effective elements it has little. In Paris, on the other hand, architects from about 1630 onwards developed house plans with great consistency and ingenuity towards ever subtler solutions of functional requirements and spatial desires. The standard elements were a *cour d'honneur*, screened off from the street, with offices and stables in wings on the right and the left, and the *corps de logis* at the back. The earliest plan of wholly symmetrical organisation is the Hôtel de Bretonvillers of about 1625–30. The first high-water marks are Mansart's Hôtel de la Vrillière of about 1635 and Levau's Hôtel Lambert of shortly after 1642, the latter with a courtyard with two rounded corners and an oval vestibule (fig. 90). A little later Lepautre's Hôtel de Beauvais (1655–60) revels in curves. Then the same reaction took place which we had seen between Vaux and the Louvre. Colbert did not like curves, he called them in 1669 "not

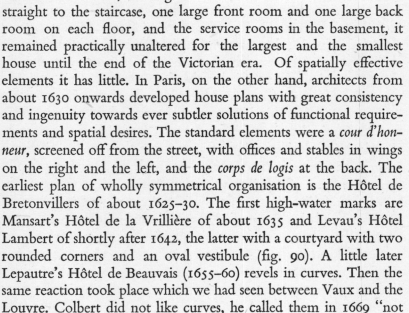

90.   LOUIS LEVAU: HÔTEL LAMBERT, PARIS, ABOUT 1645.

in the good taste, particularly in exteriors", and the *appartements* of Louis XIV's later years are of less spatial interests.

The most important development between 1700 and 1715 is concerned with interior decoration. In the hands of one of Hardouin-Mansart's chief executives, Jean Lepautre, it went more and more delicate and sophisticated. Grandeur was replaced by *finesse*, high relief by an exquisite play on the surface, and a virile deportment by an almost effeminate grace. Thus during the last years of Louis XIV's reign the atmosphere of the Rococo consolidated itself.

The Rococo is indeed of French origin, although we have introduced it in this book first in its German, that is its extreme and most brilliant spatial forms. The term Rococo is a pun, it seems, from *barocco*, alluding to the passion for those strange rock-like or shell-like formations which are typical of its ornament and have been analysed apropos Bruchsal and Vierzehnheiligen. They appear there in the fifties, but are a French invention of 1715–30—or rather an invention made in France. For the leaders of the generation responsible for the step from Lepautre's thin grace to full-blooded Rococo were without exception not properly French: Watteau the painter was a Fleming, Gilles-Marie Oppenord (1672–1742) was the son of a Dutch father, Juste-Aurèle Meissonier (1695–1750) of Provençal stock and born at Turin, Toro has an Italian name and lived in Provence, and Vassé was Provençal too. It is due to these architects and decorators that vigour re-entered French decoration, that curves of Italian Baroque derivation made their appearance once more, that ornament launched out into the third dimension again, and that the fantastic, completely original ornament of the *rocaille* was conceived. In exterior architecture less can be observed of this development than in interiors. Oppenord's and Meissoniers' designs for facades were not carried out. It is in the planning and decoration of houses that the Rococo celebrates its greatest triumphs. The Rococo is a style of the *salon*, the *petit appartement* and of sophisticated living (pl. XC). Decoration is far more graceful and as a rule considerably less vigorous than in Germany, and planning is of an unprecedented subtlety.

One difficulty in the standard Parisian *hôtel* plan which the architects liked to face and overcome was, for instance, the fact that the front towards the *cour d'honneur* and the back towards the garden should both be symmetrical in themselves and even when they did not lie on the same axis. Courtonne's Hôtel de Matignon (fig. 92) shows one very neat solution. Here and in any of the other contemporary *hôtels* the ingenious tricks of anti-chambres and cabinets and garderobes and little inner service courts should be studied, all devised to facilitate the running of a house and fill the many odd corners behind curved rooms and alcoves. The form and position of the staircase was another problem. As to its position, it had to communicate easily with vestibule and service rooms, without interfering with the smooth run of room into room and the representational splendour of vistas. The same desire for a smooth run was extended to the interaction between floor and floor, and staircase forms were chosen accordingly. It has been shown that Spain, for all we know, invented both the most popular types of Baroque staircases (fig. 91). The square one with three flights round an open well became popular in Jacobean England, where it was interpreted in timber, character-istically reduced in size to a somewhat cramped mediæval narrowness, but

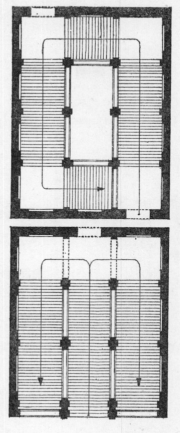

91.　THE TWO CHIEF TYPES OF BAROQUE STAIRCASES.

gorgeously decorated by Flemish or English woodcarvers (Hat-field, Audley End, etc.). Only when we come to Inigo Jones at Ashburnham House, London (perhaps by him), is the spaciousness of Spain emulated. However, Ashburnham House and a few other examples of Baroque breadth such as Coleshill, Berks (by Roger Pratt, one of Wren's early competitors), are rare exceptions in England. There are at that time exceptions in Italy too (Longhena: S. Giorgio Maggiore, Venice, 1643–45—the example from which Coleshill seems to be derived). Only Genoa took a real liking to staircases as wide, light and airy as those of Spain. France must have got to know of these through several channels. The Escorial type was taken up by Levau at the Tuileries in Paris. Since then it was

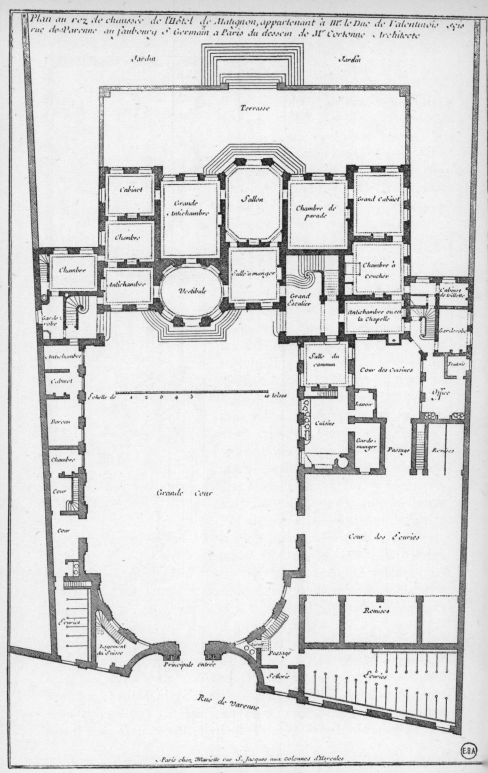

Plan au rez de chaussée de l'Hôtel de Matignon, appartenant à Mr. le Duc de Valentinois sis rue de Varenne au faubourg S. Germain a Paris du dessein de Mr Cortonne Architecte

92.   JEAN COURTONNE: HÔTEL DE MATIGNON, PARIS, BEGUN 1722.

established as the grandest of all types. The square open-well type occurs in Mansart's Blois and then with countless minor variations in the Paris *hôtels* (see e.g. fig. 92). These variations all aim at suppler, more elegant forms.

Externally the Paris *hôtels* are just as elegantly varied, though never anything like as boldly Rococo as the palaces and houses in Germany and Austria, whereas in London the exterior of the 17th- and 18th-century brick house was, except for ornamental details, almost standardised. It has no connection with the classic French style, that much is certain, although it may have had some originally with the less pretentious domestic architecture of Henri IV and later with Holland.

As for country houses, they are—at least after 1660—of minor importance in France, where the life of the ruling class was centred in the court, while in England most of the noblemen and nearly all the squires still regarded their London houses only as *pieds-à-terre*, and looked on their seats in the country as their real homes. Consequently it is here that one can expect variety and, indeed, finds it. All the more noteworthy, however, is it that about 1700, when the standardised town house had become an accepted fact, a type of smaller country house had also been introduced (clearly on the Mauritshuis pattern) that—with many and delightful minor variations—is to be found all over the countryside, in the villages round London, at Hampstead, Roehampton, Ham, Petersham, round the close at Salisbury—everywhere. They are usually built of brick with stone quoins, either completely rectangular or with two short wings on the sides, the entrance with a pediment, hood or porch, and with a larger pediment to crown the centre of the house (fig. 93). These lovable houses of mellow and undated rightness are too well known to need further description. Their origin and diffusion have however not yet been fully elucidated. The earliest example seems to be Eltham Lodge, near London, of 1663. It was designed by Hugh May, with Pratt and Webb Wren's most important competitor in the sixties. By 1685 or 1690 the type was certainly fully established. It has as a rule a generously spaced three-flight staircase with an open well and rich woodcarving and rooms of simple and straightforward shapes; of that ingenious *commodité* on which all the French 18th-century architects insisted in their writings, they have little.

Apparently, to the British, comfort was something quite different from what it was to the French. But while these houses of about 1700 are, whatever French critics might have said against them, as serviceable to-day as at the time when they were built, there are indeed certain English 18th-century country houses on a larger scale which—from our point of view at least—seem to be designed

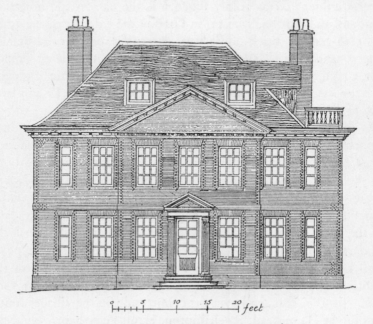

93. FENTON HOUSE, HAMPSTEAD, LONDON, 1693.

for display and not for comfort. This is an argument heard frequently against Blenheim, near Oxford (pls. xci, xcii, xciii and fig. 94), the palace which the nation presented to Marlborough. It was designed by Sir John Vanbrugh (1664–1726) in 1705. His style derives from Wren at his grandest and most Baroque—the Wren of Greenwich Hospital—but is always of a distinctly personal character. Wren never seems to forget himself. He is never carried away by forces stronger than his reason. Vanbrugh's designs are of a violence and ruthless directness that could not but offend the rationalists of his age. His family came from Flanders; his expansive temperament seems more of Rubens's country than of Wren's and Reynolds's. He studied art in France, was arrested and put into the Bastille. After his release he returned to England and began to write plays. They were a huge success. Then suddenly one finds him engaged in architectural work at Castle Howard. In 1702 he was appointed Comptroller of Works—a curious career, very different from Wren's.

Blenheim is planned on a colossal scale. One does not know whether the Palladian villa with its wings or Versailles with its *cour d'honneur* stands behind its plan. The *corps de logis* has a massive portico with giant columns between giant pillars, and a heavy attic above. The same Baroque weight characterises the side elevations, especially the square squat corner towers of the wings (pl. CXII). If in the case of Wren the term Baroque could be used only with careful qualifications, these towers would be called Baroque by anyone familiar with the work of Bernini, Borromini and the others in Italy. Here is struggle, mighty forces opposing overwhelming weights; here are fiercely projecting mouldings and windows crushed by thick-set pilasters placed too close to them; here is the deliberate discordance of the semicircular window placed against a semicircular arch right above and higher up again a segmental arch. Everything jars, and the top of the daring composition has nothing of a happy end either. Vanbrugh in the forms which crown the tower, the vases and the ball, does not accept any indebtedness to anybody. The pilasters and the windows are also highly original, but not to the same extreme degree. In some details they appear reminiscent of Michelangelo. However, the mentioning of Michelangelo makes Blenheim—the whole of the entrance front—at once appear coarse, even meaty, and certainly theatrical and ostentatious: that is Flemish as well as Baroque. Yet in spite of that Vanbrugh, seen side by side with Michelangelo or Bernini, is also a classicist. It seems a contradiction but it is not. It simply is, just as in the case of Wren, the special English twist given to the Baroque. There is very little in Wren and Vanbrugh of that plastic treatment of walls which Michelangelo had first conceived and which produced the undulating facades and interiors of Baroque buildings in Italy and Southern Germany. Movement is never in England so insinuating, nor so frantic. Spatial parts never abandon their separate existence, to merge into each other, as they do at S. Carlo or Vierzehnheiligen. The individual members, especially the solid round detached columns, also try to keep themselves to themselves. Vanbrugh's drama lies in the visible forcing of this English aloofness into the service of an overmighty plan. English Baroque is Baroque asserting itself against an inborn leaning towards the static and the sober.

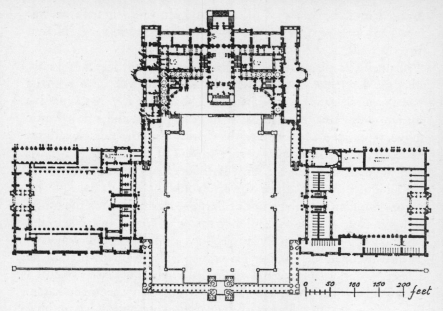

94. SIR JOHN VANBRUGH: BLENHEIM PALACE, BEGUN 1705.

The same conflict will be experienced in interiors of Wren's and Vanbrugh's time. There again spatial relations bind rooms together which are articulated and decorated according to the principles of Classicism—by panelling if they are small, by columns or pilasters if they are larger. At Blenheim there is an enormous entrance hall leading into the saloon which forms the centre of two symmetrical groups of rooms along the whole garden front, with all the doors in one axis, or as it is called, one *enfilade*, as at Versailles. But—this is of the greatest significance—the staircase, the dynamic element *par excellence*, is nothing like as prominent as it would be in a contemporary palace in France or Germany. This lack of interest in spatial dynamics is by no means a sign of meanness in planning. On the contrary, Blenheim is just as vast as the largest new palaces of the minor rulers of Germany, and just as unpractical—at least from our point of view.

However, it seems rather cheap to harp on the fact that kitchen and service rooms are far away from the dining-room—in one of the two wings in fact, opposite the other with the stables (an accepted Palladian tradition). Servants may have had to walk a long way, and hot dishes may have got cold long before they reached their destination. To us that may seem a functional error. Vanbrugh and his clients would have called such arguments extremely low. Of servants they had plenty. And what we call comfort mattered less than a self-imposed etiquette more rigid than we can imagine. The function of a building is not only utilitarian. There is also an ideal function, and that Blenheim did fulfil. However, not all Vanbrugh's contemporaries agreed that it did. There is, e.g. Pope with his famous, often quoted " 'tis very fine, But where d'ye sleep, or where d'ye dine?" What did he mean by that? Critics to-day interpret it as referring to a lack of material comfort. Pope was more philosophical than that. What, in the name of good sense, he asked for, is that a room and a building should look what they are. He disliked Vanbrugh's colossal scale and decorative splendour as unreasonable and unnatural. For "splendour", he insists, should borrow "all her rays from sense", and again:

> "Something there is more needful than expense,
> And something previous e'en to taste—'tis sense".

In this he gave expression to the feelings of his generation, the generation following Vanbrugh's. For Pope was born in 1688, whereas Vanbrugh was of almost the same age as Swift and Defoe (and Wren as Dryden).

The architecture that corresponds to Pope's poetry is that of Lord Burlington and his circle. Richard Boyle, Earl of Burlington, was some years younger than Pope (1694–1753). He went on his Grand Tour as a very young man, and brought back with him a promising young painter, William Kent. Full of the new Italian impression, he was, it seems, converted to the beauties of strict Palladianism by Colin Campbell, who in 1715 had begun to publish *Vitruvius Britannicus*, a book of illustrations of the best modern buildings of Britain. In the same year the Italian architect Leoni, who lived in England, had brought out a sumptuous English edition of Palladio. So Burlington went back to Italy in 1719, this time to study Palladio's works in and around Vicenza. Under his influence Kent turned Architect and edited at Burlington's expense in 1727 a folio of engravings from Inigo Jones's buildings and supposed buildings. These publications and Burlington's personality and propaganda set a Palladian fashion in British country houses that lasted almost unchallenged for fifty years, and with certain modifications for nearly a hundred.

The town house, however, was hardly affected. There are very few examples of Palladian influence beyond facade motifs. And where, as in a house designed by Lord Burlington himself, an attempt was made to interfere with the standardised London plan, the outcry against this imposition of the rationalist's new rules was just as pronounced as the rationalist's outcry had been against Vanbrugh's unruliness. Lord Chesterfield suggested to the owner that he should take a house opposite, so as to be able to admire his own at leisure without having to live in it.

It is the country house that became wholly Palladian by Lord Burlington's efforts. In Vanbrugh's work the variety of plans and exterior compositions had been unlimited. Now the *corps de logis* with a centre portico and isolated wings connected to the main body by low galleries became *de rigueur*. Prior Park, near Bath (pl. XCIV), is a typical example. It was designed for Ralph Allen in 1735 by the elder John Wood (*c.* 1700–54), a local architect, but, by virtue of his talent and the opportunities which he had in the most fashionable spa of England, one of the leading architects of his generation. Compared with Palladio's villas, these British derivations are larger and heavier. They also often incorporate motifs freer than Palladio would have tolerated: more variation in the shapes of rooms, or a boldly curved outer staircase into the garden (the one at Prior Park is of the 19th century). The sites, as a rule on a gentle slope, also add a quality that is absent in Palladio's work for a flat country. But more important still is the fact that Palladian country houses in Britain were designed to stand in English parks.

It seems at first contradictory that the same patrons should have wanted the formal Palladian house and the informal English garden, and that the same architect should have provided both. Yet it is a fact that William Kent, Lord Burlington's protégé, was celebrated as one of the creators of the English style in laying out grounds, and that Lord Burlington's own villa at Chiswick (about 1725), a free copy of Palladio's Villa Rotonda, was one of the earliest examples of what was called "the modern taste" in gardening. How can this have come about? Was the landscape garden just a whim? It was not; it was a conscious part of an anti-French policy in the arts. Le Nôtre's parks express absolutism, the king's absolute rulership over the country, and also Man's rulership over Nature. The active, expansive Baroque force that shapes the house, flows over into nature. Progressive English thinkers recognised this and disliked it.

Shaftesbury spoke of "the mockery of princely gardens", and Pope satirised them in his neat couplet:

"Grove nods at grove, each alley has a brother,
And half the platform just reflects the other".

Now this enforcing of architectural rule on the garden is certainly something unnatural. And so Addison wrote in *The Spectator* in 1712: "For my own part I would rather look upon a tree in all its luxuriance and diffusion of boughs and branches than when it is cut and trimmed into a mathematical figure". That profession of faith in nature not tampered with is evidently a revolt of liberalism and tolerance against tyranny; it is a Whig revolt. But the curious thing about it is that although these attacks were made in the name of nature, nature was still understood by Addison and Pope in Newton's and indeed in Boileau's sense. Boileau's objections in his *Art of Poetry* of 1674 against the Baroque of the South were that it was unreasonable and therefore unnatural. Reason and nature are still synonyms with Addison and Pope, as we have seen in Pope's comments on Blenheim.

Add to this Shaftesbury's "passion for things of a natural kind" and his idea that "the conceit or caprice of Man has spoiled their genuine order by breaking in upon (their) primitive state", and you will be near an answer to the puzzling parallelism between classicist architecture and natural gardening. The original state of the universe is harmony and order, as we see it in the ordered courses of the stars which were revealed by the new telescopes, and in the structures of organisms which were revealed by the new microscopes. "Idea or Sense, Order, Proportion everywhere", to use Shaftesbury's words once more. Now to illustrate the superiority of harmony over chaos Shaftesbury explicitly refers to the superiority of the "regular and uniform pile of some noble Architect" over "a Heap of Sand or Stones". But is not the heap of sand nature in her primitive state? That the early 18th century did not want to recognise. So we arrive at this curious ambiguity. Simple nature is order and harmony of proportion. So a natural architecture is an architecture according to Palladio. But simple nature is also, in the common speech of everybody, fields and hedgerows, and of these people were genuinely fond, at least in England. So the garden should be left as close to this simple nature as possible. Addison was the first to reach this conclusion. He exclaimed: "Why may not a whole estate be thrown into a kind of garden?", and "A man might make a pretty landscape of his own possessions". Pope followed Addison in a contribution to *The Guardian* in 1713 and, more important still, in his own miniature garden at Twickenham. However, when it came to "improving" Twickenham (to use the 18th-century term) in 1719–25—another equally remarkable thing happened. These earliest anti-French gardens were by no means landscape gardens in the later sense. They were not Pope's "Nature unadorned". Their plans with elaborately meandering paths and rills are of as artificial an irregularity as Baroque regularity had been before. Or as Horace Walpole put it in 1750: "There is not a citizen who doesn't take more pains to torture his acre and a half into irregularities than he formerly would have employed to make it as formal as his cravat". Now all that, this "twisting and twirling" (to use Walpole's words again), is evidently Rococo, and nearer in spirit to the Bruchsal Rocaille than to those gardens of the later 18th century which really tried to look like untouched nature. It is the English version of Rococo—as characteristically English as Wren's Baroque had been in comparison with Continental Baroque.

So while one remembers the grandeur and elegance of French 17th- and 18th-century architecture as urban all the way through— for the straight avenues in the park of Versailles are urban in spirit too—one should never forget in looking at the formality of English Palladian houses between 1660 and 1760 that their complement is the English garden. John Wood's Prior Park possesses such informal natural grounds. And even in the most urban developments of Georgian England such as New Edinburgh and above all Bath nature was close at hand and willingly admitted.

John Wood was the first after Inigo Jones to impose Palladian uniformity on an English square as a whole. All the squares in London and elsewhere laid out since 1660 had left it to each owner of a house to have it designed as he liked, and it was only due to the rule of taste in Georgian society that not one of these houses ever violently clashed with its neighbours. John Wood now made one palace front with central portico and secondary emphasis on the corner blocks out of his Queen Square in Bath. That was in 1728. Twenty-five years later he designed the Circus (1754–c. 1770), again as a uniform theme. His son, the younger John Wood (died 1781), in the Royal Crescent of 1767–c. 1775 (pl. xcv) broke open the compactness of earlier squares and ventured to provide as the only response to his vast semi-elliptical palace frontage of thirty houses with giant Ionic columns a spacious, gently sloping lawn. Here the extreme opposite of Versailles had been reached. Nature is no longer the servant of architecture. The two are equals. The Romantic Movement is at hand.

In London the principle of the palace facade for a whole row of houses was introduced by Robert Adam in his Adelphi (that magnificent composition of streets with its Thames front known all over Europe, which was destroyed, not by bombs, but by mercenary Londoners just before the war) and then taken up at Fitzroy Square and Finsbury Square. But Adam's work, which won international fame in the sixties and seventies—at the same moment when the English garden also began to influence Europe—should not be discussed so close to the Palladianism of the Burlington group. It is of a fundamentally different kind. As a rule this difference is expressed by placing Adam at the beginning of the so-called Classical Revival. But that is not the whole answer, for the Classical Revival is really only a part of a much wider process, the Romantic Movement. So from the renewed direct approach to Greek and Roman antiquities as well as from the English creation of landscape gardening we are led into a consideration of the central European problem of 1760–1830: the Romantic Movement.

CHAPTER VIII

Romantic Movement, Historicism and Modern Movement

FROM 1760 TO THE PRESENT DAY

THE Romantic Movement originated in England. In literature this fact is well enough known. For the arts and for architecture in particular it has yet to be established. In literature Romanticism is the reaction of sentiment against reason, of nature against artificiality, of simplicity against pompous display, of faith against scepticism. Romantic poetry expresses a new enthusiasm for nature and a self-abandoning veneration of the whole, elemental, undoubting life of early or distant civilisations. This veneration led to the discovery of the Noble Savage and the Noble Greek, the Virtuous Roman and the Pious Mediæval Knight. Whatever its object, the Romantic attitude is one of longing, that is antagonism to the present, a present which some saw predominantly as Rococo flippancy, others as unimaginative rationalism, and others again as ugly industrialism and commercialism.

The opposition to the present and the immediate past goes through all utterances of the Romantic spirit, although certain tendencies within the new movement grew out of the 18th century's Rationalism and Rococo. It has been shown for instance how the conception of the landscape garden—a truly Romantic conception—dates back to Addison and Pope, but appears at first in Rococo dress. Similarly that most popular architectural expression of Romanticism, the revival of mediæval forms, started long before the Romantic Movement proper and went through all the phases of 18th-century style, before it became wholly Romantic in character.

In fact the Gothic style had never quite died in England. There is college work in Oxford of the 17th century which is unselfconscious Perpendicular, notably the staircase up to the hall of Christ Church. Wren also used Gothic forms in some of the London City churches, and others followed him. But the beginnings of an original handling of mediæval elements, a revival and not a survival, are connected with Vanbrugh and his school. His own house at Blackheath of 1717–18 is castellated and has a fortified-looking round tower. He also introduced castellated structures into some of the grounds which he furnished or laid out. His reason for doing so was that mediæval forms suggested strength, and he always wanted to be *masculine* in his designs. Hence thick round towers and battlements occur even in in his country houses which are otherwise in the current style. However, it was not only their æsthetic qualities which tempted him in mediæval castles. He saw more in them. Not that he actually built sham ruins as the later 18th century did, but he defended the preservation of genuine ruins when he found them, because they "move lively and pleasing reflections . . . on the persons who have inhabited them (and) on the remarkable things which have been transacted in them", and because "with yews and hollies in a wild thicket" they make "one of the most agreeable objects that the best of landscape painters can invent".

Vanbrugh's austere version of mediævalism found no successors, but the two passages quoted from his memorandum of 1709 on Blenheim form the foundation of Romantic Revivalism. As will have been noticed Vanbrugh uses two arguments: the associational and the picturesque. Both were developed by theorists of the 18th century. A building is clothed in the garb of a special style, because of the meditations which that style will rouse. And a building is conceived in conjunction with the surrounding nature, because the virtuosi had discovered on the Grand Tour amid the ruins of Roman architecture in and around Rome, the truth and the picturesqueness of the heroic and idyllic landscapes of Claude Lorraine, Poussin, Dughet and Salvator Rosa. These were bought freely by English collectors and helped to form the taste of artists and gardeners, amateur and professional.

Lorraine may have been admired by Pope and Kent (who after all was a painter before he became an architect), but the gardens of Twickenham and Chiswick had nothing of the serene calm of a Lorraine landscape. The Rococo had to die, before this kind of beauty could be reproduced. The Leasowes, the garden which William Shenstone the poet had laid out for himself about 1745, was apparently amongst the first to replace the "twisting and twirling" of the earlier style by a gentler flow of curves which, together with the many memorial seats and temples which he erected, helped to rouse feelings of pleasant meditation. The great name in the history of mid-18th-century gardening is Lancelot

Brown (Capability Brown, 1715–83). His are the wide softly sweeping lawns, the artfully scattered clumps of trees and the serpentine lakes which revolutionised garden art all over Europe and America (pl. xcIII). This is no longer Rococo, it has the gentle simplicity of Goldsmith's *Vicar of Wakefield* and the chaste elegance of Robert Adam's architecture.

But Adam's is a more complex case than Brown's. Robert Adam (1728–92) is internationally known as the father of the Classical Revival in Britain. His revival of Roman stucco decoration and his delicate adaptation of classical motifs have influenced the Continent just as widely as the new English style in gardening. Yet delicacy is hardly what our present knowledge of Greece and Rome would lead us to expect from a true classical revivalist. Where in Adam's work is the severe nobility of Athens or the sturdy virility of Rome? There is in fact more severity in Lord Burlington's Palladianism and more virility in Vanbrugh than can anywhere be found in Adam. Compare, e.g., the walls and ceiling of Adam's Library at Kenwood (pl. xcvI) with those of any Palladian mansion. Adam covers his walls with dainty and exquisitely executed stucco work in a light and quick rhythm. And he loves to run out a room into a gently rounded niche screened off by two free-standing columns with an entablature above. This veiling of spatial relations, this transparency—air floating from room to apse between the columns and above the entablature—is decidedly anti-Palladian, original and spirited. It occurs again in exterior architecture in the entrance screen to the grounds of Syon House (pl. xcvII). Here too Lord Burlington would have spoken of flippancy and frippery. And Vanbrugh's centre pavilions in the wings of Blenheim Palace (pl. xcII) look, compared with Adam's screen, like boulders piled up by a giant. Adam's gracefully ornamented pilasters and the lion in profile silhouetted against the sky make Vanbrugh appear a tartar, Burlington a pedant. What Adam admired in a building is, in his own words: "the rise and fall, the advance and recess, and other diversity of forms", and "a variety of light mouldings".

Now this is eminently revealing. It is neither Baroque nor Palladian—although in the exteriors of his country houses Adam did not often depart from Palladian standards—nor is it classical. It is Rococo if anything—yet another passing and concealed appearance in England of the general European style of the mid-18th century. All the same, it is not wrong either to see in Robert Adam a representative of the Classical Revival. He did go to Rome as a young man, from there crossed over to Spalato to study and measure the remains of Diocletian's Palace, and after his return home published the results of his research as a sumptuous volume in 1763. Now these engraved folios of the monument of antiquity are quite rightly regarded as a hall-mark of the Classical Revival. Adam's was preceded by the most important of all, James Stuart's and Nicholas Revett's *Antiquities of Athens*, of which the first volume came out in 1762. The two architects had worked at the expense of the recently founded Society of Dilettanti, the London club of archeologically interested gentlemen. Six years later the temples of Pæstum were illustrated by Thomas Major. In these books the architect and the virtuoso in England could see for the first time the strength and simplicity of the Greek Doric order. For what until then, and ever since the Books of Orders of the 16th century, had been known and used as Doric, was the much slenderer variety now known as Roman, if fluted, and Tuscan, if not fluted. The short and thick proportions of the Greek Doric order, and the complete absence of a base, shocked the Palladians. Sir William Chambers, champion of Palladian traditions in the generation after Burlington and one of the founders of the Royal Academy in 1768, called it downright barbaric. Adam did not like it either. Its reappearance in the books of the sixties is memorable. It became the *leitmotif* of the severest phase or variety of the Classical Revival, that known in England as the Greek Revival. Stuart and Revett's work was paralleled in French by Le Roi's skimpier *Ruines de Grèce* of 1758 and in German by Winckelmann's classic *History of Ancient Art* of 1763—the first book to recognise and analyse the true qualities of Greek art, its "noble simplicity and tranquil greatness".

However, Winckelmann's recognition of these qualities was still more literary than visual; for he placed the Apollo Belvedere and the Laocoon, that is examples of Late Greek Baroque and Rococo, higher than any other antique statuary. Would the figures of Olympia and Aegina and perhaps even those of the Parthenon have shocked him? It is not at all unlikely. His Grecian tastes probably did not go further than say Josiah Wedgwood's. Wedgwood copied vases from those Greek examples of the 5th century which were then believed to be Etruscan, and even called his new factory up by Stoke-on-Trent Etruria. But the style of Wedgwood ware is gentle and elegant— an Adam not a Greek style. Still, there is the undeniable desire to be

Greek, the marked tendency in archeological publications to prefer the Greek to the Roman, and there is, if not in Adam, in his contemporary James Stuart, "Athenian" Stuart (1713–88), the actual copying in earnest of complete Greek structures on Northern soil and the putting up of Doric temples for Northern patrons. If this is not a genuine Greek Revival, what is? But once again, if we forget about associations and intentions and simply use our eyes, we see miniature pavilions in Doric forms placed into landscape gardens—picturesque pieces of garden furnishing. Such a Doric temple of Stuart's, e.g., graces the grounds at Hagley, near Birmingham, and close to it the same owner put up at the same time a Gothic ruin as a keeper's lodge and a rustic seat to the memory of Thomson of the *Seasons*.

The only difference between the Doric and the Gothic of Hagley is that the one is tolerably correct and the other is not. The owner, owing to his classical education, watched the one, but could not watch the other. Architects too and even country builders knew by 1760 enough of the orders and the details of antiquity to be able to reproduce a Pantheon *en miniature* or a half-broken Roman aqueduct without too many blunders. But in the case of the earliest Gothic Revival antiquarian knowledge was still scanty. Thus while the result in the Greek and Roman copies tends to be somewhat dry, the innumerable Gothic seats, hermits' cells, "umbrellos" and sham ruins (fig. 95) are charmingly naïve and lighthearted—a Gothic Rococo, as Adam's was a classical Rococo.

To Horace Walpole belongs the credit of having inspired and commissioned the first complete country house in the Gothic style: Strawberry Hill, near London, begun in 1747. Walpole was ahead of his day in insisting on correct details, especially in his interiors, where fireplaces or wall panelling were copied from engravings after mediæval tombs and screens. He evidently admired other qualities in the Gothic style than we do. In letters of 1748 and 1750 he talks of "the charming venerable Gothic" and the "whimsical air of novelty" which Gothic motifs give to contemporary buildings. And charming and whimsical Strawberry Hill is indeed with its thin, papery exterior work and the pretty gallery inside whose gilt fan-vaults and tracery have mirrors set in as panels. This playful use of Gothic forms is closer in spirit to Chippendale's Chinese furniture than to Wordsworth's feelings at Tintern Abbey or to Victorian Neo-Gothic churches. Walpole himself was against the fashion of the *Chinoiserie*; but for a generalising view of the style of 1750 a

Chinese bridge, a miniature Pantheon and a Gothic ruin all belong together. In fact we find that even Robert Adam enjoyed drawing ruins with all the Rococo sparkle of Piranesi, and occasionally designed domestic work in a mildly mediæval taste. And we also find Sir William Chambers in spite of his staunch adherence to Palladianism designing the Pagoda at Kew Gardens.

Kew had originally the most varied set of such Rococo garden extravaganzas: besides the Pagoda (which alone survives) a temple of Pan, a temple of Æolus, a temple of Solitude, a temple of the Sun, a temple of Bellona, a temple of Victory, a house of Confucius, a Corinthian colonnade, an Alhambra, a mosque, a Gothic cathedral, a ruin, various stone seats, etc. The fun of Turkish, Moorish, Gothic and Chinese in this *omnium gatherum* of exotic styles is that of Voltaire's *Zadig* and *Babouc* and of Montesquieu's *Lettres Persanes*, that is one of a sophisticated Rococo double-meaning. Not much of the solemn meditation of the Romantics could in fact be evoked by a Pagoda. When the Romantic Movement somewhat later instilled these sentiments into gardening, a good many of the current garden adornments were eliminated as unsuitable. Yet to Walpole too Strawberry Hill had associational qualities. It was, in some ways, his *Castle of Otranto*. It seems difficult to believe that; but that Beckford's mansion, Fonthill Abbey, with its vast galleries and enormous

95. GARDEN SEAT FROM P. DECKER'S " GOTHIC ARCHITECTURE
DECORATED," 1759.

193

tower had to him some of the awe-inspiring qualities of the dark Middle Ages can be appreciated from surviving illustrations. Here the eccentricity of a millionaire seems to have created something truly romantic. Fonthill was built by James Wyatt (1746–1813) from 1796 onwards. But already as early as 1772 Goethe in front of Strasbourg Cathedral had found words of passionate admiration for the Gothic spirit in architecture. "It rises like a most sublime, wide-arching Tree of God, who with a thousand boughs, a million of twigs, and leafage like the sands of the sea, tells forth to the neighbourhood the glory of the Lord, his master. . . . All is shape, down to the minutest fibril, all purposes to the whole. How the firm-grounded gigantic building lightly rears itself into the air! How filagree'd all of it, yet for eternity. . . . Stop brother, and discern the deepest sense of truth . . . quickening out of strong, rough, German soul . . . Be not girled, dear youth, for rough greatness by the soft doctrine of modern beauty-lisping."[1]

Now here the Gothic style is no longer something in the same category as Rococo, Chinese and Hindu, it stands for all that is genuine, sincere, elemental—in fact very much for what Winckelmann, and only a little later Goethe himself, saw in the art of Greece. The Greek and the Gothic were both, in the minds of serious æstheticians and artists, the salvation from 18th-century flippancy. But they could not be an effective remedy. For no healthy style can stop at the mere imitation of another. The Renaissance had not done it. The Grecians of the early 19th century did it too often. Goethe in the most classical mood of his *Iphigenia* remained essentially original. But in fact what he had praised more than anything at Strasbourg was originality in the sense of Young. And so the few architects of Goethe's era who possessed true genius used the forms of Greece and Rome with the greatest freedom. Of Greece and Rome; for an equally free and masterly style based on Gothic principles time was not yet ripe. The sense of mediæval building had not yet been sufficiently digested to allow for a revival in another than an imitative sense.

Two architects above all others must be mentioned as the creators of an original idiom of 1800: Sir John Soane in England and Friedrich Gilly in Prussia. Soane (1753–1837) had gone through apprenticeship and Royal Academy tuition, when he went to Rome in 1778.

[1] Geoffrey Grigson's translation, published in *The Architectural Review*, vol. 98, 1945.

Already amongst his earlier designs there is an amazingly personal blend of Baroque grandeur of composition with Grecian severity of detail. Soane was the first (except for Piranesi, the engraver) to understand the *terribilità* of the Greek Doric order. Then during the nineties Soane discovered that the severity which was his aim could be achieved by sheer unadorned surface—a discovery which makes his work appear so topical to-day. He had been appointed architect to the Bank of England in 1788.

The exterior, before it was converted by recent governors and directors into a podium for a piece of 20th-century commercial showiness, indicates this new and to the majority shocking austerity. The interiors, preserved though atrociously ill-treated, give an even clearer idea of his sense of surface integrity. Walls flow smoothly into vaults. Mouldings are reduced to a minimum. Arches sit on piers which they seem to touch only in points. No precedent is allowed to cramp the master's style. The Dulwich Gallery of 1811–14 (damaged by bombs but not irreparably) and Soane's own house in Lincoln's Inn Fields (pl. xcviii), built in 1812–13 and intended to be carried on to more than double its width, are his most independent designs. The ground floor of the house has severely plain arcading in front of the actual wall; the first floor repeats this unusual motif with the variation of a centre with Ionic columns supporting the thinnest of architraves, and wings where the weight of the piers is lightened by typically Soanian incised ornament. The top pavilions on the left and the right are equally original. Except for the Ionic columns there is not one motif in the whole facade that has a Greek or Roman ancestry. Here more than anywhere in architecture England approached a new style unhampered by the past, and a style moreover that possesses the crispness and precision of the dawning machine age. Soane for all we know was not in special sympathy with that age, which in most of its social and visual aspects was still sordid enough. Soane was a wilful, obstinate and irritable character, and wilful is his almost *Art Nouveau* looking ornament. But its meaning is clear. These delicate lines emphasise the planes into which they are cut, just as the lack of pediments on the flat roofs emphasise the cubic relations of such planes. From the beginning of his career Soane had been fascinated by this problem of cubic relations. He first expressed it with massive Doric columns and rustication, but later with flat surfaces of seeming skin or film or slab thinness.

96. CLAUDE NICOLAS LEDOUX: ONE OF THE CITY GATES OF PARIS, DESIGNED BETWEEN 1784 AND 1789.

The same faith in the bare surface but not the same elegance appears with a much more aggressive force in the work of a few French architects of the time of the Revolution. Claude Nicolas Ledoux (1736–1806) has only within the last fifteen years been rediscovered. He was an eccentric, cantankerous and quarrelsome. But his designs since 1776 are amongst the most original ever conceived by any architect, original sometimes to the verge of mania: a completely spherical house, a pyramidal house, fantastic projects for vast community buildings. His planning is as boldly Baroque as Soane's. His predilection for the squat Doric column also connects him with Soane (fig. 96). He was no doubt influenced by England, and the publication of his work in 1804 may have influenced England in turn.

Friedrich Gilly (1772–1800), the Soane of Germany, was certainly inspired by Ledoux. He had his training in Berlin, one of a small group of young architects who about 1790 discovered the force of the true Doric order in Italy. Gilly himself however never saw Italy, and went to Paris and London only after he had designed one of the two masterpieces which are left us to bear witness of his genius —left, however, only in drawings. Neither was ever carried out. The first is the National Monument to Frederick the Great (1797), the second a National Theatre for Berlin—clearly a conception of the Goethe age (pl. xcix). The Doric portico without a pediment is a strong and grave opening. The semicircular windows, a favourite motif of the revolutionary architects of Paris, though imported from England, add strength to strength, and the contrast between the semicylinder of the auditorium walls and the cube of the stage is functionally eloquent and æsthetically superb. Here again we are close to a new style of the new century.

Why is it then that a hundred years had to pass before an original "modern" style was really accepted? How can it be that the 19th century forgot about Soane and Gilly and remained smugly satisfied with the imitation of the past? Such a lack of self-confidence is the last thing one would expect from an epoch so independent in commerce, industry and engineering. It is the things of the spirit in which the Victorian age lacked vigour and courage. Standards in architecture were the first to go; for while a poet and a painter can forget about their age and be great in the solitude of their study and studio, an architect cannot exist in opposition to society. Now those to whom visual sensibility was given saw so much beauty destroyed all around by the sudden immense and uncontrolled growth of cities and factories that they despaired of their century and turned to a more inspiring past. Moreover the iron-master and mill-owner, as a rule self-made men of no education, felt no longer bound by one particular accepted taste as the gentleman had been who was brought up to believe in the rule of taste. It would have been bad manners to build against it. Hence the only slightly varied uniformity of the English 18th-century house. The new manufacturer had no manners, and he was a convinced individualist. If, for whatever reasons, he liked a style in architecture, then there was nothing to prevent him from having his way and getting a house or a factory or an office building or a club built in that style. And unfortunately for the immediate future of architecture he knew of a good many possible styles, because—as we have seen—some sophisticated and leisurely *cognoscenti* of the 18th century had explored for fun certain out-of-the-way architectural idioms, and a set of Romantic poets was revelling in nostalgic fantasies of the distant in time and space. The Rococo had reintroduced alien styles, the Romantic Movement had endowed them with sentimental associations. The 19th century lost the Rococo's lightness of touch and the Romantics' emotional fervour. But it stuck to variety of style, because associational values were the only values in architecture accessible to the new ruling class.

We have seen Vanbrugh's defence of ruins for associational reasons. Sir Joshua Reynolds in his thirteenth *Discourse* of 1786 made the same point more neatly. He explicitly counts amongst the principles of architecture "that of affecting the imagination by means of association of ideas. Thus," he continues, "we have naturally a veneration for antiquity; whatever building brings to our remembrance ancient customs and manners, such as the castles of the Barons of ancient Chivalry, is sure to give this delight."

Hence on the authority of the late President of the Royal Academy the manufacturer and merchant could feel justified in placing associational criteria foremost. Visual criteria his eyes were not trained to appreciate. But the eyes of architects were; and it was a grave symptom of a diseased century that architects were satisfied to be story-tellers instead of artists. But then painters were no better. They too, to be successful, had to tell stories or render objects from nature with scientific accuracy.

Thus by 1830 we find a most alarming social and æsthetic situation in architecture. Architects believed that anything created by the pre-industrial centuries must of necessity be better than anything made to express the character of their own era. Architects' clients had lost all æsthetic susceptibilities, and wanted other than æsthetic qualities to approve of a building. Associations they could understand. And one other quality they could also understand and even check: correctness of imitation. The free and fanciful treatment of styles developed into one of archeological exactitude. That this could happen was due to that general sharpening of the tools of historical knowledge which characterises the 19th century. It is in truth the century of Historicism. After the system-building 18th century, the 19th appears to an amazing extent satisfied with, say, a historical and comparative study of existing philosophies to the study of metaphysics, ethics, æsthetics, etc., themselves. And so it was in theology and philology too. Similarly architectural scholarship abandoned æsthetic theory and concentrated on historical research. Thanks to a subdivision of labour which architecture, like all other fields of art, letters and science, took over from industry, architects were always able to draw from a well-assorted stock of historical detail. No wonder that little time and desire were left for the development of an original style of the 19th century. Even with regard to Soane and Gilly we have to be careful not to overestimate their originality and "modernity". Soane did a great deal that is more conventional than his own house. There are even some Gothic designs by him. And Gilly drew and published in detail the grandest of the mediæval castles of the German knights in East Prussia. Exquisite as these drawings are, the attitude that made Gilly spend so much time on them is only partially romantic and patriotic. Antiquarian ambition is at least as conspicuous in these careful renderings. The case of Girtin's and Turner's early water colours is very similar. They are the transition (though still a romantic transition full of creative power) between the polite 18th-century engravings of Athens and Pæstum and the voluminous 19th-century books on cathedral antiquities and mediæval details.

Amongst such books the transition can also be noted: the earliest are still rather sketchy, while later they became more and more thorough and as a rule rather dull. In actual buildings we find exactly the same development from the elegant and whimsical but sometimes inspired to the learned but sometimes deplorably pedestrian. Strawberry Hill stands for Rococo-Gothic, Robert Adam for a Rococo-Classical Revival. The next generation is characterised by John Nash (1752–1835). Nash had nothing of the intransigent creative fury of Soane. He was light-handed, careless, socially successful and artistically conservative. His frontages of old Regent Street and most of his palace-like facades round Regent's Park, planned and carried out between 1811 and about 1825, are still of an 18th-century suppleness. What makes them memorable is the way in which they form part of a brilliant town-planning scheme, a scheme linking up the Picturesque of the 18th century with the Garden City ideas of the 20th. For these vast terraces face a landscape park, and a number of elegant villas are placed right in the park— the fulfilment of what had been foreshadowed in the juxtaposition of houses and lawn in the Royal Crescent at Bath. While the Regent Street–Regent's Park frontages are almost entirely classical, Nash built with the same gusto Gothic if required. He had a nice sense of associational propriety; as shown in his choice of the Neo-Classical for his town house and of the Gothic for his country mansion (complete with Gothic conservatory). Moreover he built Cronkhill, in Shropshire (1802), as an Italianate villa with a round-arched loggia on slender columns and with the widely projecting eaves of the Southern farmhouse (Roscoe's *Lorenzo Medici* had come out in 1796), he built Blaise Castle, near Bristol (1809), in a rustic Old-English cottage style with barge-boarded gables and thatched roofs (one is reminded of the *Vicar of Wakefield*, Marie Antoinette's dairy in the Park of Versailles, and Gainsborough's and Greuze's sweet peasant children), and he continued the Brighton Pavilion in a Hindu fashion, first introduced just after 1800 at Sezincote, in the Cotswolds, where the owner, because of personal reminiscences, insisted on the style. "Indian Gothic" was the eminently characteristic contemporary name of the style.

So here, in the early years of the 19th century, the fancy-dress ball of architecture is in full swing: Classical, Gothic, Italianate,

Old-English. By 1840 pattern-books for builders and clients include many more styles: Tudor, French Renaissance, Venetian Renaissance and others. That does not however mean that at all moments during the 19th century all these styles were really used. Favourites changed with fashion. Certain styles became associationally branded. A familiar example is the Moorish synagogue. Another is the perseverance of the battlemented castle for prisons. An account of architecture from 1820 to 1890 is bound to be one of the coming and going of period styles.

On the Classical side 1820–40 is characterised by the most correct Neo-Greek. Fancy had left the treatment of antiquity even earlier than that of the Middle Ages. The results are competent, and in the hands of the best architects of a noble dignity. The British Museum, begun in 1824 by Sir Robert Smirke (1780–1867), is amongst the best examples in Britain (pl. c), or would be if its front with its grand Ionic order of the Erechtheum in Athens could been seen from a distance; Carl Friedrich Schinkel (1781–1841), Gilly's pupil, is the greatest, most sensitive and most original representative on the Continent (fig. 97), William Strickland (1787–1854) probably the most vigorous in the United States.

For now, with the Greek Revival, America can no longer be left out of the picture of Western architecture. American building had been colonial to the end of the 18th century; colonial as the latest Gothic, Renaissance and Baroque buildings of the Spanish and the Portuguese in North, Central and South America. The Greek Revival in the United States is also still closely dependent on European, especially English examples, but national qualities, such as a remarkable stress on engineering technique, sanitary installation and equipment in general, now come to the fore. The ideological background of the strict Neo-Greek is the liberal humanism of the educated classes in the early 19th century, the spirit of Goethe, i.e. the spirit which created our first public museums and art galleries, and our first national theatres, and which is responsible for the reorganisation and the broadening of education.

On the Gothic side the corresponding development leads back to the Romantic Movement. Young Goethe's enthusiasm for Strasbourg had been a revolutionary genius's worship of genius. To the generation after his, the Middle Ages became the ideal of Christian civilisation. Friedrich Schlegel, one of the most brilliant of Romantic writers and one of the most inspired Gothicists, became a convert

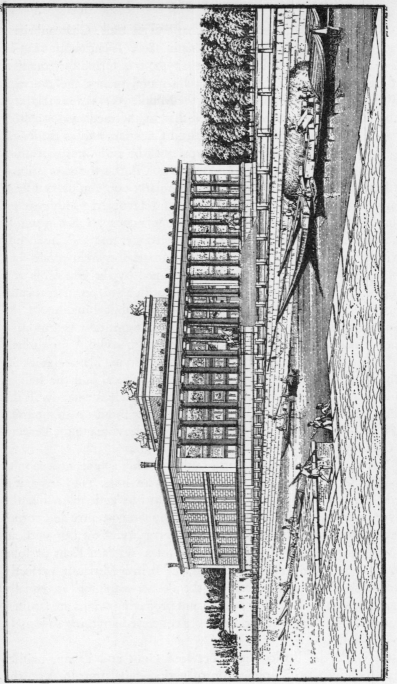

97. CARL FRIEDRICH SCHINKEL: THE OLD MUSEUM (ALTES MUSEUM), BERLIN, 1822–30.

to the Roman Catholic church. That was in 1808. Châteaubriand had written his *Génie du Christianisme* in 1802. Then, about 1835 in England, Augustus Welby Pugin (1812–52) transferred the equation of Christianity and Gothic into architectural theory and practice. With him, to build in the forms of the Middle Ages is a moral duty. And he went further. He contended that, as the mediæval architect was an honest workman and a faithful Christian, and as mediæval architecture is good architecture, you must be an honest workman and a good Christian to be a good architect. In this the associational attitude appears fatefully extended. Similarly contemporary Classicists began to brand the architect who favoured Gothic as an obscurantist and, worse still, his work as popery. On the whole the arguments of the Gothicists proved stronger and had, in an unexpected way, a more beneficial effect on art and architecture, but the æsthetic value of the buildings designed by the Classicists was higher. The Houses of Parliament, begun in 1836, are æsthetically more successful than any later large-scale public building in the Gothic style (pl. CI). The competition—a significant symptom—had demanded designs in the Gothic or Tudor style. A monument of national tradition had to be in a national style. The architect Sir Charles Barry (1795–1860) preferred the Classical and the Italian. But Pugin worked with him and was responsible for nearly all the detail inside and outside. Hence the building possesses an intensity of life not to be found in other architect's endeavours in the Perpendicular style.

Yet even Pugin's Gothic turns out to be only a veneer, as soon as the Houses of Parliament are examined as a whole. They have, it is true, a picturesque asymmetry in their towers and spires, but the river front is, in spite of that, with its emphasised centre and corner pavilions a composition of Palladian formality. You can without much effort visualise it with porticoes of a William Kent or John Wood type. And strangely enough, the British Museum, perfectly Greek as it appears, reveals to the deeper-searching an equally Palladian structure. Centre portico and projecting wings are familiar features. The Athens of Pericles never conceived anything so loosely spread-out.

So while the battles raged between Goth and Pagan, neither realised how all this application of period detail remained on the surface. Moral arguments and associational tags were freely used, but architecture as a job of designing to fulfil functions remained unheeded—or at least undiscussed. Even to-day in such cases as the British Museum and the Houses of Parliament people think much too much of æsthetics and too little of function. Yet it should not be forgotten that to build a palace for democratic government and a palace for the instruction of the people was equally new. In fact to erect public buildings, specially designed as such, had been extremely rare before 1800. There were town halls of course, and London had the Royal Exchange. Somerset House also had been intended for Government offices and learned societies from the beginning. But these were exceptions. If one takes the 19th century on the other hand, and tries to pick out the best examples of town architecture of all dates and all countries, a number of churches will have to be included, palaces rarely, private houses of course; but the vast majority of what one would collect are Governmental, municipal and later private office buildings, museums, galleries, libraries, universities and schools, theatres and concert halls, banks and exchanges, railway stations, department stores, hotels and hospitals, i.e. all buildings erected not for worship nor for luxury, but for the benefit and the daily use of the people, as represented by various groups of citizens. In this a new social function of architecture appears, representative of a new stratification of society. But the work in evolving plan forms for these new uses was more often than not anonymous, or at least appears so to us. The Renaissance library had been a hall of two or three aisles. The Renaissance hospital had been almost exactly identical in plan. Both came without essential modifications, from the monastic buildings of the Middle Ages. Now schemes were worked out for special library stores with stacking apparatus. For hospitals systems were tried of groups of separate wards and separate buildings for each kind of disease. For prisons the star-plan was invented (Pentonville) and accepted. For banks and exchanges the glass-covered centre hall or court proved the most serviceable solution. For museums and galleries a specially good system of lighting was essential, for office buildings the most flexible ground plan. And so every new type of building required its own treatment.

But the academician architects were too busy with new trimmings for facades to notice much of all that. When the struggle between Classicists and Gothicists began to subside, other styles took their place. In the mediæval field the generations before Pugin had been all for Perpendicular. To Pugin and those who followed him, notably Sir George Gilbert Scott, Perpendicular was anathema. Gothic had now to be of the 13th and early 14th century to be right, and Scott and his colleagues never minded replacing a genuine Perpendicular window by an imitation earlier one when they had to restore a church. Their archæological knowledge sharpened and on the whole their imitations grew in sensitivity as the century progressed. The change from Perpendicular to Early English belongs to the thirties. In the last quarter of the century Bodley's and especially Pearson's work (St. Augustine's, Kilburn, London ; St. John's, Red Lion Square, London ; Cathedral, Truro) are the most refined. When it comes to originality, however, these accomplished revivalists were far surpassed by such characters as William Butterfield and James Brooks. Butterfield's detail is original to the extreme of harshness and demonstrative ugliness (All Saints', Margaret Street, London; St. Alban's, Holborn, London), and Brooks's plans occasionally abandon all dependence on English Gothic precedent.

No other country took so whole-heartedly to the Gothic Revival in all its tendencies and shades as England. France kept away from it for a long time and has only a few Neo-Gothic churches of the first order (and Gau, the architect of Ste. Clotilde, was born at Cologne). In Germany the change from Schinkel's sometimes romantic and sometimes free functional treatment of Gothic form to the archæological phase is connected with the effort to complete Cologne Cathedral, after the original plan had been found in 1841. Since then good Gothic churches and later on public buildings appeared from Hamburg to Vienna.

In the opposite camp of the Southerners the grand style of the Italian High Renaissance *palazzi* replaced the chastity of the Neo-Greek. The first European Neo-Renaissance palace is Klenze's Beauharnais Palace, in Munich, of 1816. Munich after that produced a number of excellent examples in the thirties (National Library by Gärtner, 1831). So did Dresden, thanks to Gottfried Semper (Opera, 1837). In London the style makes its appearance with Sir Charles Barry's Travellers' and Reform Clubs (1829 and 1837). What helped to popularise the Renaissance style must have been its plasticity as against the flatness of Neo-Classical and the thinness of Neo-Perpendicular form. Also it represented a more substantial prosperity, and this, as is well known, was the ideal of the leading classes during the Victorian age (pl. CII).

Then, already shortly after 1831, France rediscovered her native

Early Renaissance, and Paris rebuilt its 16th-century town hall with picturesque gables and playful pilasters. To this corresponded in England a revival of Elizabethan and Jacobean forms, especially for country houses. Their associational value was of course national; their æsthetic appeal lay in a still livelier play of ornaments on surfaces. Apparently the underground tendency, covered up by changing period costumes, was towards the *mouvementé* and spectacular, the flamboyant style of Disraeli and the pompousness of Gladstone. Thus about 1850–60 Italianate forms became also more and more exuberant, until a Neo-Baroque was reached. Charles Garnier's Opera in Paris of 1861–74 is one of the earliest and best examples (pl. CIII). Another is Poelaert's enormous Law Courts at Brussels (1866–83). In England there is little of this *Second Empire* style. A revival of Palladianism in its most Baroque form took its place, and a strong inspiration from the Wren of Greenwich Hospital. Then with a slight sobering of form and a marked influence from a Classical Re-revival in America (McKim, Mead and White) a character-istically prosperous Edwardian Imperial style was arrived at (Selfridge's). In Germany the late 19th- and early 20th-century Neo-Baroque goes under the name of Wilhelmian; in Italy it has disgraced Rome with the national monument to King Victor Emmanuel II.

However, by the time these buildings were designed, a reaction had come and spread against so superficial—truly superficial—a conception of architecture. It did not originate with the architect. It could not; because it concerned problems of social reform and of engineering, and architects were not interested in these. Most of them loathed the industrial development of the age just as heartily as the painters. They did not see that the Industrial Revolution, while destroying an accepted order and an accepted standard of beauty, created opportunities for a new kind of beauty and order. It offered to the imaginative new materials and new manufacturing processes, and opened up a vista towards architectural planning on an undreamt-of scale.

As for new materials, iron, and after 1860 steel, made it possible to achieve spans wider than ever before, to build higher than ever before, and develop ground plans more flexible than ever before. Glass, in conjunction with iron and steel, enabled the engineer to make whole roofs and whole walls transparent. Reinforced concrete, introduced at the end of the century, combines the tensile strength of steel with the crushing strength of stone. Architects knew little of these things. They left them to the engineers. For about 1800, in connection with the growing subdivision of competencies, the architect's and the engineer's had become different jobs for which a different training was provided. Architects learnt in the offices of older architects and in schools of architecture, until they set up in practice themselves doing what the civil-servant-architect had done in the 17th century, but now chiefly for private clients instead of the State. Engineers were trained in special university faculties or (in France and Central Europe) special technical universities. The most perfect examples of early iron architecture, the suspension bridges, such as Brunel's Clifton Bridge, designed in 1829-31 and begun in 1836, are the work of engineers, not of architects. Paxton who conceived the Crystal Palace of 1851 was a landscape gardener used to the iron and glasswork of conservatories. The men who introduced iron stanchions into the construction of American warehouses and occasionally, in the forties and fifties, opened whole fronts by glazing the whole interstices between the stanchions, are mostly unknown or undistinguished as architects. And in France, where a few trained and recognised architects (Labrouste: Geneviève Library, 1845-50) used iron conspicuously—even occasionally for a whole church interior (St. Eugéne, Paris, begun 1854), they were attacked and ridiculed by the majority.

In all this a fundamentally unsound conception of architecture as a social service is apparent. This was first recognised by Pugin, who saw only one remedy: the return to the old faith of Rome. Then shortly after him, John Ruskin preached in *The Seven Lamps of Architecture* (1849) that a building must be truthful first of all. And a little later he began to realise that to achieve this, thought had to be given to social as well as æsthetic problems. The step from theory to practice was taken by William Morris (1834-96). He had undergone the influence of Ruskin and the Pre-Raphaelites, had actually been for a time a pupil of Rossetti, and also of one of the most conscientious Neo-Gothic architects. But he was not satisfied with either painting or architecture as he saw them practised, i.e. painting as the art of making easel pictures for exhibitions, and architecture as writing-desk and drawing-board work.

And whereas Ruskin kept his social activities apart from his æsthetic theory, Morris was the first to link up the two in the only way they could be successfully linked up. Instead of becoming a painter or an architect, he founded a firm for designing and making furniture, fabrics, wallpaper, carpets, stained glass, etc., and got his Pre-Raphaelite friends to join him. Not until the artist becomes a craftsman again, this was his belief, and the craftsman an artist, can art be saved from annihilation by the machine. Morris was a violent machine-hater. He attributed to mechanisation and sub-division of labour all the evils of the age. And from his point of view he was right. The solution he found was æsthetically sound, though socially not in the long run adequate. To build up a new style on design was sound, to try to build it up in opposition to the technical potentialities of the century was just as much escapism as the Classicist's disguising of a town hall as a Greek temple. The forms which Morris & Co. chose for their products were inspired by the late Middle Ages, as was Morris's poetry. But Morris did not imi-tate. He recognised Historicism as the danger it was. What he did was to steep himself in the atmosphere and the æsthetic principles of the Middle Ages, and then create something new with a similar flavour and on similar principles. This is why Morris fabrics and wallpapers will live long after all applied art of the generation before his will have lost its significance.

Morris's social-æsthetic theory as it was embodied in the many lectures and addresses he delivered from 1877 onwards will keep its life in history too. By trying to revive the old faith in service, by indicting the contemporary architect's and artist's arrogant indiffer-ence to design for everyday needs, by discrediting any art created by individual genius for a small group of connoisseurs, and by forcing home with untiring zest the principle that art matters only "if all can share it", he laid the foundation of the Modern Movement.

What Morris did for the philosophy of art and for design, Richardson in the United States and Webb and Norman Shaw in Britain did concurrently for the æsthetics of architecture. Henry Hobson Richardson (1838–86) unquestionably still belongs to the era of period revivals. He studied in Paris and returned to New England deeply impressed by the power of the French Romanesque style. He continued to make use of it for churches, public and office buildings (Auditorium, Chicago)—but no longer just for imitative or associational reasons. He saw that these plain massive stone sur-faces and mighty round arches could convey emotional contents more suited to our own age than any other familiar to him. And he and his followers designed country houses in the eighties freer and

98. ROBERT NORMAN SHAW: STORES AND INN AT THE BEDFORD PARK GARDEN SUBURB, CHISWICK, 1878.

bolder than any Europe did at the same time—or should one say Europe with the exception of Philip Webb in England? Webb (1830–1915) liked plain brick walls, and introduced into them the plain slender windows of the William and Mary and Queen Anne period, remaining nevertheless in sympathy with the sturdy honest building traditions of the Gothic and Tudor styles. The Red House at Bexley Heath, near London, his first work, designed for (and with) Morris in 1859 shows already a combination of pointed arches and long segment-headed sash windows.

The picturesque possibilities of a mixture of motifs derived from widely different styles were more readily taken up by Richard Norman Shaw (1831–1912). He had a much lighter touch, a quicker imagination, but a less discriminating taste. In a professional career extending over more than forty years he never ceased to try the contemporary appeal of new period styles. Thus he went in for half-timbered Tudor country houses, then for the many-gabled brick architecture of the Dutch Renaissance, then for a very restrained Neo-Queen Anne, or rather Neo-William and Mary, and finally joined in the pompous Edwardian Imperial. He enjoyed, however, nothing more than playing with motifs of different centuries (fig. 98). By combining a few Tudor and a few 17th-century motifs with others of his own invention, he achieved a lightness and animation that makes Morris designs appear gloomy.

Norman Shaw's influence on the architectural profession was immediate and very widespread. A generation of architects came from his studio to whom he left the freedom of following Morris's ideas, while following his own forms. They and some closer disciples of Morris founded the Arts and Crafts Movement. Once one knows what Morris taught, the name becomes self-explanatory. More and more original interpretations of architectural traditions were worked out by the members of this group, almost exclusively in designs for town and country houses. Lethaby, Prior, Stokes, Ricardo are amongst the most noteworthy names. They are little known nowadays, but the freshness of their approach was unique in the Europe of about 1885 to 1890. In America, however, the country houses of Richardson and his followers in the seventies and eighties had already achieved a synthesis of novelty with comfort and ease which England only reached in the early works of the most brilliant architect and designer of his generation: Charles F. Annesley Voysey (1857–1941). Voysey was neither connected personally with Shaw nor with Morris. His fabrics, wallpapers, furniture and metal-work especially, so novel and so graceful, had an effect no less revolutionising than Morris's. In his buildings he appears just as dainty and lovable (fig. 99). Of period detail little is kept, but no effort is made to eliminate a general period flavour. In fact it is just the effortless, unaffected nature of Voysey's architecture that gives it its charm. Moreover, going more closely into it, one will be struck by the boldness of bare walls and long horizontal bands of windows. In such buildings of the nineties England came nearest to the idiom of the Modern Movement.

For the next forty years, the first forty of our century, no British name need here be mentioned. Britain had led Europe and America in architecture and design for a long time; now her ascendancy had come to an end. From Britain the art of landscape gardening had spread, and Adam's and Wedgwood's style, in Britain the Gothic

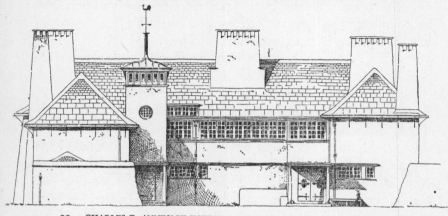

99.   CHARLES F. ANNESLEY VOYSEY: HOUSE AT COLWALL, MALVERN, 1893.

Revival had been conceived, to Britain the degradation of machine-produced applied art was due, to Britain the constructive reaction against it. The domestic revival of Morris, Norman Shaw and Voysey was British; British was the new social conception of a unified art under architectural guidance, and British the first achievements of design completely independent of the past. They are to be found in the work of Arthur H. Mackmurdo's Century Guild about 1885 and then in that of Voysey and some architects influenced by him, Baillie Scott, C. R. Ashbee and above all Charles Rennie Mackintosh (1869–1928).

Art Nouveau, the first novel style on the Continent, and in fact a style, it seems now, desperately set on being novel, drew its inspiration from English design. It started in Brussels in 1893 and had by 1895 become the *dernier cri* amongst the young artists and architects of Germany, Austria and France. Of Continental buildings designed between 1760 and the years of Art Nouveau not many have so far been mentioned in this chapter. All that was of importance either happened in Britain or could at least be followed just as easily in Britain as abroad.

The position changed a few years before 1900. The stage reached by Britain at that moment was one of truly contemporary design, but of a free traditionalism (as against the earlier more pedantic Historicism) in architecture. The step that had to be taken to recover a genuine style was that from Voysey's designs to buildings equally bold. And the British character was (and is) all against such drastic steps, so uncompromising an attitude, so logical a procedure. Thus progress in Britain stopped for thirty years. Voysey's Tudor traditionalism was followed by a Wren and Georgian traditionalism, equally pleasant in domestic architecture, but feeble if not painfully inflated-looking in representational buildings.

The first private houses in which the new, original style of the 20th century can be recognised are Frank Lloyd Wright's (born 1869), built in the nineties in the neighbourhood of Chicago. They have the freely spreading ground plans, the interweaving of exteriors and interiors by means of terraces and cantilevered roofs, the opening up of one room into another, the predominant horizontals, the long window bands that are familiar in to-day's houses. Also at Chicago, and as early as the eighties and nineties, the first buildings were erected with steel skeletons (William Le Baron Jenney: Home Insurance Company, 1884–85) and facades not disguising them (Holabird and Roche: Marquette Building, 1894). If a period style was still used for external detail it usually was Richardson's severely plain American Romanesque. As against this American priority in the appreciative use of steel, France was the first country to design in a genuine concrete character. (A. de Baudot: St. Jean de Montmartre, begun 1894, and buildings of *c.* 1900–5 by Tony Garnier, born 1869, and Auguste Perret, born 1873).

Then, between 1905 and 1914, Germany became the most important country. Here the liaison of design and architecture was most successful. Peter Behrens (1868–1938) designed factories and their products. The *Werkbund* was founded to be a meeting-place of progressive manufacturers, architects and designers. And while in the United States and France the pioneers remained solitary, in Germany, twenty years ago, a style independent of the past had been accepted by quite a large public. In 1914, Walter Gropius (born 1883) showed the world, at an exhibition in Cologne, a factory so completely of to-day in every detail that it might be mis-dated by anybody (pl. CIV). It had a flat roof, again the general stress on horizontals, and two staircases entirely encased in curved glass so that the skeleton and the interior workings were proudly exposed. It will at once be recognised that in this motif as in the floating ground plan of Wright (and later on of Le Corbusier), and as incidentally also in the fantastic American highways intersections with wide areas given up to nothing but traffic bands on different levels, the eternal passion of the West for spatial movement once more expresses itself.

So by 1914 the leading architects of the younger generation had courageously broken with the past and accepted the machine-age in all its implications: new materials, new processes, new forms, new problems. Of these the most important is symbolised to an extent that probably future civilisations will find as obscure as we find Avebury Circle and the Kennet Avenue, by the American traffic crossings just mentioned: namely the problem of modern town-planning. It has been said before that one of the greatest changes brought about by the Industrial Revolution was the sudden growth of cities. To cope with this, architects should have concentrated on the adequate housing of the vast new working-class populations of these cities and on the planning of adequate routes of traffic for the worker to get to his job and back every day. But they were interested in facades and nothing else; and so in a way were municipalities of the 19th century. New public buildings cropped up everywhere. They were as splendid as money could buy them. Take Manchester Town Hall, Glasgow University, the Law Courts in Birmingham, London County Hall, or take the series of magnificent but characteristically unrelated monuments along the Ringstrasse in Vienna: the Gothic Town Hall, the Classical Houses of Parliament, the Renaissance museums, etc., one cannot say that Governments and city councils failed in their undeniable duty to give representational architecture a chance.

Where they failed was in their infinitely greater duty to provide decent living conditions for their citizens. One may say that this was an outcome of the philosophy of liberalism, which had taught them that everybody is happiest if left to look after himself, and that interference with private life is unnatural and always damaging; but while this explanation will satisfy the historian, it could not satisfy the social reformer. He saw that 95 per cent of the new houses in industrial towns were put up by speculative builders as cheaply as the scanty regulations would allow, and acted as best he could. If he was a man like William Morris, he preached a mediævalising socialism and escaped into the happier world of handicraft. If he was like Prince Albert and Lord Shaftesbury, he founded associations for improving by private generosity the dwellings of the artisan and labourer. If however he was an enlightened employer himself, he went one step further and commissioned an estate to be designed and built to a more satisfactory standard for his own workers. Thus Sir Titus Salt founded Saltaire, near Leeds, in 1853. It looks very drab now, but it was pioneer work. Lever Brothers began Port Sunlight in 1888 and Cadbury's Bourneville in 1895. These two were the first factory estates planned as garden suburbs. From them—and Bedford Park, near London, which had been designed as early as 1875 by Norman Shaw on the same principle, though for private tenants of a wealthier class—the garden suburb and the garden city movement spread, another British contribution to the pre-history of modern European architecture.

Now in connection with this movement, architects re-entered the domain of town-planning. The greatest town-planning scheme between 1830 and 1880 had been the work of an administrative genius, Baron Haussmann, Napoleon III's prefect of the Seine Department. His long, wide and straight roads all through the centre of Paris were drawn for the sake of civic magnificence and military security, but also for easier traffic to such focal points as railway stations. Haussmann was, however, not interested in housing, in the slums that developed behind his new facades, nor did he extend his appreciation of traffic to the railways themselves.

But this problem, too, could not in the long run be neglected by the architect, once he accepted it as his job to design whole estates and suburbs. These new estates of small houses in their own gardens took a great deal of space. They were only possible right outside the built-over areas of towns. So the question of well-

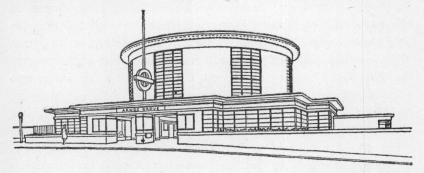

100. CHARLES HOLDEN: ARNOS GROVE STATION, OF THE LONDON UNDERGROUND, 1932.

organised road and rail traffic became imperative. This question until then had been in the hands of the business man and again the engineer. Both had shown themselves staggeringly obtuse to architectural values. Some of the best vistas of London were cut into by railway bridges: the approach to St. Paul's, e.g., and the views down the Thames. Station buildings themselves, except for a few early ones such as old Euston and King's Cross, and except for the bewildering splendour of Gilbert Scott's Early English St. Pancras Station, were mean and untidy—at least in Britain. This unwillingness to accept the care for decent design as a public duty still applied quite universally to British big business and public services thirty years ago. The first to set an example of what immense improvements personal initiative can achieve was Frank Pick, to whom London owes a transport system beautifully designed from the station building down to the lighting standards and the litter baskets.

Frank Pick must be mentioned in a history of architecture as the prototype of the 20th-century patron. A Medici, a Louis XIV, are impossible in an age such as ours. The new Mæcenas is an administrator, a worker himself, with a house not much bigger than yours and mine, a cottage in the country, and a car far from spectacular. But as Managing Director of the London General Omnibus and the London Underground Companies, Pick saw that to assemble artists and architects round such a vast business enterprise would be to bring Morris's ideals up to date. So before the first World War he began to reform the lettering used, had one of the best modern type-faces designed especially for his purpose and impressed it so deeply on the minds of millions that a revolution in British lettering ensued. Concurrently he started a campaign for better posters, and again succeeded in establishing Britain in the front rank of modern poster art. And when in the twenties and thirties many new stations had to be built, he realised that the Continent had evolved a style more suited than contemporary English Neo-Georgian to express the synthesis of function and civic dignity that was his ideal. So he found the right architect in Mr. Charles Holden, and the London Underground stations (fig. 100) became the most perfect examples in London of the style of to-day, serviceable, uncompromisingly modern, and yet in keeping with the quiet distinction of the Georgian brick house.

Those who are doubtful about the blessings of the Modern Movement in architecture often say that the strongest argument against it is the very fact that its most representative examples are stations, factories, office buildings and the like. Now this is certainly not an accident. It would not be possible to find anything like the same number of good contemporary buildings for private luxury as for workaday use. But then, does not the architect to-day build for a population with nothing like the leisure for luxuries which patrons of the Baroque enjoyed? Must that not change the style, if it is a genuine style? Moreover, as has already been said, nearly every building that is designed nowadays serves masses and not individuals. Must not therefore our style be one adapted to mass production, not only in the sense of production in masses but also for masses?

Thus, if the new style is bare, if it goes straight to the point, there are good reasons for it. The ground had first of all to be cleared of the weeds of 19th-century sham ornamentation. Once that had been done, all available energy had to be devoted to research into function. What during the 19th century had been done slowly and anonymously, now became the central task of the architect. If you have to build a soap factory, you must know how soap is being made. If your job is to design a nursery-school, you must find out all about nursery-school work. You cannot accept any plan on authority; it must be evolved anew every time from fundamentals. This Back-to-Fundamentals attitude with regard to function encouraged the same attitude to form. Again no authority was accepted, and again —after the first Art Nouveau flourish of unshackled imagination— the basic principles were rediscovered. This happened—a very hopeful sign—not only in architecture, but also in painting and sculpture. Cubism and then abstract art were the outcome, the most architectural art that had existed since the Middle Ages. In architecture, sheer proportion at last took its legitimate place again. No mouldings, no frills were permitted to detract one's attention from true architectural values: the relation of wall to window, solid to void, volume to space, block to block. I need not here go into more detail about things which belong to our own day and not to history yet.

The one fact that matters to the historian already now, and the one that he can state without falling into the rôle of counsel for the defence or for prosecution, is that the Modern Movement is a genuine and independent style. This fact is full of promise. For over a hundred years no style in that sense had existed. As Western civilisation had become more and more subdivided, it had lost its faculty to create a language of its own. An atomised society cannot have an architectural style. Can we not take it then that the recovery of a true style in the visual arts, one in which once again building rules, and painting and sculpture serve, and one in which form is obviously representative of character, indicates the return of unity in society too? Granted that this new style often looks rather forbidding and seems to lack human warmth. But is not the same true of contemporary life? Here, too, amenities to which we have been used are being replaced by something more exacting and more elementary.

Beyond stating this the historian should not go. Whether the new social and architectural attitude heralds a last phase of Western civilisation or the dawn of a new, whether the style of the future will be at all similar to our own, and whether we shall like it—all this it is not for the historian to foretell. His job is done when he has applied the principles of historical analysis as far into the problems of the present day as they can safely be applied.

Bibliography

GENERAL

A. Michel: Histoire de l'Art, 18 vol., Paris, 1905–29.
Sir Banister Fletcher: A History of Architecture, 13th ed., London, 1946.
R. Sturgis: Dictionary of Architecture and Building, 3 vol., New York, 1901–2.
Talbot F. Hamlin: Architecture through the Ages, New York, 1941.
Fiske Kimball and G. H. Edgell: A History of Architecture, New York, 1918.
Wasmuths Lexikon der Baukunst, 5 vol., Berlin, 1929–37.
U. Thieme and F. Becker: Allgemeines Lexikon der bildenden Künstler, 32 vol., Leipzig, 1907 *seqq.*
M. S. Briggs: The Architect in History, Oxford, 1927.
G. Dehio and F. von Bezold: Die kirchliche Baukunst des Abendlandes, 10 vol., Stuttgart, 1884–1901.

BRITAIN

W. Godfrey: The Story of Architecture in England, 2 vol., London, 1928.
F. Gibberd: The Architecture of England from Norman Times to the present Day, 5th ed., London, 1944.
N. Lloyd: A History of the English House, London, 1931.
H. Avray Tipping: English Homes, 9 vol., London, 1920–37.

FRANCE

C. Enlart: Manuel d'archéologie française, 2nd ed., 4 vol., Paris, 1919–32.
P. Lavedan: L'architecture française, Paris, 1944.

GERMANY

G. Dehio: Geschichte der deutschen Kunst, 2nd ed., 6 vol., Berlin, 1921–31.

HOLLAND

F. Vermeulen: Handboek tot de Geschiedenis der Nederlandsche Bouwkunst, 3 vol., The Hague, 1928–41.
A. W. Weiszman: Geschiedenis der Nederlandsche Bouwkunst, Amsterdam, 1912.
H. E. van Gelder (and others): Kunstgeschiedenis der Nederlanden, 2nd ed., Utrecht, 1946.

ITALY

A. Venturi: Storia dell'Arte Italiana, 21 vol., Milan, 1901 *seqq.*
M. Salmi: L'Arte Italiana, 3 vol., Florence, 1943–44.
C. A. Cummings: A History of Italian Architecture, 2 vol., New York, 1901.

SPAIN

B. Bevan: A History of Spanish Architecture, London, 1938.
Marques de Lozoya: Historia del Arte hispanico, 4 vol., 1931–45.

MIDDLE AGES

EARLY CHRISTIAN AND BYZANTINE

O. M. Dalton: East Christian Art, Oxford, 1925.
O. Wulff: Altchristliche und Byzantinische Kunst (Handbuch der Kunst-
wissenschaft), 2 vol., Neubabelsberg, 1914–18.
D. Talbot Rice: Byzantine Art, Oxford, 1935.
C. Diehl: Manuel d'Art Byzantin, 2nd ed., Paris, 1925–26.
L. Bréhier: L'Art Byzantin, Paris, 1924.

MEDIÆVAL : GENERAL

W. R. Lethaby: Mediæval Art from the Peace of the Church to the Eve
of the Renaissance, London, 1904.
A. Kingsley Porter: Mediæval Architecture, its origins and development,
2 vol., New York, 1909.
P. Frankl: Die Frühmittelalterliche und Romanische Baukunst (Handbuch
der Kunstwissenschaft), Neubabelsberg, 1926.
A. W. Clapham: Romanesque Architecture in Western Europe, Oxford,
1936.
H. R. Hahnloser: Villard de Honnecourt, Vienna, 1935.

BRITAIN

F. Bond: An Introduction to English Church Architecture, 2 vol.,
London, 1913.
C. E. Power: English Mediæval Architecture, 2nd ed., 3 vol., London,
1923.
E. S. Prior: A History of Gothic Art in England, London, 1900.
E. S. Prior: The Cathedral Builders in England, London, 1905.
T. F. Bumpus: The Cathedrals of England and Wales, London, 1905.
K. Escher: Englische Kathedralen, Zurich, 1929.
A. Hamilton Thompson: The Ground-Plan of the English Parish Church,
Cambridge, 1911.
A. Hamilton Thompson: The Historical Growth of the English Parish
Church, Cambridge, 1913.
J. C. Cox: The English Parish Church, London, 1914.
F. E. Howard: The Mediæval Styles of the English Parish Church,
London, 1936.
A. Hamilton Thompson: Military Architecture in England during the
Middle Ages, London, 1912.
G. Baldwin Brown: The Arts in Early England. Vol. 2: Anglo-Saxon
Architecture, 2nd ed., London, 1925.

BIBLIOGRAPHY

A. W. Clapham: English Romanesque Architecture, 2 vol., Oxford, 1930–34.

S. Gardner: A Guide to English Gothic Architecture, Cambridge, 1922.

J. Bilson: Les origines de l'architecture gothique, and Les premières croisées d'ogives en Angleterre, *Revue de l'Art Chrétien*, 1901 and 1902.

C. Enlart: Du Rôle de l'Angleterre dans l'Evolution de l'Art Gothique, Paris, 1908.

FRANCE

R. de Lasteyrie: L'Architecture Réligieuse en France à l'Époque Romane, 2nd ed., Paris, 1929.

J. Baum: Romanesque Architecture in France, 2nd ed., London, 1928.

C. Martin: L'Art Roman en France, 3 vol., Paris, c. 1910–14.

J. Evans: The Romanesque Architecture of the Order of Cluny, Cambridge, 1938.

E. Gall: Die Gotische Baukunst in Frankreich und Deutschland, vol. 1, Leipzig, 1925.

R. de Lasteyrie: L'Architecture Réligieuse en France à l'Epoque Gothique, 2 vol., Paris, 1926–27.

C. Martin and C. Enlart: L'Art Gothique en France, 2 vol., Paris, c. 1913–25.

L. Schürenberg: Die Kirchliche Baukunst in Frankreich zwischen 1270 und 1380, Berlin, 1934.

E. Mâle: L'Art Réligieux du XIIe Siècle en France, Paris, 1922.

E. Mâle: L'Art Réligieux du XIIIe Siècle en France, Paris, 1902 (English translation, 1913).

ITALY

P. Toesca: Storia dell'Arte Italiana, vol. I, Turin, 1927.

A. Kingsley Porter: Lombard Architecture, 2 vol., Newhaven, 1915–17.

G. T. Rivoira: Lombardic Architecture, 2nd ed., Oxford, 1934.

C. Ricci: Romanesque Architecture in Italy, London, 1925.

C. Martin and C. Enlart: L'Art Roman en Italie, 2 vol., Paris, c. 1911–24.

M. Salmi: L'Architettura Romanica in Toscana, Milan, 1927.

W. Paatz: Werden und Wesen der Trecento-Architektur in Toskana, Burg, 1937.

SPAIN

V. Lampérez y Romea: Historia de la Arquitectura Cristiana Española en la Edad Media, 2nd ed., Madrid, 1930.

G. G. King: Pre-Romanesque Churches of Spain, Bryn Mawr, 1924.

M. Gomez-Moreno: El arte romanico español, Madrid, 1934.

G. E. Street (revised by G. G. King): Some Account of Gothic Architecture in Spain, London, 1914.

E. Lambert: L'Art Gothique en Espagne, Paris, 1931.

RENAISSANCE, MANNERISM AND BAROQUE IN ITALY

J. Burckhardt: Geschichte der Renaissance in Italien, 5th ed., Esslingen, 1912.

W. J. Anderson and A. Stratton: The Architecture of the Renaissance in Italy, London, 1927.

C. von Stegmann and H. von Geymüller: Die Architektur der Renaissance in Toskana, 12 vol., Munich, 1909.

A. Haupt: Renaissance Palaces of Northern Italy and Tuscany, London, 3 vol., c. 1931.

D. Frey: Architettura della Rinascenza, Rome, 1924.

J. Baum: Baukunst und dekorative Plastik der Frührenaissance in Italien, Stuttgart, 1920.

C. Ricci: Baukunst der Hoch- und Spätrenaissance in Italien, Stuttgart, 1923.

G. Giovannoni: Saggi sull'Architettura del Rinascimento, Milan, 1931.

N. Pevsner: The Architecture of Mannerism, *The Mint,* 1946.

N. Pevsner: Gegenreformation und Manierisums, *Repertorium für Kunstwissenschaft,* vol. 46, 1925.

C. Gurlitt: Geschichte des Barockstils in Italien, Esslingen, 1887.

A. E. Brinckmann: Die Baukunst des 17 and 18 Jahrhunderts in den Romanischen Ländern (Handbuch der Kunstwissenschaft), Neubabelsberg, 1919 *seqq.*

C. Ricci: Baroque Architecture and Sculpture in Italy, London, 1912.

T. H. Fokker: Roman Baroque Art, 2 vol., Oxford, 1938.

Brunelleschi: H. Folnesics, Vienna, 1915.
  L. H. Heydenreich, *Jahrbuch der preussischen Kunstsammlungen,* vol. 52, 1931.
Michelozzo: L. H. Heydenreich, *Mitteilungen des Kunsthistorischen Instituts in Florenz,* vol. 5, 1932, and *Festschrift für Wilhelm Pinder,* Leipzig, 1938.
Alberti: M. L. Gengaro, Milan, 1939.
  R. Wittkower, *Journal of the Warburg and Courtauld Institutes,* vol. 4, 1941.
Bramante: C. Baroni, Bergamo, 1941.
Raphael: T. Hofmann, 4 vol., Zittau, 1900–14.
Michelangelo: J. A. Symonds, 2 vol., London, 1893.
  H. Thode: Kritische Untersuchungen, 6 vol., Berlin, 1902–13.
Michelangelo's Laurenziana Library: R. Wittkower, *The Art Bulletin,* vol. 16, 1934.
Giulio Romano: E. Gombrich, *Jahrbuch der Kunsthistorischen Sammlungen in Wien,* N.F., vols. 8 and 9, 1935–36.
Serlio: W. B. Dinsmoor, *The Art Bulletin,* vol. 24, 1942.
Palladio: A. M. della Pozza, Vicenza, 1943.
  F. Burger, Die Villen des Andrea Palladio, Leipzig, c. 1909.
  R. Wittkower, *Journal of the Warburg and Courtauld Institutes,* vol. 7, 1944.

Bernini: S. Fraschetti, Milan, 1900.
Borromini: E. Hempel, Vienna, 1924.
   H. Sedlmayr, Munich, 1939.

16TH TO 18TH CENTURY IN BRITAIN, FRANCE, GERMANY AND SPAIN

BRITAIN

T. Garner and A. Stratton: Domestic Architecture of England during the Tudor Period, 2nd ed., 2 vol., London, 1929.
J. A. Gotch: Early Renaissance Architecture in England, London, 1914.
J. A. Gotch: The English House from Charles I to George IV, London, 1918.
S. E. Rasmussen: London, the Unique City, London, 1937.
J. Summerson: Georgian London, London, 1946.

Inigo Jones: J. A. Gotch, London, 1928.
Wren: G. Webb, London, 1937.
   L. Weaver, London, 1923.
   Wren Society, 20 vol., London, 1924-44.
   Bicentenary Memorial Volume, published by the Royal Institute of British Architects, London, 1923.
Lord Burlington: R. Wittkower, *Archæological Journal*, vol. 102, 1945.
Wood: M. A. Green, Bath, 1914.
Adam: J. Swarbrick, London, 1915.
   A. T. Bolton, 2 vol., London, 1922.

FRANCE

Sir Reginald Blomfield: A History of French Architecture 1494–1774, 4 vol., London, 1911–21.
F. Kimball: The Creation of the Rococo, Philadelphia, 1943.
L. Hautecœur: Histoire de l'Architecture classique en France, vol. 1, parts 1 and 2, Paris, 1943.
A. E. Brinckmann: Die Baukunst des 17 und 18 Jahrhunderts in den Romanischen Landern (Handbuch der Kunstwissenschaft), Neubabelsberg, 1919 *seqq.*
H. Rose: Spätbarock, Munich, 1922.
L. Hautecœur: Les Grands Palais de France, Le Louvre et les Tuileries, Paris, *c.* 1924.
L. Hautecœur: L'Histoire des Châteaux du Louvre et des Tuileries . . ., Paris and Brussels, 1927.
G. Brière: Le Château de Versailles, 2 vol., Paris, 2c. 1910.
P. de Nolhac: Versailles et la Cour de France, 10 portfolios, Paris, 1925–30.
G. Gébelin: Les Châteaux de la Loire, Paris, 1947.
J. Vacquier and Jarry: Les Vieux Hôtels de Paris, 22 portfolios, Paris, 1910–34.
   Pillement: Les Hôtels de Paris, 2 vol., Paris, 1941–45.

A. Blunt: François Mansart, London, 1941.

GERMANY

W. Pinder: Deutscher Barock, 2nd ed., Königstein, 1924.

S. Sitwell: German Baroque Art, London, 1927.

M. Hauttmann: Geschichte der kirchlichen Baukunst in Bayern, Schwaben und Franken, 1550–1780, Munich, 1924.

SPAIN

A. Byne and M. Stapley: Spanish Architecture of the Sixteenth Century, New York, 1917.

O. Schubert: Geschichte des Barocks in Spanien, Esslingen, 1908.

19TH AND 20TH CENTURIES

S. Giedion: Spätbarocker und Romantischer Klassizismus, Munich, 1922.

C. Hussey: The Picturesque, London, 1927.

N. Pevsner: The Genesis of the Picturesque, *The Architectural Review*, vol. 96, 1944.

Sir Kenneth Clark: The Gothic Revival, London, 1928.

N. Pevsner: Pioneers of the Modern Movement, from William Morris to Walter Gropius, London, 1936.

S. Giedion: Space, Time and Architecture, Harvard, 1941.

T. E. Tallmadge: The Story of Architecture in America, London, 1928.

J. M. Richards: An Introduction to Modern Architecture, Pelican Books, 3rd ed., 1945.

Soane: A. T. Bolton, London, 1927.

Nash: J. Summerson, London, 1935.

Ledoux: G. Levallet-Haug, Paris, 1934.
   M. Raval and Moreux, Paris, 1946.

Gilly: A. Oncken, Berlin, 1935.

Schinkel: A. Grisebach, Leipzig, 1924.

William Morris: J. W. Mackail, 2nd ed., London, 1922.
   A. Vallance, London, 1897.

H. H. Richardson: H. R. Hitchcock, New York, 1936.

Norman Shaw: Sir Reginald Blomfield, London, 1940.
   N. Pevsner, *The Architectural Review*, vol. 89, 1941.

P. Webb: W. R. Lethaby, London, 1935.

F. L. Wright: H. R. Hitchcock, In the Nature of Materials, New York, 1942.

Some Technical Terms Explained

*Only less familiar architectural terms are included, and only those which
have not already been explained in the places where they first occurred
in the text. Note.—Bracketed references refer to drawings illustrating
technical terms in this appendix.*

Ambulatory: Aisle round an apse or a circular building.

Arcade: Group of arches on columns or pillars.

Architrave: Bottom member of an entablature (C.3).

Attic: Low story above main cornice.

Basilica: Church with aisles and a nave higher than the aisles.

Bay: Vertical unit of a wall or facade; also compartments into which a
nave is divided.

Caryatid: Sculptured figure used as a support.

Clerestory: Upper part of church nave with windows above the roofs of
the aisles.

Cornice: Projecting top portion of an entablature or any projecting top
course of a building (A.3 and C.4).

Cross: Cf. Greek cross.

Cross Rib: (E.1).

Drum: Circular or polygonal structure on which a dome is raised (B.1).

Entablature: The horizontal top part of an order of classical architecture.
It is supported by columns and consists of architrave, frieze and
cornice (C.5).

Greek Cross: Cross with all four arms of equal length.

Jamb: Vertical part of the masonry of a door or window (D.1).

Lantern: Small open or glazed structure crowning a dome or a roof (B.2).

Lierne: A decorative rib in a Gothic vault which does not spring from the
wall and does not touch the central boss (E.5).

Metope: Panel filling the space between triglyphs (C.1). *See* Triglyph.

Mullion: Vertical division of a window.

Narthex: Porch in front of the nave and aisles of a mediæval church.

Ogee Arch: (D).

Pediment: Triangular or segmental upright front end of a roof of moderate pitch (A.1).

Plinth: Projecting base of a building or a column.

Quoins: Corner stones at the angle of a building (A.2).

Ridge Rib: (E.3).

Rustication: Wall treatment with large freestone blocks, either smooth
with recessed joints, or with a rough, rock-like surface and recessed
joints.

Solar: Chamber on an upper floor.

Spandrel: Space between the curve of an arch; the vertical drawn from its springing and the horizontal drawn from its apex (C.6).

String-course: Projecting horizontal band along the wall of a building (A.4).

Tierceron: Rib inserted in a Gothic vault between the transverse and diagonal ribs (E.4).

Transom: Horizontal division of a window.

Transverse Rib: (E.2).

Triforium: Wall passage between the arcade of a church nave and the clerestory, or between the gallery and the clerestory. It opens in arcades towards the nave. The arcading can also be blind, with no wall-passage behind. Some writers call the gallery a triforium.

Triglyph: Vertical grooved member of the Doric frieze (C.2).

Voussoir: A wedge-shaped block forming part of the arch of a door or window (D.2).

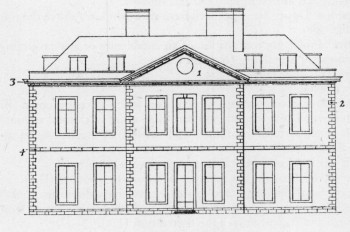

A.—QUEEN ANNE HOUSE.

1. Pediment.	3. Cornice.
2. Quoins.	4. String-course.

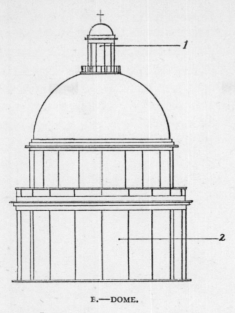

E.—DOME.

1. Lantern.   2. Drum.

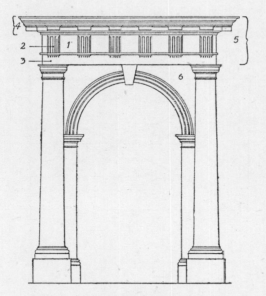

C.—CLASSICAL DETAILS.

1. Metope.   4. Cornice.
2. Triglyph.   5. Entablature.
3. Architrave   6. Spandrel.

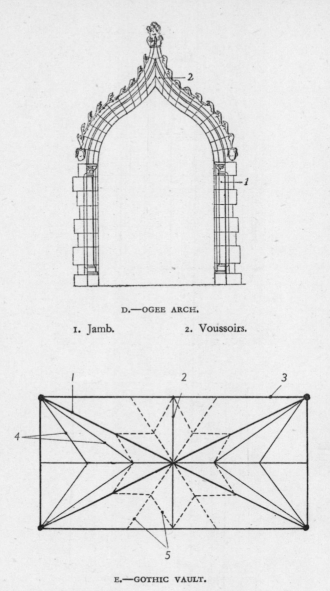

D.—OGEE ARCH.

1. Jamb.   2. Voussoirs.

E.—GOTHIC VAULT.

1. Diagonal Rib.   4. Tiercerons.
2. Ridge Rib.   5. Liernes.
3. Transverse Arch.

American Postscript

THE most obvious difference between the history of architecture in the United States and in Western Europe is that American architecture as part of Western architecture is less than four hundred years old, whereas in England, in France, in Italy, in Germany, in the Netherlands, in Spain, one coherent and unbroken development runs through the last thousand years and more. During these ten or eleven centuries every new step of importance was taken within the compass of no more than fifteen hundred miles across from the North Sea to Sicily and from Ireland and Galicia to West Prussia and Bohemia. In this territory, less in extent than the United States, Charlemagne restored a Roman Empire and, against his will, helped to raise the first monuments of a youthful Western spirit, the Cluniacs in France and the Saxon Emperors in Germany evolved the Romanesque style, in the Île de France ingenious masons devised the Gothic system; English, Spanish, German, Italian masons somewhat later modified it to suit their growing national consciousness, Italy revolted against it for a new purity, scientific order and grace, then for a newer gravity and solemnity and then for a forced, self-tormenting artificiality, in her Early Renaissance, High Renaissance and Mannerism.

All this—this mighty drama of the birth, adolescence, virile maturity and first symptoms of ageing of the West—had taken place before any buildings of Western character existed in the United States. And even if we take the whole of the Americas there is only a faint echo here and there —say in the belated rib-vaults of some friars' churches in Mexico—of posthumous Western Gothic. Otherwise Mannerism is the first European style reflected on American soil.

Prehistory, on the other hand—in the sense in which we use the term in Europe for the Mediterranean before the advent of historic styles first in Egypt and Asia Minor, then in Greece and the Hellenistic States, and then in Rome and the Roman Empire, and for the North roughly up to the coming of Roman and in some parts Carolingian civilisation—applies in the Americas to everything before Columbus, before Cortez, before Pizarro, before Raleigh, the Pilgrim Fathers and Penn.

Thus not even the shortest outline of prehistoric art and architecture could afford to omit Aztec, Maya and Inca temples and the artifacts of North American Indians, but an outline of Western architecture can, it is my contention, do without any mention of buildings in America prior to the 18th, or indeed the 19th, century. In a book in which the severe Mannerism of Herrera and his followers in Spain appears only in a few lines, it would be as perverse to devote space to the ruin of Tecali—the "purist" Franciscan church in Mexico, dated 1569—as it would be to choose Dalmatian examples to discuss Venetian architecture or Tortosa in Syria to discuss French Gothic church building.

Again, the *incunabula* of New England's domestic architecture, while they are rightly treasured by New Englanders and treated with all the affectionate respect and care with which the English should treat (and often don't) their heritage of farm- and manor-house all up and down a country altogether not so much bigger than New England, can have no place in a brief textbook. What America, during the 17th century, did in the way of house-building, has all "the charm of sincere effort, naïve ignorance and unskilful execution", as Talbot Hamlin says, but it is not one of the essential tributary forces to the main stream of architectural development.

However, with the 18th century emphasis changes. American architecture is still Colonial, that is primarily dependent on colonising countries—England, Spain and Portugal, and up to a point France—but dependence is no longer complete and aesthetic quality certainly no longer necessarily provincial. The Sanctuary of Ocotlan at Tlaxcala, in Mexico, or the church of the Third Order of St. Francis at Bahia, in Brazil, may be somewhat barbaric and sensational, but so is much of the Churrigueresque in Spain. And as this riotous superabundance, this overcrowding with clamorous detail is part and parcel of Pyrenean Baroque, it would have been no less legitimate to illustrate it from Mexican or Brazilian examples than from the Cartuja of Granada, as I have done. It is true that certain features in America may be due less to Spanish and Portuguese precedent than to Indian workmen, for whom the wildly distorted and elaborately intertwined decoration of Aztec and Inca temples was still alive and valid. Indian influence as early as about 1500 has been assumed (p. 74) to explain Portuguese Manueline ornament. But there it was European artists impressed by the achievements of the natives; now it is the natives themselves transforming European patterns.

In North America during the same decades a similar change of balance can be observed, but with eminently significant modifications. Prosperity was just as firmly established in North as in Central and South America, but instead of the Roman Catholic social pattern of mission and skilled native labour, there grew in the North a system of secular land ownership and Protestant town civilisation. The style of architecture was as English as it was Pyrenean in the South. Local variation on the home themes was as conspicuous. But as in the future United States both patrons and builders were Western by origin and traditions, and often even by birth, these variations were the outcome of climatic rather than racial conditions. Red Indian ingenuity was, alas, expelled and by degrees eradicated. Thus the colonial style of North America, the Colonial Style *par excellence*, is wholly English Georgian. The most notable American modifications are due to the prevalent use of timber as a building material. Wood accounts for the slimness of the columns, and wood also for the cheerful colour schemes. A warmer climate permits terraces, porches and loggias, and the wide spaces, only gradually to be populated, a more generous siting, the preservation of many trees and, in the little towns, the planting of those venerable avenues and greens which now give to Salem, Nantucket, Savannah and so on, and even to what is left of the oldest manufacturing towns of New England, their delightful garden-city character.

Still, while a short general history of architecture could illustrate Christ Church, Philadelphia, or one of the churches of Charleston instead of an English church, or Salem or Nantucket as particularly carefully preserved specimens of the Georgian country town, there is certainly no necessity to do so. What there is of differences between American and English Georgian does not go beyond the differences say between Bavarian and Dresden Rococo. And as far as quality goes, while Mexican Baroque may be regarded in some ways as the climax of Spanish Baroque, even the best examples of American Colonial can hardly be placed upon the same level as Vanbrugh's or Adam's works.

This last remark and all else I have so far ventured to say about America is, I think, borne out by the published views of American scholars. When it comes to the early 19th century, however, I am a little at variance with at least some of the most distinguished architectural historians in the United States. Mr. Hamlin, the author of the best general history of architecture that I know, has as Chapters 2 and 3 of his immensely knowledgeable *Greek Revival Architecture in America* (Oxford University Press, 1944), "The Birth of American Architecture", dealing chiefly with Latrobe, and "American Architecture comes of Age", dealing with Mills, Strickland and the other Greek Revivalists. So the contention is that the Greek Revival is the first national American style. I fail to see that. There is to my mind no more that separates Latrobe from Soane, or Mills and Strickland from Smirke and Hamilton than there is between the 18th-century country houses of Virginia and Louisiana and those by Robert Adam or Henry Holland. So the relation between Europe and America cannot, I think, be regarded as much different in 1820 from what it had been in 1770. America developed away from delicacy towards a new grandeur and severity during these fifty years; but so did England, France and Germany.

Thomas Jefferson was enthusiastic about Nîmes, when he saw it in the 1780's, and the result was an architectural style ranging from the imitation of that sober Palladianism which Paris at that very moment was evolving from English precedent (Monticello, Capitol Richmond—cf. Clérisseau, and especially Ledoux and his group of French architects) to a much more naïve imitation of Roman detail (University of Virginia). Latrobe, Ramée, Mangin were themselves of French origin. Latrobe had passed through English training, Ramée had worked in Germany (and his son edited the second volume of Ledoux's *Architecture*). When Latrobe left England to settle in America in 1796, he could just have seen designs and perhaps more of Soane's revolutionary work at the Bank of England and at Tyringham. They would account for the most striking innovations in Latrobe—for instance, his determined change from Tuscan to Greek Doric, and also for some of the details inside North America's most beautiful church, Latrobe's Baltimore Cathedral of 1805–18. Here for once is true

first presented themselves to an amazed Europe. For now, in the eighties, the United States reached the front of architectural creativeness. Up to the end of the 18th century America had been Colonial, between 1800 and 1880 it was one of the many provinces of the West. Now it had become one of the few centres of progress—unnoticed, it must be said, by the most successful American or European architects and critics of the day. Official, generally accepted architecture in America was, it must not be forgotten, still as imitative in 1890 and 1920 as it was in England. Sullivan was no more widely acknowledged than Voysey or Mackintosh. Growing American importance was however reflected in the fact that academic architecture of the United States now influenced England, and no longer English academic architecture America. The Edwardian Imperial style of Britain and the Dominions (p. 205) derived a considerable amount of encouragement, if not more, from the Classical Re-Revival which in the United States had followed the Chicago Exhibition of 1893, and indeed sometimes taken forms grander, vaster and simpler than in England.

Of the Chicago Exhibition Sullivan said that the damage wrought by it would last for half a century. The prognostication has proved accurate, if we accept the Modern Movement as the only truthful expression of the spirit of our age. It had won a great victory in the Middle West just before 1893, and Chicago might have become the international centre of early modern architecture, if it had not been for the "World's Fair." For Chicago was the birthplace of the steel-skeleton skyscraper and the peculiar, wholly original idiom worked out by Sullivan and his pupil Frank Lloyd Wright (born 1869).

The skyscraper had been conceived for reasons of commercial pride and lack of space, independent of the skeleton technique, but could only be developed if a method of building was found obviating the immense thickness of load-bearing masonry walls which a building of twelve or twenty stories otherwise demands. Who exactly invented the skyscraper has proved a question most tempting to American research, but one which *per se* can never be wholly answered. There were on the one hand Viollet-le-Duc's prophetic remarks, and on the other the iron framework inside factories in England and France. Buffington may well have been stimulated by them as early as 1882 into some vague and tentative thought of the possibility of steel skyscrapers, but it is certain now that he did not get to grips with the constructional problems involved until Le Baron Jenney had completed his Home Assurance Building at Chicago in 1886 (p. 210). Buffington's patent dates from 1888, and was by then already obsolete. The first complete steel-frame skyscraper is Holabird and Roche's Tacoma Building of 1887–88. The most popular period style to express the boldness of these wholly American structures was Richardson's Neo-Romanesque. With its squareness and bareness and with what little it had of completely flat decoration it was indeed a suitable disguise, if disguise was felt to be needed. But some of the buildings of about 1890 to 1900—in steel-frame as well as masonry—already exhibit quite an independent aesthetic attitude, for instance Root's Monadnock Block, Holabird and

Roche's Marquette Building, Sullivan's Guarantee Building at Buffalo, and—more amazingly up-to-date than any of the others—Sullivan's Carson, Pirie Scott and Company Building at Chicago (of 1899–1903). In this building there is already the long horizontal window band as the one and only dominant motif of the facade, and there is an almost complete absence of ornament. No European country had at that moment gone as far in the preparation of the style of to-day as the Middle West.

And no European country had at the same date private houses to compare with those of the United States. There again the initiative goes back to Richardson and such amazingly free, comfortable, rustic compositions of his as the F. L. Ames Gate Lodge at North Easton, Mass., of 1880, and the Stoughton House at Cambridge, Mass., of 1882. Early Sullivan houses followed, and some of them were designed by Frank Lloyd Wright while he worked in Sullivan's office. The Winslow House at River Forest (1893) shows his personal style in the making, the houses since *c.* 1900 show it complete, with their cantilevered-out slab roofs, spacious terraces and rooms floating into each other. Their first publication in Germany in 1910 and 1911 helped towards the elaboration of the Continental modern style exactly as much as the more familiar houses of Voysey, Baillie Scott and Mackintosh. France and Austria, on the other hand, in their contribution of 1900–05 (Garnier, Perret, Loos, Hoffmann) seem to have been independent of America.

I have found it necessary in the foregoing pages to mention European architects left out of the chapters dealing with European architecture. This applies, for instance, to Loos and Hoffmann, and to Labrouste and Lefuel. My reason is that with the known history of architecture in the United States being virtually compressed into two hundred years, each trend assumes a greater importance than a corresponding trend in the longer history of building in Europe. All the interest we spend over here on Greek and Roman, Romanesque and Gothic, Renaissance and Baroque goes in the United States into the achievement of these two centuries.

This has another consequence, and one I want to point out in conclusion. With intensity of interest goes intensity of research. In Britain architectural research has not been very intensive during the last thirty years or so. After Prior and Lethaby, Bilson, St. John Hope and Hamilton Thompson mediæval research of an international outlook has all but stopped. Renaissance research is as scarce as everywhere. So it is on the English 17th and 18th centuries chiefly that consistent intelligent work is done. In the United States, thanks to a much more firmly and widely established system of teaching the history of art and architecture in the universities and colleges, and thanks to a national penchant towards doing things thoroughly and with international documentation, once they are being done at all, architectural research is infinitely more active and successful.

This is especially noticeable, if we compare books brought out between the two wars on matters referring to American architecture of the 18th and 19th centuries in America, with books on English architecture of the same period in England. I can only enumerate a few. First of all the State guides of the Federal Writers' Project (1937, etc.), uneven in quality, but on the whole far more alive and architecturally comprehensive than English county guidebooks. Then there is the work of such scholars as Mr. Fiske Kimball and Mr. Talbot Hamlin. On British Georgian and Greek Revival architecture no such detailed handbooks and papers as theirs are yet in existence. Again regional surveys comparable with Mr. Henry-Russell Hitchcock's of Rhode Island, to mention only one of several, are absent in England. So are books dealing with the interaction of social and architectural matters as soundly and attractively as Mr. John Coolidge's *Mill and Mansion*. Finally there are monographs on the architects of 1760 to 1900. We have books (of varying standard) on Adam, Soane, Wyatt, Nash and Pugin, and on Webb and Norman Shaw. But where are modern biographies of Vanbrugh and Hawksmoor, of Gibbs and Chambers, and then of Barry, Scott, Burges, Street, Brooks, Pearson, Sedding, Voysey, Mackintosh and so forth? In America not everyone of the leaders has his book yet either—a Life of Latrobe for instance, a Life of Strickland, a Life of Downing are still sorely needed—but between the wars, and particularly in the last ten years, monographs have come out on McIntire, Jefferson, Bulfinch, Mills, Town and Davis, Upjohn, Richardson, Burnham, McKim, Goodhue, not to say anything of additional papers in the magazines.

Why should an American Postscript to a small and unpretentious book end with a list of publications referring to architects and works hardly appearing in the text? The answer is that there is a lesson in it for the British as well as the Americans. One reason not yet sufficiently stressed for the more coherent progress of architectural research in the United States is that America is prouder of her achievements than Britain, or at least more attached to them. This leads to a most laudable seriousness in research even on such initially unpromising looking topics as the development of architecture in Victorian Detroit (B. Pickens), whereas in England what attention is paid to Victorian buildings and design is still, with a very few exceptions, of the whimsical variety.

On the other hand, there is in the American concentration on local, regional and national architecture the danger of parochialism. Things are regarded as peculiarly American, because all their antecedents, phases and particulars are by now far better known in America than in Europe. Thus English or Continental precedent is disregarded because not familiar. Even Mr. Hamlin's exemplary integrity and thoroughness have not always protected him from this unevenness of judgment.

If that is so with the scholars, may there not be quite an acceptable reason in offering to the laymen in America a brief outline of architectural events on our side of the Atlantic?

INDEX

I. ATHENS, THE PARTHENON, BEGUN IN 447 B.C.

II. ROME, BASILICA OF MAXENTIUS, c. A.D. 310–20.

III. RAVENNA, S. APOLLINARE NUOVO, EARLY 6TH CENTURY.

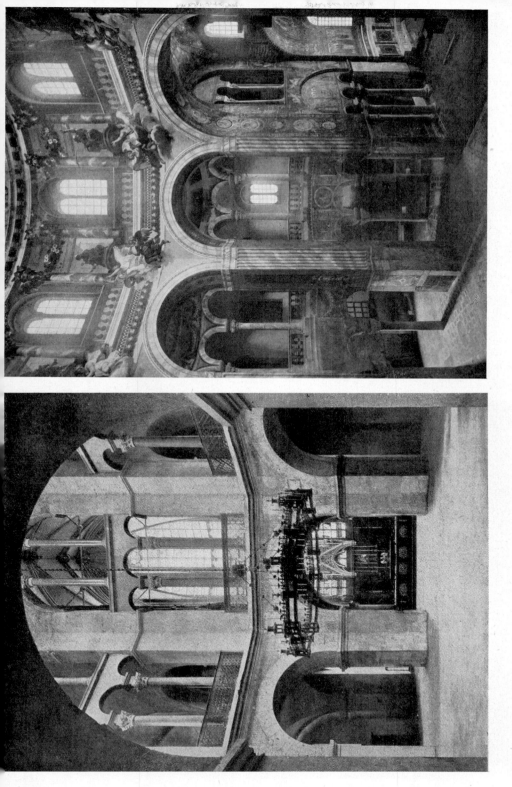

IV (TOP). RAVENNA, S. VITALE, COMPLETED IN 547.

V. AACHEN, CATHEDRAL (THE CHAPEL OF CHARLEMAGNE'S PALACE), CONSECRATED IN 805.

VI, VII.   S. MARIA DE NARANCO, BUILT AS A ROYAL HALL SHORTLY BEFORE 848.

VIII.   EARL'S BARTON, NORTHAMPTONSHIRE, 10TH OR EARLY 11TH CENTURY.

IX (TOP).   CASTLE HEDINGHAM, ESSEX, 12TH CENTURY.

X.   WINCHESTER CATHEDRAL, NORTH TRANSEPT, *c.* 1080–90.

XI.   DURHAM CATHEDRAL, THE NAVE, EARLY 12TH CENTURY.

XIIa (TOP).   JUMIÈGES, ABBEY CHURCH, BEGUN *c.* 1040.

XIIb.   TOULOUSE, ST. SERNIN, THE NAVE, EARLY 12TH CENTURY.

III. CLUNY, ABBEY CHURCH, FROM THE EAST, ACCORDING TO PROFESSOR CONANT'S RECONSTRUCTION, LATE 11TH TO EARLY 12TH CENTURY.

XIV. TOULOUSE, ST. SERNIN, FROM THE EAST. CHOIR CONSECRATED IN 1096. THE TOWER OVER THE CROSSING DATES FROM THE 12TH AND 13TH CENTURIES.

XV.   ANGOULÊME CATHEDRAL, EARLY 12TH CENTURY.

XVI.   PÉRIGUEUX, ST. FRONT, *c.* 1125–50.

XVII. VÉZELAY, CHURCH OF THE MAGDALEN, EARLY 12TH CENTURY.

XVIII.   AUTUN, ST. LAZARE, EARLY 12TH CENTURY.

XIX.   ST. GILLES, *c.* 1150.

XX.   COLOGNE, HOLY APOSTLES, *c.* 1200 (SEVERELY DAMAGED IN THE SECOND WORLD WAR).

XXI. WORMS CATHEDRAL, c. 1175–1250.

XXII. MILAN, S. AMBROGIO, PROBABLY SECOND QUARTER OF THE 12TH CENTURY.

XXIII. FLORENCE, S. MINIATO AL MONTE; GROUND FLOOR SECOND HALF OF THE 11TH CENTURY, UPPER PARTS LATER.

XXIV.   ST. DENIS, CHOIR AMBULATORY, 1140–44 (THE PIER ON THE RIGHT IS OF *c.* 1235).

XXV.   LAON CATHEDRAL, NAVE, LAST QUARTER OF THE 12TH CENTURY.

XXVI. PARIS, NOTRE DAME, NAVE, DESIGNED *c.* 1185. THE EAST BAY SHOWS A RECONSTRUCTION OF THE
ORIGINAL ARRANGEMENT OF THE WINDOWS.

XXVII.   AMIENS CATHEDRAL, NAVE, BEGUN IN 1220.

XXVIII.   RHEIMS CATHEDRAL, THE WEST FRONT, BEGUN *c.* 1225.

XXIX.   RHEIMS CATHEDRAL, FROM THE NORTH, BEGUN IN 1211 ; CHOIR, TRANSEPTS AND NAVE 13TH CENTURY,
TOWERS 15TH CENTURY.

XXX.   LINCOLN CATHEDRAL, FROM THE NORTH, CHIEFLY 1192–1280.

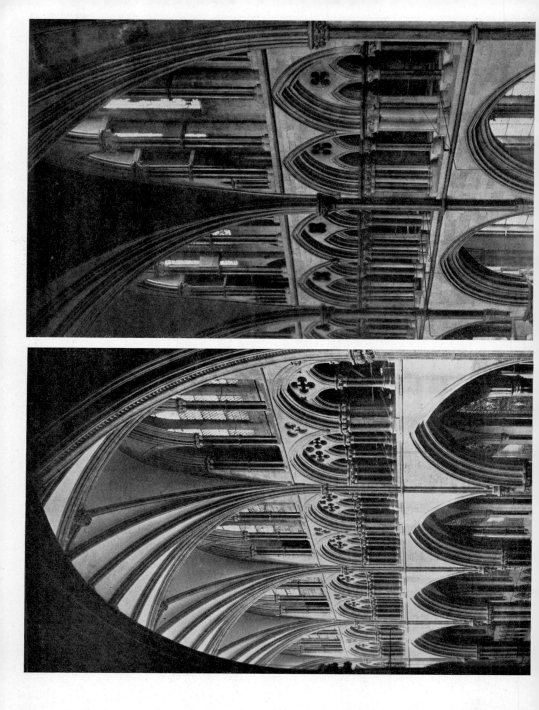

XXXIa (TOP). LINCOLN CATHEDRAL, THE CHOIR, BEGUN IN 1192.

XXXIb. LINCOLN CATHEDRAL, THE NAVE, ROOFED IN 1233.

XXXII.   LINCOLN CATHEDRAL, THE ANGEL CHOIR, BEGUN IN 1256.

XXXIII.   SALISBURY CATHEDRAL, CHAPTER-HOUSE,
c. 1275.

XXXIV.   SOUTHWELL MINSTER, CAPITAL FROM THE
CHAPTER-HOUSE, LATE 13TH CENTURY.

XXXV.   BRISTOL CATHEDRAL, CHOIR AISLE, 1298–1332.

XXXVI. ELY CATHEDRAL, FROM THE LADY CHAPEL, 1321–49.

XXXVII (TOP). GLOUCESTER CATHEDRAL, THE CHOIR, 1337–77.
XXXVIII. GLOUCESTER CATHEDRAL, THE VAULT OF THE CHOIR.

XXXIX.   PENSHURST PLACE, KENT, BEGUN *c.* 1341.

XL.   COVENTRY, ST. MICHAEL'S, 15TH CENTURY (DESTROYED IN THE SECOND WORLD WAR).

XLI.   SWAFFHAM, NORFOLK, TIMBER ROOF, 1454 OR LATER.

XLII (TOP). CAMBRIDGE, KING'S COLLEGE CHAPEL, BEGUN 1446, MAINLY EARLY 16TH CENTURY.

XLIII. VALLADOLID, ST. PAUL'S, *c.* 1490–1515. DESIGNED BY SIMÓN DE COLONIA.

XLIV.   NUREMBURG, ST. LAWRENCE, CHOIR, 1445–72 (SEVERELY DAMAGED IN THE SECOND WORLD WAR).

XLV.   STRASSBURG CATHEDRAL, PORTAL OF ST. LAWRENCE. BY JAKOB OF LANDSHUT, 1495.

XLVI (TOP).   FLORENCE CATHEDRAL, BEGUN 1296, BUILT CHIEFLY FROM 1357 ONWARDS. PRINCIPA
ARCHITECTS : ARNOLFO DI CAMBIO AND FRANCESCO TALENTI.

XLVII.   FILIPPO BRUNELLESCHI : STO. SPIRITO, FLORENCE, BEGUN 1435.

XLVIII. FILIPPO BRUNELLESCHI : FOUNDLING HOSPITAL, FLORENCE, BEGUN 1419.

XLIX. LUCIANO LAURANA (?) : COURTYARD OF THE DUCAL PALACE, URBINO, *c.* 1470–75.

L. LEONE BATTISTA ALBERTI : S. FRANCESCO, RIMINI, BEGUN 1446.

LI (RIGHT). LEONE BATTISTA ALBERTI : PALAZZO RUCELLAI, FLORENCE, 1446–51.

LII (ABOVE). RAPHAEL : PALAZZO VIDONI CAFFARELLI, ROME, c. 1515–20.

LIII. DONATO BRAMANTE: THE TEMPIETTO OF S. PIETRO IN MONTORIO, ROME, 1502.

LIV.   ANTONIO DA SAN GALLO : PALAZZO FARNESE, ROME, 1530–46. THE TOP FLOOR BY MICHELANGELO.

LV.   BALDASSARE PERUZZI : PALAZZO MASSIMI ALLE COLONNE, ROME, BEGUN 1535.

LVI.   GIULIO ROMANO : THE ARCHITECT'S OWN HOUSE AT MANTUA, *c.* 1544.

LVII.   ANDREA PALLADIO : PALAZZO CHIERICATI, VICENZA, BEGUN IN 1550.

LVIII.   ANDREA PALLADIO : VILLA ROTONDA, OUTSIDE VICENZA, BEGUN *c.* 1567.

LIX.   MICHELANGELO : ANTEROOM TO THE LAURENZIANA LIBRARY, FLORENCE, BEGUN IN 1526.

LX.   GIORGIO VASARI : THE UFFIZI PALACE, FLORENCE, BEGUN IN 1570.

LXI.   GIACOMO VIGNOLA : CHURCH OF THE GESÙ, ROME, BEGUN IN 1568.

I.   MICHELANGELO : THE DOME OF ST. PETER'S IN ROME, DESIGNED 1558–60, COMPLETED BY GIACOMO DELLA
PORTA 1588–90.

LXIII. ST. PETER'S IN ROME, WITH THE FRONT AND NAVE BY CARLO MADERNA, 1607–c. 1615, AND THE
COLONNADES BY BERNINI, BEGUN IN 1656. THE VATICAN PALACE APPEARS ON THE RIGHT.

LXIV (TOP).   FRANCESCO BORROMINI : S. CARLO ALLE QUATTRO FONTANE, ROME, BEGUN IN 1633.

LXV.   FRANCESCO BORROMINI : S. CARLO ALLE QUATTRO FONTANE, ROME, THE FRONT, BEGUN IN 1667.

LXVI.   PIETRO DA CORTONA : S. MARIA DELLA PACE, ROME, BEGUN IN 1656.

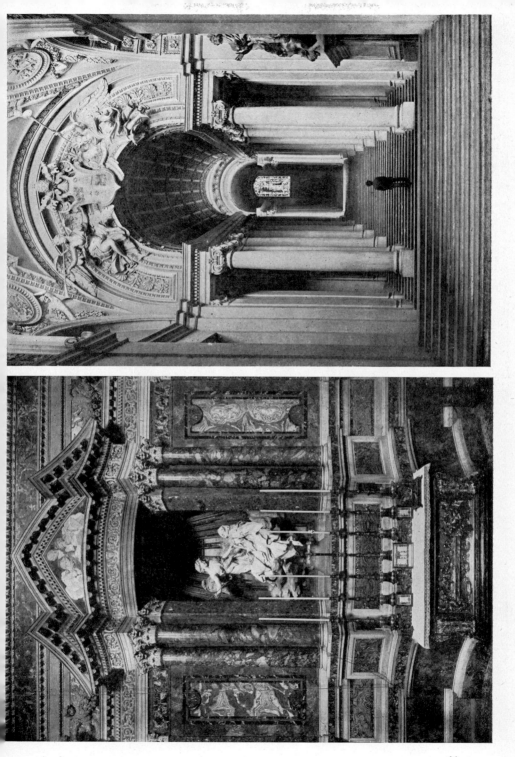

LXVII (TOP).   GIANLORENZO BERNINI : THE SCALA REGIA IN THE VATICAN PALACE, ROME, *c.* 1660–70.

LXVIII.   GIANLORENZO BERNINI : ALTAR OF ST. TERESA AT S. MARIA DELLA VITTORIA, ROME, 1646.

LXIX (TOP). NARCISO TOMÉ : THE TRASPARENTE IN TOLEDO CATHEDRAL, COMPLETED IN 1732.

LXX. LUIS DE ARÉVALO AND F. MANUEL VASQUEZ : SACRISTY OF THE CHARTERHOUSE (CARTUJA), GRANADA 1727-64.

LXXI.   COSMAS DAMIAN AND EGID QUIRIN ASAM : ST. JOHN NEPOMUK, MUNICH, 1730–c. 1750.

LXXII.   JOHANN BALTHASAR NEUMANN : VIERZEHNHEILIGEN, 1743–72.

LXXIII (TOP). JAKOB PRANDTAUER : THE MONASTERY OF MELK ON THE DANUBE, 1702–36.

XXIV. MATTHÄUS DANIEL PÖPPLEMANN : THE ZWINGER AT DRESDEN, 1709–19 (BADLY DAMAGED IN THE SECOND WORLD WAR).

LXXV. JOHANN BALTHASAR NEUMANN : STAIRCASE IN THE ELECTORAL PALACE AT BRUCHSAL, DESIGNED 1730.
GROUND FLOOR.

LXXVIa (TOP). JOHANN BALTHASAR NEUMANN : STAIRCASE IN THE ELECTORAL PALACE AT BRUCHSAL, DESIGNED 1730. HALF-WAY BETWEEN GROUND FLOOR AND UPPER FLOOR.

LXXVIb. JOHANN BALTHASAR NEUMANN : STAIRCASE IN THE ELECTORAL PALACE AT BRUCHSAL, DESIGNED 1730. A LITTLE HIGHER UP THAN LXXVIa.

LXXVII.   JOHANN MICHAEL FEICHTMAYR : STUCCO CARTOUCHE, BRUCHSAL, 1752.

LXXVIII.   CAMBRIDGE : KING'S COLLEGE CHAPEL, SOUTHERN LUNETTE OF THE WEST SIDE OF THE CHOIR SCREEN,
1532–36.

LXXIX.   BLOIS : THE CASTLE, WING OF FRANCIS I, 1515–*c.* 1525.

LXXX.   PIERRE LESCOT : SOUTH-WEST PAVILION IN THE LOUVRE COURTYARD, PARIS, 1546.

LXXXI. BURGHLEY HOUSE, NORTHANTS, CENTRE PAVILION IN THE COURTYARD, 1585.

LXXXII.   LONGLEAT, WILTSHIRE, BEGUN IN 1567.

LXXXIII.   INIGO JONES : QUEEN'S HOUSE, GREENWICH, BEGUN IN 1616.

LXXXIV.   FRANÇOIS MANSART : THE ORLÉANS WING OF BLOIS CASTLE, 1635–38.

LXXXV.   JACOB VAN CAMPEN : THE MAURITSHUIS, THE HAGUE, 1633–35.

LXXXVI.   CLAUDE PERRAULT : THE LOUVRE, PARIS, EAST FRONT, BEGUN IN 1665.

LXXXVII.   JULES HARDOUIN-MANSART : ST. LOUIS DES INVALIDES, PARIS, 1675–1706.

LXXXVIII.   SIR CHRISTOPHER WREN : ST. PAUL'S CATHEDRAL, LONDON, 1675–1710.

LXXXIX.   SIR CHRISTOPHER WREN : ST. STEPHENS, WALBROOK, LONDON, 1672–78.

XC.   GERMAIN BOFFRAND : SALON DU PRINCE IN THE HÔTEL DE SOUBISE, PARIS, *c.* 1737.

XCI.   SIR JOHN VANBRUGH : BLENHEIM PALACE, BEGUN IN 1705.

XCII.   SIR JOHN VANBRUGH : BLENHEIM PALACE, GATE PAVILION OF THE KITCHEN WING, 1708–09.

XCIII.   BLENHEIM PALACE FROM THE AIR, THE GROUNDS LAID OUT BY LANCELOT BROWN.

XCIV.   JOHN WOOD THE ELDER : PRIOR PARK, NEAR BATH, BEGUN IN 1735.

XCV.   JOHN WOOD THE YOUNGER : ROYAL CRESCENT, BATH, BEGUN IN 1767.

XCVI.   ROBERT ADAM : KENWOOD, NEAR LONDON, THE LIBRARY, 1767-69.

XCVII. ROBERT ADAM : SYON HOUSE, NEAR LONDON, THE ENTRANCE SCREEN, 1773.

XCVIII.   SIR JOHN SOANE : DESIGN FOR THE ARCHITECT'S OWN HOUSE, LINCOLN'S INN FIELDS, LONDON, 1813.

XCIX.   FRIEDRICH GILLY : PLAN FOR A NATIONAL THEATRE, BERLIN, 1798.

C.   SIR ROBERT SMIRKE : THE BRITISH MUSEUM, LONDON, 1823–47.

CI.   SIR CHARLES BARRY AND A. W. N. PUGIN : THE HOUSES OF PARLIAMENT, LONDON, BEGUN IN 1835.

BARRY : THE REFORM CLUB, LONDON, BEGUN IN 1837.

GARNIER : THE OPERA, PARIS, 1861–74.

CIV.   WALTER GROPIUS : MODEL FACTORY AT THE " WERKBUND " EXHIBITION, COLOGNE.

CII.   SIR CHARLES BARRY : THE REFORM CLUB, LONDON, BEGUN IN 1837.

CIII.   CHARLES GARNIER : THE OPERA, PARIS, 1861–74.

CIV.   WALTER GROPIUS: MODEL FACTORY AT THE "WERKBUND" EXHIBITION, COLOGNE, 1914.